Towards a Happy Family

Shaykh Ḥabīb al-Kāẓimī

AL-BURĀQ

Copyright

ISBN: 978-1-956276-45-9
Printed and published by al-Burāq Publications.
Translated by Safa Muhawesh. Where needed, context and transliterations were added. Some minor edits were made to the translated Arabic text.

Ordering Information
We offer discounts and promotions for wholesale purchases, non-profit organizations, and other educational institutions. Contact us at the email below for further information.

www.al-Buraq.org
publications@al-Buraq.org

First Edition | December 2023

Dedication

The publication of this book was made possible through the generous support of our donors.

Please recite *Sūrat al-Fātihah* and ask God for the Divine reward (*thawāb*) to be conferred upon the donors and also the souls of all the deceased in whose memory their loved ones have contributed graciously towards the publication of *Towards a Happy Family.*

We begin by giving all praise and thanks to God ﷻ for giving us the *tawfiq* to translate this book. He has guided us, and without Him, we would not have been guided to the straight path embodied by the Prophet Muḥammad ﷺ and the Ahl al-Bayt عليهم السلام.

This book is dedicated to all the scholars, martyrs, and believers who worked tirelessly to promote the pure Muḥammadan path.

We also want to thank and appreciate all believers worldwide and acknowledge the team that helped al-Burāq Publications complete this work, spending countless hours to make its publication possible. Please recite Sūrat al-Fātiḥah on behalf of them, their families, and their marḥūmīn.

This book is dedicated in honor of the following individuals. Please remember them in your prayers, and may God ﷻ have mercy on them and their loved ones.

Ali Ftouni
Ali Hammoud
Ali J. Husain
Alya Agemy
Amir Rizk
Ansia Naqvi
Arif Raza
Ayoub A. Shah
Bande Khuda
Dua M
Farzana Rizvi
Feroz Naqvi
Hajj Ahmad Fouani
Hajj Hassan Sobh
Hajj Sami Ftouni
Hajji Amneh Sobh-Ftouni
Hajji Hiam Hojeije
Hajji Imane Srour
Intissar Bazzi
Kassem Baydoun
Mahmoud Tiba
Mubeen Jafri
Murtaza Rizvi
Rayhana Hammoud
Sajida Fatima
Sakina S. Ali
Sami Saleh
Sayyed Khaled M. Abdallah
Sayyid Rūḥullāh Khumaynī
Sayyid Sobh H. Sobh
Shahīd Ibrahim Hadi
Syed Abul Hassan Bokhari
Syed Mohammed H. Bokhari
Tammy Gharbi
Turfah Sobh
Zahraa Hammoud

Duʿāʾ al-Ḥujjah

اللهم كن لوليك الحجة بن الحسن صلواتك
عليه وعلى آبائه في هذه الساعة وفي كل
ساعة وليا وحافظا وقائدا وناصرا ودليلا
وعينا حتى تسكنه أرضك طوعا وتمتعه فيها طويلا

O God, be, for Your representative, the Ḥujjat (proof), son of al-Ḥasan, Your blessings be upon him and his forefathers, in this hour and in every hour: a guardian, a protector, a leader, a helper, a proof, and an eye - until You make him live on the Earth, in obedience (to You), and cause him to live in it for a long time.

Terms of Respect

The following Arabic phrases have been used throughout this book in their respective places to show the reverence the noble personalities deserve.

عزّ وجلّ

Used for God, meaning:
Exalted and Sublime (Perfect) is He

صلى الله عليه وآله

Used for Prophet Muḥammad, meaning:
Blessings from God be upon him and his family

عليه السلام

Used for a man (singular) of a high status, meaning:
Peace be upon him

عليها السلام

Used for a woman (singular) of a high status, meaning:
Peace be upon her

عليهما السلام

Used for men/women (dual) of high status, meaning:
Peace be upon them both

عليهم السلام

Used for men and women (plural) of high status, meaning:
Peace be upon them all

عجّل الله تعالى فرجه الشريف

Used for Imām Muḥammad al-Mahdī, meaning:
May God hasten his return

قدس سره

Used for a deceased scholar, meaning:
May his resting [burial] place remain pure

Transliteration Table

The method of transliteration of Islāmic terminology from the Arabic language has been carried out according to the standard transliteration table below.

ء	ʾ	ر	r	ف	f
ا	a	ز	z	ق	q
ب	b	س	s	ك	k
ت	t	ش	sh	ل	l
ث	th	ص	ṣ	م	m
ج	j	ض	ḍ	ن	n
ح	ḥ	ط	ṭ	و	w
خ	kh	ظ	ẓ	ه	h
د	d	ع	ʿ	ي	y
ذ	dh	غ	gh		
Long Vowels					
ا	ā	و	ū	ي	ī
Short Voweles					
ـَـ	a	ـُـ	u	ـِـ	i

Table of Contents

The Bottom Line for a Happy Family 297

Foreword

بسم الله الرحمن الرحيم

In the Name of God, the Beneficent, the Merciful

Allāhumma ṣalli ʿalā Muḥammadin wa ʿalā āli Muḥammad

In the grand tapestry of human existence, few endeavors are as profound and sacred as the quest for a harmonious and joyful family life. The institution of the family, where love, understanding, and compassion reside, stands as the bedrock of our societies. We find solace, support, and the potential for enduring happiness within these familial bonds.

Towards a Happy Family, authored by the erudite and insightful Shaykh Ḥabīb al-Kāẓimī, is a monumental work that beckons readers to embark on a transformative journey toward realizing a contented and blissful family life. Drawing inspiration from the teachings of the Fourteen Infallibles عليهم السلام, this book offers a set of guidelines and a profound philosophy that can illuminate the path to lasting happiness within the familial realm.

The wisdom and teachings of the Fourteen Infallibles عليهم السلام, revered figures within the Shīʿa Islām tradition, have been a source of enlightenment and guidance for countless generations. In *Towards a Happy Family*, Shaykh Ḥabīb al-Kāẓimī distills this wisdom into easily digestible tidbits, offering readers a profound yet accessible roadmap to nurturing a thriving and joyous family.

As we delve into these pages, we shall encounter the rich tapestry of familial experiences and the sagacious counsel of the Imāms. We are reminded that the foundations of a happy family are laid in the subtlest of gestures and the quietest of moments. From communication and empathy to trust and understanding, the book illuminates the virtues that underpin the most serene households.

Our homes are a sanctuary where we find shelter, the warmth of companionship, the laughter of children, and the understanding of partners. A happy family is, in essence, a garden where love, patience, and respect are the seeds, and the teachings of the Twelve Imāms provide the nurturing soil.

This book is more than a mere guide; it explores the core principles that make a family flourish. It is a testament to the profound impact of the Twelve Imāms' ﷺ teachings on the fabric of familial bonds.

We hope this book serves as a source of inspiration, reflection, and transformation. It is an invitation to explore the depths of our souls and the dynamics of our families, ultimately leading us to build bridges of love and resilience that will withstand the trials of time.

In closing, we thank Shaykh Ḥabīb al-Kāẓimī for his dedication to assembling this remarkable work. We invite readers to embark on this enlightening journey, guided by the wisdom of the Twelve Imāms ﷺ, towards the radiant shores of a truly happy family.

In shāʾAllāh, this book finds a place in your hearts and homes as you pursue the profound and timeless quest for family happiness. Together, we can build a world where families thrive, and love reigns supreme.

Shaykh Odeh Muhawesh
October 20, 2023

Preface

In the Name of God, the Beneficent, the Merciful.

All praise is due to God, the Lord of the Worlds. May God's blessings be upon Muḥammad and his immaculate Household.

Family is the first building block of human society; its well-being and integrity are the well-being and integrity of society. Hence, Islāmic law paid meticulous attention to the formulation of this block and its maintenance and protection from anything that could harm it. We see in the Noble Qur'ān that there is a call to protect the family after the call to protect one's soul, as God ﷻ says:

﴿يَٰٓأَيُّهَا ٱلَّذِينَ ءَامَنُوا۟ قُوٓا۟ أَنفُسَكُمْ وَأَهْلِيكُمْ نَارًا وَقُودُهَا ٱلنَّاسُ وَٱلْحِجَارَةُ﴾

﴿yā-'ayyuhā lladhīna 'āmanū qū 'anfusakum wa-'ahlīkum nāran waqūduhā n-nāsu wa-l-ḥijāratu﴾

﴿O you who have faith! Save yourselves and your families from a Fire whose fuel will be people and stones﴾[1]

The human soul does not find rest and tranquility in a family atmosphere free from disturbances and chaos. Narrations and experiences have shown that when the devil loses hope in trying to misguide a person, he provokes the family atmosphere against this person to remove them from tranquility and stability. Mental distraction is one of the biggest obstacles in spiritual wayfaring, through which the submission humans were created for is accomplished.

A person's immediate community- including their parents, relatives, neighbors, co-workers, and those they must interact with-

---

[1] Sūrat al-Taḥrīm, Verse 6.

is in the second circle surrounding a person after their family. Thus, the heedful and mindful person must be an effective agent in the refinement and education of those in this circle or to repel the harm they cause by kind and good treatment. The Divine order came with a call to guide this class, which was among the closest classes to the Holy Prophet ﷺ through God's ﷻ words:

﴿وَأَنذِرْ عَشِيرَتَكَ ٱلْأَقْرَبِينَ﴾

﴿*wa-'andhir 'ashīrataka l-'aqrabīna*﴾

﴿*Warn the nearest of your kinsfolk*﴾[2]

It is noticeable in this area that some, out of a desire to devote themselves to worship, need to pay more attention to this aspect of worship and submission to God ﷻ. In turn, they unknowingly commit a violation against the orders of the Lord. As a result of their violation, some divine bestowals are taken away from them, or they are kept away from getting more because complete submission to God ﷻ includes all forms of obedience, and it is how the righteous servants of God ﷻ achieve their ranks. Just as ideological belief is an indivisible unit, practical faith is similarly interrelated, and the Noble Qur'ān referred to this practical faith as the sum and collection of a person's good deeds (*al-ṣāliḥāt*).

In this book, by God's grace, we sought to highlight the basis of dealing with others, whether in the small family circle or the large community. When a person masters dealing with others, he can clarify the atmosphere with them and even positively influence them, ensuring avoiding harm from others. This, in turn, helps one

[2] Sūrat al-Shu'arā', Verse 214.

to free themselves, enabling them to devote themselves to their internal reform,

﴿يَوْمَ لَا يَنفَعُ مَالٌ وَلَا بَنُونَ﴾

﴿*yawma lā yanfaʿu mālun wa-lā banūna*﴾

﴿إِلَّا مَنْ أَتَى ٱللَّهَ بِقَلْبٍ سَلِيمٍ﴾

﴿*illā man ʾatā llāha bi-qalbin salīmin*﴾

﴿*the day when neither wealth nor children will avail, except him who comes to God with a sound heart,*﴾[3]

May God ﷻ help us and protect us against the malice of our souls and the evils of our deeds by the right of the most honorable servants to Him, Muḥammad, and his immaculate and purified Household.

Shaykh Ḥabīb al-Kāẓimī

[3] Sūrat al-Shuʿarāʾ, Verses 88-89.

Advices

1. Comparing

One factor that can lead to frustration in a marriage, or even to the deterioration of a marriage, is dissatisfaction with one's spouse. This can happen when a spouse compares their husband or wife to the person they envisioned themselves married to, an issue that can arise from either party. For example, a man could be married to a devout woman yet be unsatisfied with her because she does not match the image of the perfect woman he created - one who may not exist. This comparison could stem from various factors, including an illicit previous relationship or a previous relationship that - although legitimate - did not work out for any number of reasons, such as a conflict between his significant other and his family. This could leave the man spending his marriage measuring and comparing his unfortunate wife to some other woman who could be happily married or even dead by that point!

The situation could be exacerbated should the man share his feelings with his wife, leaving her with unimaginable heartbreak. Conversely, the wife could be the one doing the comparison. She may have met and grown attached to another man during her school years, could have her own imaginary perfect man, or could have had an engagement that did not work out before her current marriage, leaving her living constantly comparing and measuring her husband to others. It is no secret that this behavior is irrational, causing one to miss out on the blessings bestowed upon them in exchange for something not meant to be. It is also unbefitting for a believer who should strive to embody the mercy and kindness of God ﷻ.

2. Balancing

No marriage is perfect in every aspect, as spouses are not like two halves of an apple, asked to come together to make a single, whole apple. Instead, the husband is one kind of fruit and the wife another, with no similarity in size, taste, color, or even the environment they belong to. So, as two halves, each entirely different from the other, their differences are completely normal. When disagreements arise, there must be a balance between the positives and the negatives; issues should be handled objectively, and, if needed, the couple should refer to a religious expert or their families to help them resolve issues. As the Qur'ān states:

﴿وَإِنْ خِفْتُمْ شِقَاقَ بَيْنِهِمَا فَابْعَثُوا حَكَمًا مِّنْ أَهْلِهِ وَحَكَمًا مِّنْ أَهْلِهَآ﴾

﴿wa-'in khiftum shiqāqa baynihimā fa-b'athū ḥakaman min 'ahlihī wa-ḥakaman min 'ahlihā﴾

﴿If you fear a split between the two of them, then appoint an arbiter from his relatives and an arbiter from her relatives﴾[4]

Seeking the assistance of an arbitrator or a religious scholar with insight into marriage matters may also be helpful. If a solution cannot be reached, divorce may be the answer. However, it is one of the most undesirable acts permitted by God ﷻ.

Unfortunately, some women abuse "divorce" without pondering its implications or consequences, as if throwing the word around will solve their problems. A woman's respect and the sanctity of her

[4] Sūrat al-Nisā', Verse 35.

marriage decreases when the word is repeated whenever conflict arises.

3. Role Models

The absence of righteous role models for men and women today is noticeable. A man may take a famous athlete as his role model, and a woman may adopt adoration for a celebrity she sees in the media, one whose real-life shows little resemblance to what she portrays on screen.

A believer should be well-acquainted with their goals in life and strive continuously to achieve them, drawing inspiration from the legacy of pious believers before them. A believing woman can find a role model from amongst the many righteous women in history, one of the most prominent of which is Āsiya, the wife of the Pharaoh who reigned at the time of Prophet Mūsā عليه السلام.

Āsiya has an enduring legacy; married to a man who claimed to be God, killed male children, and took the females as slaves, she was able to reach a degree of spiritual nearness to God ﷻ so lofty that He mentioned her in the Noble Qur'ān, setting her beautiful prayers as an example to others. Āsiya lived in a heavily guarded palace and was likely denied access to religious scholars who could guide her on her spiritual journey. Despite her situation, she never stopped striving to reach spiritual perfection. Just as Maryam عليها السلام ascended to a spiritual nearness to God ﷻ so high that He would send food from the heavens to her whenever she entered the chapel, Āsiya achieved a similar state of spirituality.

When she beseeched God ﷻ to build her a home in the heavens near Him:

﴿رَبِّ ٱبْنِ لِي عِندَكَ بَيْتًا فِي ٱلْجَنَّةِ﴾

﴿*rabbi bni lī ʿindaka baytan fī l-jannati*﴾

﴿*My Lord! Build me a home near You in paradise*﴾[5]

And this house built for her in paradise is undoubtedly unlike any other house.

4. Containment

A parent's concern for their children's moral righteousness should be no less than their concern for their children's health. For example, a parent may be so unwilling to bear seeing their daughter inflicted with a rash that they are willing to travel far to find her treatment, yet they do not move a finger when they see the early signs of moral corruption in their child!

While parents must monitor their children and guard against their corruption, they must be careful about the methods they employ. Interrogation and accusation should be avoided. For example, if a father looks through his son's web browsing history with his son present and finds content that he disapproves of, hurling insults and shaming him is counterproductive and could make the problem worse. Instead, he should guide his son gently, using the teaching style of Imāms al-Ḥasan and al-Ḥusayn عليهما السلام as an example.

---

[5] Sūrat al-Taḥrīm, Verse 11.

The Imām ﷺ once saw an old man making wuḍū' (ablution). They noticed he was making some mistakes and wanted to show him the correct method, so they decided to make wuḍū' in front of him and allow him to judge which one made better. With this ingenious method, they taught the man the correct way of making wuḍū' without embarrassing him! Parents should adopt similar methods in raising their children and gently tackle issues that arise.

5. Propensity for Excellence

The nature of a woman's life, specifically raising her children and managing her household, could prevent her from reaching the same level of education as a man, leading to an intellectual and cultural disparity between spouses. It is unfair to a husband who discovers such a disparity to become proud and feel a sense of superiority over his wife.

A woman's preoccupation with attending to her children and household could hinder her education. However, it could distract from her relationship with God ﷻ, causing her to stop trying to advance her spiritual and cultural development. A man must appreciate that his wife may have endured intellectual and spiritual deprivation so that she could be there for him and his children, who will ultimately carry on his name and are a source of pride for him, and so that her husband can fulfill his dreams in life!

Moreover, not all knowledge automatically elevates a person's status; knowledge truly counts when it imparts a sense of responsibility, obligation, and God's wariness upon a person. A woman with good deeds and the tireless effort she pours into raising her children could achieve a level of transparency and closeness to God ﷻ that surpasses what can be gained in a university or other educational institution.

A woman who is God-fearing and keeps away from what is prohibited, even when it is pleasurable, is knowledgeable and virtuous. However, one who elevates on the ladder of knowledge while increasingly moving away from God ﷻ is a person who has no weight or value. For knowledge not accompanied by God-wariness, even knowledge of religious matters could degrade a person in the eyes of God.

6. The Miracle of Marriage

Marriage is a sign that shows God's ﷻ greatness, power, and magnificent creation. One of the ways this is accomplished is through the miraculous creation of a human being. Spouses should take time to watch scientific videos showing the stages of fetal development. After the amazing union between an egg cell and a sperm cell, the first cell that carries genetic traits is formed. The rest of the body's cells are formed from that cell, grouping into what will eventually become bones, the liver, eyes, nerves, etc., until the whole body is created.

It is truly mind-blowing how these cells form and specialize for each organ with such precision! It is even more astonishing when the soul enters the body during the fourth month of pregnancy, and the mother begins to feel her baby's movements! Human creation is one of God's ﷻ greatest signs, whose many secrets remain a mystery to the scientific world. God ﷻ attributes the creation of humanity to Himself, saying in the Qur'ān:

﴿هُوَ ٱلَّذِي يُصَوِّرُكُمۡ فِي ٱلۡأَرۡحَامِ كَيۡفَ يَشَآءُۚ﴾

﴿huwa lladhī yuṣawwirukum fī l-'arḥāmi kayfa yashā'u﴾

﴿It is He who forms you in the wombs [of your mothers] however He wishes﴾[6]

7. Dualism

The nature of this life is that it is filled with affliction. Problems are endless; no one is free from worry about health, family, finances, or even one's destiny in the afterlife. The solution is to take a dualist approach to our problems, separating between the spiritual and earthly worlds. What is being harmed, be it through words or actions, is one's character - a component of their physical being. On the other hand, a person's spiritual personality is concerned only with the Lord of the Worlds and cannot be harmed by matters of this world. The soul, therefore, should not be poured into trivial matters.

Think about it like this. If a wealthy merchant grew tired of dealing with other people's problems and sought a quaint, blissful life, the merchant could construct a three-story building. The first level would be dedicated to his business and its issues and managed by a person hired for this task. The second level would be reserved for his family. The third level would be his own, a quiet place to reflect and a reprieve from the stresses of work and family. Anyone arriving at the building for business would be directed to the first level, where signs would be posted to prevent them from ascending to the second or third level. This method would allow the

[6] Sūrat Āl 'Imrān, Verse 6.

merchant to keep his business running, his family life thriving, and his inner self at peace. He would be relieved of dealing with the stresses of his business as that task would be delegated to the person hired to complete it. Like the merchant, we can approach our problems by compartmentalizing them, approaching our material, worldly problems by addressing them, and not allowing them to preoccupy our entire being.

8. The Keys

To influence a person, especially a child, one must do so through one's heart. It is known that large safes can be opened with small keys. Similarly, each person has a key; if it can be identified, their heart can be unlocked and opened to the divine guidance they are meant for.

Unfortunately, relationships between parents and their children are not ideal, often lacking closeness and intimacy. A friendship between a father and son is rare, the type of relationship wherein the son feels sadness when his father is away from home. Instead, children are often happy in their father's absence, awaiting the chance to do what they want, whether it be allowed or not. There are even those who, deep within their heart, wish for their father's death so that they can inherit his wealth. It is, therefore, essential to befriend your child and address them on their level as the Holy Prophet ﷺ did with his grandsons عليهما السلام.

The Prophet ﷺ used to kneel to allow his grandsons, Imāms al-Ḥasan and al-Ḥusayn ﷺ, to ride on his back, saying:

> "What a good ride you have!"[7]

It has been narrated that the Prophet ﷺ said:

> "One who has a child has to behave in a childlike manner with them."[8]

And as a child grows into their formative teenage years, the nature of a parent's dialogue with that child should evolve. They should be spoken to in their language, and their hearts reached through methods they can relate to.

9. Truth Sessions

For a married couple to address any deficiencies in their marriage, honest sessions may be necessary, although they must be done calmly. They should take advantage of special occasions to hold these meetings, including wedding anniversaries, birth anniversaries of the infallible ﷺ, or during Ramaḍān.

One of the best opportunities to hold these family sessions is during a visit to one of the holy shrines. Just as the head of the household thinks about his family's financial situation, he often thinks about their righteousness and whether they are on the right path. He may find that, at home, his opinions and advice are

---

[7] al-Mīrzā al-Nūrī, *Mustadrak al-Wasā'il wa-Mustanbaṭ al-Masā'il*, Vol. 15, p 173.

[8] al-Ḥurr al-ʿĀmilī, Shaykh Muḥammad b. al-Ḥasan, *Wasā'il al-Shīʿa*, Vol. 21, p 486, ḥadīth 27659.

ignored as his family is preoccupied with school, work, etc. However, the serenity and tenderness achieved during a visit to a holy place make such a visit an ideal time to be honest with one's wife and children about areas that could be improved, ultimately improving family dynamics.

So, what stops a father, who cannot bear to see his son embarking on a dangerous path, from advising him in the presence of an infallible? What stops him from getting a commitment from his son not to go back to his negative ways with the blessing of an infallible ﷺ?

10. Suppressing Anger

In a state of anger, a person loses control of himself as Shayṭān takes control, leading him to use obscene and abusive language. To remove a believer from the state of anger, Prophet Muḥammad ﷺ advised:

> "If one of you is angry when he is standing, let him sit down so the anger will leave him. Otherwise, let him lie down."[9]

It is also recommended to prostrate with humility to God ﷻ. How beautiful it is when a believer speaks to their Lord while in prostration, showing restraint from their anger, even when it is justified, and hoping that God ﷻ will grant them the same on judgment day! Doing so is one of the best manifestations of a whispered prayer. It is likely to be accepted and answered as the

[9] Rayshahrī, Āyatullāh Muḥammad, *Mīzān al-Ḥikmah*, Vol. 3, p. 2269.

believer remembers to turn to their Lord, showing that they are swallowing their anger to attain nearness to God ﷻ.

It was narrated:

> "There is none from the potions swallowed by the servant more beloved to God ﷻ than the potion of anger swallowed while repelling it in his heart, either by patience or forbearance.[10]

Furthermore, in a ḥadīth Qudsī (divine narrative), God ﷻ says:

> "O son of Ādam, remember Me during your anger, and I will remember you during My anger."[11]

It was also narrated that the Prophet ﷺ advised one of his wives to say the following when she was angry:

> "O God, forgive my sins, remove the anger from my heart, and protect me from the trials of misguidance."[12]

11. Heart Pollutants

Looking at that which is forbidden leads to pollution of the heart. Frequently looking at pornographic images and videos leads to an abnormal increase in desires and a hormonal imbalance. While the reaction is involuntary, it can cause early puberty. This is prevalent

---

[10] Kulaynī, Shaykh Muḥammad b. Ya'qūb, *al-Kāfī*, Vol. 1, p. 111.

[11] Rayshahrī, Āyatullāh Muḥammad, *Mīzān al-Ḥikmah*, Vol. 2, p. 973.

[12] Majlisī, 'Allamah Muḥammad Bāqir, *Biḥār al-Anwār*, Vol. 70, p. 273.

in youth who delve deeply into this world, sometimes reaching puberty at twelve.

Even a grown man can become ill due to a hormonal imbalance. No longer satisfied with the lawful means available, he may resort to multiple marriages and forbidden relationships instead.

Today, committing the forbidden takes only a person's determination and can be carried out easily, without obstacles. Therefore, a woman who sees that her husband has become involved with the forbidden should stop him, even if only for her interest. Otherwise, if she chooses to stay silent to get along, she should know she will be the first victim in this battle, even before the man himself. Thus, she should make her position against this behavior known and discourage and dissuade her husband from continuing down this path, even if only using her words.

12. Arrows of the Night

When a woman who was brought up by gentle and merciful parents who spoiled her moves in with her husband, who does not follow his religion nor does he show her love and compassion (she could also be facing problems with her mother-in-law), it is as though she has fallen into Hell! While some women decide to endure those difficulties for the sake of their children, others cannot bear such living and prefer to separate no matter the consequences, giving up all their belongings and sometimes even their children.

It is a tragedy when one reaches such a level that no one can bear to live with them. Even if such a person prays the night prayer from the beginning of the evening until sunrise, would it be enough to raise their standing in the eyes of God ﷻ? How could he find comfort and sleep when someone is praying and complaining about him to God ﷻ? He should consider that whenever this poor woman thinks of the child she had to leave behind, she feels pain and a fire in her heart and sends an arrow that does not miss towards her husband during the night in the form of her plea to God ﷻ to give her justice from her oppressive husband.

13. Three Places

One of the ways to control and decrease anger, especially towards one's wife and children, is for a believer to remind himself that anger is the doing of the accursed Shayṭān and to seek refuge in God ﷻ from him because Shayṭān is most likely to have control over the sons of Ādam in three places:

The first is at the time of sexual desire: when one is alone with a woman (who is not his wife or forbidden in marriage to him), then Shayṭān is their third. We have often seen involuntary action taken by believers alone with a woman, even if it is a small forbidden action because he has no self-control.

The second is at the time of anger: anger is another time a person loses control over themselves because

> "Shayṭān flows through the son of Ādam as blood flows through the veins."[13]

---

[13] al-Aḥsā'ī, Ibn Abī Jumhūr, *'Awālī al-La'ālī al-'Azīziyya fil-Aḥādīth al-Dīniyya*, Vol. 1, p. 274.

Imām Muḥammad al-Bāqir ﷺ, warned us about anger and gave us a remedy for it when he said:

> "Indeed, this anger is a spark lit by Shayṭān in the heart of the son of Ādam...and when one of you becomes angry, his eyes become red, his veins expand, and Shayṭān goes into him... Therefore, if one of you fears that for himself, let him stay still (not act upon his anger), and Shayṭān's harm will leave him then."[14]

The third is at the time of worship: thus, we have been told to seek refuge in God ﷻ from Shayṭān before reading the Noble Qur'ān and praying.

14. Prizes

A person who does not control himself and is plagued with the curiosity of seeing, hearing, and speaking loses many divine blessings while also being punished.

If divine blessings can be lost from deeds that are not prohibited, how many blessings are lost when one sins? There are narrations, however, that give hope to the souls of believers, such as the ones that mention the reward God ﷻ gave to a believer in this world when he struggles against himself and lowers his gaze.

The greater and more difficult the struggle, the greater the reward! What a difference there is between the struggle of an old man lowering his gaze and that of a young, single man who resists temptation when he finds himself alone with a beautiful woman!

---

[14] Kulaynī, Shaykh Muḥammad b. Ya'qūb, *al-Kāfī*, Vol. 2, p. 304, ḥadīth 12.

Some of these struggles are hard on the soul but can be the reason for great horizons opening for a person. As one narration states:

> "Whoever looks at a woman then raises his sight towards the sky, his sight will not return to him until God ﷻ marries him to a ḥūr al-ʿayn (a maiden in paradise)."[15]

There is another prize that is also acquired before the hereafter, as is explained in this narration:

> "No one preserves himself from sin like the one who lowers his gaze, for when the eyesight is turned away from that which God ﷻ prohibited, the heart witnesses greatness and glory."[16]

15. Changing Perspective

Anger is undoubtedly a destructive pest in a person's life, and there are great blessings in avoiding it and overcoming it by addressing its causes.

Among the known factors that lead to anger are feelings of contempt and arrogance. The way to treat those feelings is to change how we view others and remember that though one may seem corrupt and hypocritical on their exterior, only God ﷻ knows what is inside them. A believer is instructed to view all others as better than themselves, as things are judged by how they end. A person may be a hypocrite, but only God ﷻ knows their ultimate fate.

---

[15] al-ʿAsqalānī, Ibn Ḥajar, *Fatḥ al-Bārī fī Sharḥ Ṣaḥīḥ al-Bukhārī*, Vol. 3, p. 166.

[16] Majlisī, ʿAllamah Muḥammad Bāqir, *Biḥār al-Anwār*, Vol. 101, p. 41

Did anyone predict that Ḥurr b. Yazīd would become one of the supporters of the Master of Martyrs, Imām al-Ḥusayn ﷺ? While some may seem to have a corrupt and hypocritical exterior, a person who appears righteous may be harboring their hypocrisy internally. Therefore, the Prophet ﷺ said:

> "God, The Blessed, and Sublime has embedded four things in four other things: He has embedded His pleasure in His obedience. Therefore, you should not underestimate obedience to God. It may cause God's pleasure when you do not know it. God ﷻ has embedded His wrath in disobeying Him. Therefore, you should not underestimate any disobedience to God. It may cause God's wrath while you do not know about it. God has embedded His response in supplications. Therefore, you should not underestimate any supplications. It may cause God to respond to you while you do not know about it. God has embedded His friends among His servants. Therefore, you should not belittle anyone since he may be a friend of God, and you may not know it."[17]

16. Compensation

Some parents have children with mental or physical disabilities. Some of these disabilities are caused by negligence, such as the parents taking medication harmful to a fetus. Suppose the parents were careful to follow prevailing medical advice to ensure a healthy pregnancy and to follow the spiritual advice recommended to be

[17] Majlisī, ʿAllamah Muḥammad Bāqir, *Biḥār al-Anwār*, Vol. 68, p. 177, ḥadīth 17.

performed before and during the pregnancy, such as giving charity. In that case, these disabilities are a result of divine predestination.

In such cases, the parents need a substantial charge of faith (*imān*) to remain patient and content with what God ﷻ has given them. They should remember what God ﷻ said:

﴿هُوَ ٱلَّذِي يُصَوِّرُكُمۡ فِي ٱلۡأَرۡحَامِ كَيۡفَ يَشَآءُ﴾

﴿huwa lladhī yuṣawwirukum fī l-'arḥāmi kayfa yashā'u﴾

﴿It is He who forms you in the wombs [of your mothers] however He wishes﴾[18]

Therefore, He willed for a particular child to be born blind, paralyzed, or with some other handicap, and a believer surrenders to the will and wish of their Creator.

How beautiful would it be for a parent to intend to serve and take care of their disabled child to gain nearness to God's ﷻ? The care a parent gives to this child is the closest one can get to sincerity in seeking nearness, as they are not motivated by the hope that one day, they will get financial or social benefits from their child.

On the contrary, a child's disabilities could cause mental, emotional, and physical exhaustion for their parents. They could serve as a limiting factor in their lives for many years. Their patience over those years guarantees the rise of their levels with God ﷻ. In addition, God ﷻ gives special compensation to those inflicted with

[18] Sūrat Āl ʿImrān, Verse 6.

disabilities in this life. He, without a doubt, will not forget their parents and those who gave them a hand of help and compassion.

17. The Divine Blessing

He who blessed the progenies of Ibrāhīm عليه السلام and the Prophet ﷺ will also bless your family and progeny with the condition that you offer Him a sacrifice as Ibrāhīm عليه السلام and other righteous servants have done. Offering a sacrifice means successfully enduring God's tests. For example, Ibrāhīm عليه السلام only attained the position of Imāmate after he passed through a series of divine trials and tribulations:

﴿وَإِذِ ٱبْتَلَىٰٓ إِبْرَٰهِـۧمَ رَبُّهُۥ بِكَلِمَٰتٖ فَأَتَمَّهُنَّۖ قَالَ إِنِّي جَاعِلُكَ لِلنَّاسِ إِمَامٗاۖ قَالَ وَمِن ذُرِّيَّتِيۖ قَالَ لَا يَنَالُ عَهۡدِي ٱلظَّٰلِمِينَ﴾

﴿wa-ʾidhi btalā ʾibrāhīma rabbuhū bi-kalimātin fa-ʾatammahunna qāla ʾinnī jāʿiluka li-n-nāsi ʾimāman qāla wa-min dhurriyyatī qāla lā yanālu ʿahdī ẓ-ẓālimīn[a]﴾

﴾When his Lord tested Ibrāhīm with certain words and he fulfilled them, He said, 'I am making you the Imam of mankind.' Said he, 'And from among my descendants?' He said, 'My pledge does not extend to the unjust.'﴿[19]

From time to time, the believer will be tested by how they control their anger their desires, or through other tests. If they are willing to sacrifice and surrender themselves and their valuables to prove

[19] Sūrat al-Baqarah, Verse 124.

their worthiness in their service to God ﷻ, God ﷻ will choose them and draw them nearer.

It was narrated in a ḥadīth Qudsī (divine ḥadīth) that God ﷻ said:

> "If I am obeyed - I become pleased; if I am pleased - I bless; there is no end to My Blessings."[20]

The treasuries of the heavens and the earth are in the hands of the Lord of the worlds; He opens them to whomever He wishes. However, He wishes, whenever He wishes, and with whatever He wishes!

18. Arguing in Front of the Children

If there is no way for a couple to avoid an argument, they should have it in a locked room, away from their children and other family members, as doing otherwise will have severe consequences.

A man could spend the entire night arguing loudly with his wife as they scream and utter obscenities at each other, yet they could make up in the end, and no one would know a thing about it. An even bigger disaster is when those secrets, revealed during a couple's argument, manage to escape the confines of the family home, especially when those arguments occur in front of their children.

Some instances of juvenile delinquency, especially in girls, result from being raised in a tense family atmosphere and deprived of parental affection. When their home does not feel safe, children often throw themselves into Shayṭān's lap at the first opportunity. On Judgment Day, when their folders of reckoning are opened,

---

20 Qiṣaṣ ul-Anbiyā', p. 512.

and the parents are told: with your arguments and actions, you drove your children to corruption and immorality, what will their reply be?

19. Moderation

Among a man's duties is to support his family financially. However, spending on one's family should be reasonable and appropriate as it could lead to financial hardship and poverty. The wise man is the one who is moderate in his spending and strives to ensure a pleasant, decent living for his family in the future.

In addition to financial difficulties that are derived from being wasteful, God ﷻ tells of another frightful consequence of wasteful spending in the Qur'ān:

﴿إِنَّ ٱلْمُبَذِّرِينَ كَانُوٓا۟ إِخْوَٰنَ ٱلشَّيَـٰطِينِ ۖ وَكَانَ ٱلشَّيْطَـٰنُ لِرَبِّهِۦ كَفُورًا﴾

﴾'inna l-mubadhdhirīna kānū 'ikhwāna sh-shayāṭīni wa-kāna sh-shayṭānu li-rabbihī kafūra^n^﴿

﴾Indeed the wasteful are brothers of satans, and Shayṭān is ungrateful to his Lord﴿[21]

This expression, unmatched in the Noble Qur'ān, was not even used to describe major sins such as adultery, drinking alcohol, and even disbelief! The word brother suggests a state of extreme closeness; when it is said that someone is the brother of justice, a state of coherence and conformity is understood, meaning that

---

[21] Sūrat al-Isrā', Verse 27.

person is closely associated with justice. Similarly, the "brother of Shayṭān" implies a person is associated with Shayṭān.

A wasteful person is associated with Shayṭān because waste and excessive spending is the entry point for Shayṭān into the kingdom of existence, wherein he can wreak havoc on other aspects of someone's life.

20. The Ranks of a Person

Every person has two ranks. The first is a practical one and is a person's current rank. The other is a theoretical rank possible for a person to attain where they can maximize their potential.

We are like farmers who pass by a tree in an orchard and find that it has only produced ten pieces of fruit while we expected it to produce one hundred. Had we watered the tree and kept it safe from pests and disease, it would have easily produced the expected fruit. Therefore, a farmer straddles the line between hope and regret, hope stemming from the tree's capacity to produce fruit and regret over the reality that the harvest is much smaller than it could have potentially been had efforts to care for the crop been multiplied since the growing season began.

It is, therefore, incumbent upon a believer to lessen the gap between their actual and theoretical ranks as much as possible. The fortunate believer is the one whose practical rank is very close to his theoretical rank. The day of judgment is the day of regret; as said to a person on that day, you would have been on this level if you had done or did not do so.

Our reality is one thing, and the level we could have reached could be entirely different. Therefore, believers should strive to raise their level and never give up, claiming it is too late.

21. Concealing Disagreements

A man may tolerate disagreements with his wife and prefer to continue his relationship with her even if that relationship has soured. He may not resort to divorce because it may damage his reputation, adversely affect his family, or because he may be afraid to be alone and worry that no woman will accept him in his old age, unless only for his money.

Not rushing to divorce is a positive choice, as his patience to endure the hurt his wife may have caused is conducive to reaching spiritual perfection.

However, one should not degrade their spouse in front of their children. The disagreement of a married couple is not the fault of their children, so why should they have to endure their parents' arguments and live through the emotional turmoil of feeling torn between them?

It is no secret that the deterioration of a family unit is a significant cause for children, especially daughters, to go astray. Concealing disagreements from one's children is not considered hypocrisy as it leads to a greater good. If a person can say what they usually would not say when trying to resolve a problem between two people, why can't parents do that as well?

22. The Purpose of Ḥijāb

Today, there seems to be a gradual movement to undermine the ḥijāb by distorting its true purpose. The intent of the ḥijāb is not to cover the body; instead, it is meant to shield those who wear it from lustful looks. Nevertheless, what good is the ḥijāb if it becomes an attractive accessory instead of a barrier?

These days, designers are turning the ḥijāb into a fashion statement by marketing clothes to women who wear it that accentuate the details of a woman's body. Unfortunately, some women of faith are attracted to this type of clothing even though it cannot be considered a ḥijāb.

A woman of faith wears the ḥijāb to please God ﷻ, not to please others. A woman's charm and beauty are for her husband to see and enjoy and are not something to parade and display in public. One who highlights and presents her beauty for others is, in a way, trying to attract the attention of men and inviting them towards her as if she is desperate for their lust! This is not befitting of a faithful woman considered the mother of future generations.

23. The Color of Faith

If a married couple can accomplish submission to God ﷻ in a manner that He loves and approves and that couple colors their life with faith, then they are preparing the foundation for divine blessings to enter their life. The Lord of the Worlds is indeed the Generous, but there must be a receptive foundation for His outflowing generosity, as was the case with God's ﷻ blessings of Ibrāhīm ؑ and his family.

When God ﷻ saw the submission to His order from all of the members of his family: Ibrāhīm ﷺ, who left his wife and child in a barren valley, his wife, who remained patient and surrendered to the desolation, and Ismāʿīl ﷺ, whom God ﷻ knew could surrender to the divine order for sacrifice in the future, then He bestowed His blessings upon them.

The Ibrāhīmic pilgrimage with its various rituals: the well of Zamzam, Ḥijr Ismāʿīl, and the jogging of Hājar- is a commemoration to the family of Ibrāhīm ﷺ that continues year after year throughout the centuries. Prophet Muḥammad ﷺ is also from the progeny of Prophet Ibrāhīm ﷺ.

24. The Highest Degree

A man who views his relationship with his wife and children as eternal will likely put up with deprivation and hurt from them and strive to raise their religious and spiritual levels.

If his wife needs to learn about the religious guidelines and needs to follow them better, he should teach and show her how to follow them. He should also take her to the holy sites, Friday prayers, and gatherings to commemorate the Prophet ﷺ and his household ﷺ. He should do so because he strives to reach higher spiritual levels himself and wants his wife and children to do the same, and the benefit is one on the Day of Judgment. On the Day of Judgment, God ﷻ will look at the levels earned by all family members and unite them all at the highest level attained by any of them. It has been reported that the Prophet ﷺ said:

> "When a household member enters paradise, the rest of his family will follow."

When asked:

> "How so?"

The Prophet ﷺ answered:

> "He intercedes on their behalf, and his intercession is accepted until he includes the family's servant, so he says: My Lord! My servant shielded me from the heat and cold, and his intercession for the servant is accepted."[22]

25. The Light of Prayer in the Home

The sanctification of prayer and urging family members to perform their prayers on time significantly impact a family. This, in addition to reciting the Noble Qur'ān, especially when that recitation is accompanied by contemplating its words, is of great importance.

In the Noble Qur'ān, God ﷻ advised His Prophet ﷺ by saying:

﴿وَأْمُرْ أَهْلَكَ بِالصَّلَوٰةِ وَاصْطَبِرْ عَلَيْهَا﴾

﴾*wa-'mur 'ahlaka bi-ṣ-ṣalāti wa-ṣṭabir 'alayhā*﴿

﴾*And bid your family to prayer and be steadfast in maintaining it. We do not ask any provision of you: it is We who provide for you, and to Godwariness belongs the ultimate outcome [in the Hereafter]*﴿[23]

[22] Majlisī, 'Allamah Muḥammad Bāqir, *Biḥār al-Anwār*, Vol. 8, p. 56, ḥadīth 67.

[23] Sūrat Ṭā Ḥā, Verse 132.

A home that gives special attention to prayer is divine and blessed. How beautiful it is for a person of faith known to be just (not committing minor or major sins) to make their prayers at home as a group with their family!

Even a just person of faith can miss many blessings by not taking advantage of the benefits of congregational prayer.

Imām 'Alī ؏ said:

> "The house in which the Qur'ān is recited and God, The Noble and Grand, is remembered will receive numerous Divine blessings, the Angels will be present, and the devils will be distanced from there. In addition, that house will shimmer for the people of the sky just like the stars shimmer for the people on earth..."[24]

26. Real Beauty

The word 'beauty' appeals to the general public, especially women. This is because a woman, by her feminine nature and instincts, sees that her beauty is her capital.

This way of thinking is often encouraged when she sees men flocking toward the outward beauty of other women. However, this external beauty tied to the material world is only a matter of the coordination of body parts and symmetry in facial features. It is known that beauty is a relative matter and that external beauty is as fleeting as the days pass. This is contrary to internal beauty, which is tied to the world of souls (spiritual world?). This internal beauty

---

[24] al-Ḥurr al-'Āmilī, Shaykh Muḥammad b. al-Ḥasan, *Wasā'il al-Shī'a*, Vol. 6, p. 199, ḥadīth 7725.

is given to the believer, especially one committed to performing the night prayer.

As is understood from the narrations of Ahl al-Bayt عليهم السلام, this internal beauty is real and cannot be compared to the beauty of the face, the fairness of the skin, the softness of the hair, and the like. This is because it is an eternal beauty that does not fade but is earned. One does not have a hand in the external beauty they are given, but the beauty of internal spirituality is a choice.

27. Change in Nature

The effort a parent invests into raising a child may only sometimes bear fruit, as was the case with Prophet Nūḥ's عليه السلام son, some of the Imāms عليهم السلام, and the children of some righteous believers. This is because a child's bad choices and behavior can lead to a change in their nature.

For example, a person addicted to looking at something forbidden to them takes on a lustful nature. Similarly, one who is quick to become upset will develop an angry nature.

Some parents exert much effort into raising their first child but become discouraged after they perceive that no good came of it, leading them to put less effort into raising their other children, with whom those efforts could have paid off. However, a believer should always strive to create the appropriate atmosphere for their children to excel without expecting a particular result.

It is like how a teacher fulfills his duty in the classroom, yet some students fail the final exam. The failure of the students is not the criteria by which a teacher is evaluated; instead, they are judged by the extent of their efforts and skills. The more quarrelsome the students are and the more professional and accurate in work the teacher is, the more they deserve an award!

28. Working According to Duty does not Result

People of faith may suffer from having a child stray from the path of righteousness, even if they did not neglect their responsibilities in raising them. Such a parent may feel hopeless and leave their children to do as they wish. However, a person of faith must remember to try to save their child and not become discouraged if the result could be better. As God ﷻ said:

﴿وَأَن لَّيْسَ لِلْإِنسَٰنِ إِلَّا مَا سَعَىٰ﴾

﴾*wa-'an laysa li-l-'insāni 'illā mā sa'ā*﴿

﴾*that nothing belongs to man except what he strives for*﴿[25]

Take Prophet Nūḥ (a), for example, whose son fell into corruption. Prophet Nūḥ (a) did not stop trying to guide and advise him; he tried to save his son even at the time of the flood, as God ﷻ tells us:

﴿وَنَادَىٰ نُوحٌ ٱبْنَهُۥ وَكَانَ فِى مَعْزِلٍ يَٰبُنَىَّ ٱرْكَب مَّعَنَا وَلَا تَكُن مَّعَ ٱلْكَٰفِرِينَ﴾

﴾*wa-nādā nūḥun-i bnahū wa-kāna fī ma'zilin yā-bunayya rkab ma'anā wa-lā takun ma'a l-kāfirīna*﴿

[25] Sūrat al-Najm, Verse 39.

﴾*Nūḥ called out to his son, who stood aloof, 'O my son! 'Board with us, and do not be with the faithless!'*﴿[26]

Some of our Imāms ﷺ also suffered from having corrupt children. Therefore, we should emulate our prophets and imāms and fulfill our duties, leaving the rest to The Lord of the Worlds, who knows His servants best.

29. Retrieving the Child from the Laps of Vices

A righteous parent can bring their child back to their senses, especially with intense prayers for their deliverance. A specific act of worship called 'Aʿmāl Umm Dāwūd' addresses this exact scenario. 'Aʿmāl Umm Dāwūd' is typically performed in the middle of the month of Rajab and is best performed to retrieve one's child from the laps of vices and corruption.

Umm Dāwūd was a mother who endured much suffering after an oppressive government imprisoned her son. Today, many fathers, like Umm Dāwūd, have lost their sons after they moved to a Western country and fell into their prison of whims and passions. Those fathers strive to save their sons in the same way that Umm Dāwūd struggled to save hers.

Another act of worship a parent can do on behalf of their child is to regularly perform a special prayer called the Prayer of the Children. This prayer consists of two rakaʿāt: Sūrat al-Qadr is read after Sūrat al-Fātiḥah in the first rakʿāh, and in the second rakʿāh, Sūrat al-Kawthar is read after Sūrat al-Fātiḥah. Prayer of the Children is performed at night and during the day for the parents. Moreover, it is always also beneficial for parents to repeat this verse:

---

[26] Sūrat Hūd, Verse 42.

﴿رَبَّنَا هَبْ لَنَا مِنْ أَزْوَاجِنَا وَذُرِّيَّاتِنَا قُرَّةَ أَعْيُنٍ وَاجْعَلْنَا لِلْمُتَّقِينَ إِمَامًا﴾

﴿rabbanā hab lanā min 'azwājinā wa-dhurriyyātinā qurrata 'a'yunin wa-j'alnā li-l-muttaqīna 'imāma^{n}*﴾*

﴿'Our Lord! Give us joy and comfort in our spouses and offspring, and make us imāms of the Godwary.'﴾[27]

30. Persistence in the Spiritual Journey

Many of us strive to attain a marriage like that of Prophet Muḥammad ﷺ to the Mother of the Believers, Sayyidah Khadījah ؑ, or like that of Imām 'Alī ؑ to his wife Sayyidah Fāṭimah al-Zahrā' ؑ, but how many of us are successful in attaining that? The house of Imām 'Alī ؑ was the most honorable in history, containing four of the infallible People of the Cloak (Ahl al-Kisā'). In contrast, the Prophet's ﷺ house contained only one infallible person, the Prophet ﷺ himself. When the Prophet ﷺ visited the home of Imām 'Alī ؑ, the chain was complete, and the five People of the Cloak were under one roof.

While we can never reach the status of the Prophet ﷺ and his household, if we acknowledge that fact and strive to emulate them as much as possible, we have a better chance of reaching spiritual perfection. This is because the one who realizes that the path ahead of them is long will be more steadfast in their spiritual journey, as opposed to one who thinks they have reached the peak of their spirituality, leaving them content with the status quo.

---

[27] Sūrat al-Furqān, Verse 74.

31. Religious Orientation

Differences in religious orientation between spouses can become a contention in their marriage. For example, a woman who strives to achieve a spiritual closeness to God ﷻ that can only be gained through adherence to precautions (*iḥtiyāṭ*) in all her actions, constant self-monitoring, and performing her night prayers. Suppose her husband is only interested in adhering to the bare minimum of his religious duties and delays his prayers until the last moment. In that case, that couple is creating an environment rife with disagreement.

When the woman from the example above wakes up in the middle of the night to perform her night prayer, her husband may object and complain that this may affect her ability to work during the day.

A new phenomenon has also arisen recently, which can lead to disagreements between spouses over differences in Marjiʿ al-Taqlīd (religious authority). Even though taqlīd is a matter of personal conviction, this has nothing to do with marital life.

Sure, one can discuss why they believe their spouse should reconsider the Marjaʿ they follow, but if their spouse is not convinced, they should let them continue with the Marjaʿ of their choosing.

32. Careful Balancing and Minding the Parameters

Generally, Islām calls for women to limit their contact with men and vice versa. However, due to compelling circumstances, a woman sometimes has to deal with men in the public sphere.

When this is the case, it is necessary to be mindful of the parameters Islām sets for dealing with the opposite sex.

Interaction between non-married men and women should only be to the extent that serves the purpose of their interaction and fulfills that obligation, not more than is required. It is like starving, where eating dead animals (not lawfully slaughtered) becomes permissible, yet they should only eat enough to keep them alive.

It has been narrated that the Prophet ﷺ said:

> "Certainly, when a man is alone with a woman (who is not his wife or otherwise forbidden to him in marriage), Shayṭān is their third."[28]

Shayṭān will not give up until he gets them involved in sin or vice. Therefore, wise person protects themselves and avoids putting themselves in those situations first!

A faithful woman should take our Sayyidah Fāṭimah ؑ as her role model. Sayyidah Fāṭimah ؑ said:

> "Nothing is better for a woman than for her not to see a [stranger] man and for him not to see her."[29]

For this is the natural state.

[28] al-Shawkānī, Muḥammad b. ʿAlī, *Nayl al-Awṭār Sharḥ Muntaqa al-Akhbār*, Vol. 9, p. 227.

[29] al-Mīrzā al-Nūrī, *Mustadrak al-Wasā'il wa-Mustanbaṭ al-Masā'il*, Vol. 14, p. 289, ḥadīth 16741.

33. A Good Upbringing

A father who wants to raise righteous children should not think only of his material happiness and of enjoying a woman's beauty and wealth but should choose a wife with a good, righteous upbringing.

When one wants to buy agricultural land, one will likely consider two important factors: the fertility of the land and the abundance of its water. If a person sees land adorned with seasonal flowers and roses - which are only alive for a short period - and buys that land based on its seasonal beauty, they will buy land that is not fertile in the long term. Therefore, just as one who wants to grow crops should buy fertile land, one who wants righteous offspring should marry a righteous woman. There is a narration that the Prophet ﷺ said:

> "Beware of a nice plant growing in waste."

When asked to elaborate, the Prophet ﷺ answered:

> "A beautiful woman brought up in a bad family."[30]

Some plants grow on top of animal manure, and while they may look nice, they are rooted in waste. A believer should never be deceived by a beautiful exterior and overlook the ugliness of what is inside!

---

[30] Nayshābūrī, Muḥammad b. Ḥasan al-Fattāl, *Rawḍat al-Wā'iẓīn wa Baṣīrat al-Mutta'iẓīn*, Vol. 2, p. 375.

34. The Correct View

One of the most common complaints from women is that their husbands look at other women when they are out in public together. Unfortunately, in some cases, the woman may neglect her appearance and not fulfill her marital duties. Thus, she may tacitly encourage her husband to look at other women.

When a woman beautifies herself for everyone - whether when attending a wedding or family gathering - except for her poor husband, who may only see her in her kitchen-stained or ragged clothes, it is only natural for him to seek that beauty outside the home!

When some women enter a state of increased religiosity and grow spiritually and culturally, they reduce their intimate relationship to animalistic actions, leading the husband to distance himself from home. Therefore, we must examine these issues and view them from different angles. We must remember that every action to seek God's ﷻ pleasure is holy, even if it appears otherwise on the exterior.

35. The Islāmic Approach

God ﷻ wants His servants to follow the path of marriage, and the narrations that urge believers to marry are numerous. Suppose a person shows reluctance to get married or avoids marriage altogether for the sake of freeing themselves for worship. In that case, they are straying from the Islāmic approach and the practices of the Prophet ﷺ.

It is known that a believer becomes closer to God ﷻ when he enters the blessed family establishment of marriage. It has been narrated that Imām Ja'far al-Ṣādiq ؑ said:

> "Three women came to the Messenger of God ﷺ; one said: my husband does not eat meat, another said: my husband does not use perfume, and another said: my husband does not approach me.
>
> Then, (protesting the men's behavior), he, ﷺ, hastily went to the pulpit and, after praising God, ﷻ said:
>
>> "What has happened to some groups of my followers that they do not eat meat, do not use perfume, and avoid approaching their wives?... Surely, I eat meat, use perfume, and approach my wives, so he who turns away from my way of life is not of me."[31]

36. Excellence and Superiority

When a couple discusses family issues that may arise, dialogue should be meaningful, logical, and aimed at reaching solutions. It should not be just for argument or to prove one's victory over the other!

A man has been given guardianship when managing family affairs, but his wife may be superior to him in intellect and logic!

---

[31] Majlisī, 'Allamah Muḥammad Bāqir, *Biḥār al-Anwār*, Vol. 22, p. 124, ḥadīth 94.

Women have shown better understanding, accuracy, and intellect than men in some fields. Reason, logic, and human thought are not exclusive to men or women. That is why when some men who hold a position of importance want to consult someone regarding an issue, they often consult their wives, who may lack formal education but are naturally logical, reasonable, and analytical. Reason cannot be obtained with a college degree.

37. Consequences of Actions

Some marry hoping that God ﷻ will make them richer, as He promised to do so in the Noble Qur'ān:

﴿إِن يَكُونُوا۟ فُقَرَآءَ يُغْنِهِمُ ٱللَّهُ مِن فَضْلِهِۦ ۗ وَٱللَّهُ وَٰسِعٌ عَلِيمٌ﴾

﴿'in yakūnū fuqarā'a yughnihimu llāhu min faḍlihī wa-llāhu wāsi'un 'alīmun﴾

﴿If they are poor, God will enrich them out of His grace, and God is Bounteous, Knowing﴾[32]

However, they may never attain those riches as marriage is a single factor in the many that determine one's wealth and is contingent on the level of sin that those seeking it engage in.

The consequences of our actions appear in this life (before barzakh) and in the hereafter. Those actions not only affect a person, but as some narrations state, they can even affect their natural surroundings.

[32] Sūrat al-Nūr, Verse 32.

Some of the consequences of our actions, be they positive or negative, include some sins that have negative consequences; a house in which the Qur'ān is recited appears to people in Heaven as stars that light up the night just as the stars light up for people on earth, a believer who sins during the day could be deprived of the ability to perform the night prayer which would then lead to a decrease in their sustenance, and affection and compassion between a couple is taken away as a result of their sins. As such, each action affects a person's life and manifests in this life and the hereafter.

38. Consequences of Extravagance and Waste

The consequence of extravagance and waste has two dimensions: material and moral. Extravagance not only leads to poverty but to brotherhood with Shayṭān! Despite the severity of this consequence, it is not enough for some people, who may forget about its consequences as soon they become enamored with its glitz.

Therefore, transcending the material world is the primary remedy to avoid wasteful and extravagant. This will only happen once a person undergoes an internal change and reaches a state of asceticism in which they turn away from materialism.

When a couple can reach this state and agree upon a conceptual vision in which none of what others have impressed them, as long as they have what they need, their vision will become practical behavior that manifests in their contentment with life. In that state, the couple will avoid falling into extravagance and waste and close one of the doors, leading to decreased sustenance.

39. Softening the Heart

When a person falls into a conflict with another person and engages in an internal struggle to be good to those who have harmed them - as in the verse that mentions repelling an evil deed with one that is better- the animosity between them will turn into a close friendship. Accordingly, the Lord of the Worlds will soften their hearts towards each other, a feat not beyond the ability of the Merciful, who holds the hearts of his servants in his hands.

This can be likened to a sailboat that can cut through the water on its own, albeit slowly. When the winds pick up in the direction the sailboat is headed, it moves much faster!

When a believing man and woman disagree and have practiced the principle of repelling an evil deed with one which is better, they would not need to go to court or refer to experts because the Lord of the Worlds will resolve the issue between them.

40. The Moral Dimension

The way to keep the spark in a marriage alive and raging is to emphasize its moral dimension, thereby creating the tranquility, affection, and compassion pointed to in the Noble Qur'ān and knowing that the relationship is eternal.

A believer's relationship with a non-believing woman, no matter how beautiful she may be, is a temporary one because it ends at the time of death - when she would be destined for Hell and him for Heaven. On the other hand, when a believing man and a woman form a relationship, God ﷻ will reunite them on Judgement Day, as He promised in the Qur'ān:

﴿وَٱلَّذِينَ ءَامَنُواْ وَٱتَّبَعَتۡهُمۡ ذُرِّيَّتُهُم بِإِيمَٰنٍ أَلۡحَقۡنَا بِهِمۡ ذُرِّيَّتَهُمۡ وَمَآ أَلَتۡنَٰهُم مِّنۡ عَمَلِهِم مِّن شَيۡءٖۚ كُلُّ ٱمۡرِيِٕۭ بِمَا كَسَبَ رَهِينٞ﴾

﴿wa-lladhīna 'āmanū wa-ttaba'athum dhurriyyatuhum bi-'īmānin 'alḥaqnā bihim dhurriyyatahum wa-mā 'alatnāhum min 'amalihim min shay'in﴾

﴿The faithful and their descendants who followed them in faith—We will make their descendants join them, and We will not stint anything from [the reward of] their deeds﴾[33]

Believers will also ask for their servants to join them. Therefore, one who views his wife as an eternal friend instead of a friend in this life only, as well as his immortal life partner, not a life partner in this world only, will undoubtedly form a deeper relationship with his wife, and the attraction between them will increase.

41. The Nature of Women

As most women naturally have more free time than men and are not as predisposed to daily problems, they tend to be more influential in marital life than their husbands. This is because a man usually has dozens of pressing matters, such as problems at work, issues with those around him, personal worries, and family life. On the other hand, the wife's attention is usually focused on family matters. As such, having more mental free space than men combined with the emotional composition that distinguishes her from a man enables a woman to play an effective role in the family.

[33] Sūrat al-Ṭūr, Verse 21.

The verse:

﴿أَوَمَن يُنَشَّؤُاْ فِي ٱلۡحِلۡيَةِ وَهُوَ فِي ٱلۡخِصَامِ غَيۡرُ مُبِينٖ﴾

﴿'a-wa-man yunashsha'u fī l-ḥilyati wa-huwa fī l-khiṣāmi ghayru mubīn^in^﴾

﴿'What! One who is brought up amid ornaments and is inconspicuous in contests?'﴾[34]

shows that a woman was not created to feud and engage in rivalry and can, therefore, be an element of absorption for family trauma.

42. The Major Guardianship

A believing mother, with her significant role in the fulfillment of God's ﷻ, will for the existence of one of His servants, the physical and mental harm she endures during her pregnancy, the pains of labor and childbirth, the two years of breastfeeding, and the great effort she spends in caring for and educating her child until they are independent, God ﷻ, the Appreciative, the Rewarder of good works, appreciates her efforts.

Women have to appreciate this advantage and gift they have been given. The child is attributed to her; she is their mother, but God ﷻ is the real owner. If a mother asks God ﷻ for His help in attaining spiritual perfection, as she was a reason for the existence of one of His servants whom she cared for as a fetus in her womb and an infant in her lap, and asks her Lord that He similarly nurtures her soul with care and education, for she too is a like a fetus in the

---

[34] Sūrat al-Zukhruf, Verse 18.

world of souls lacking perfection, beauty, functional organs, as well as being a distorted soul; if she pleaded to God ﷻ in this way, then she will be put under the Major Guardianship!

43. Ways of Care

During their wives' pregnancy, some husbands limit their care to the fetus's health by paying attention only to the mother's nutrition and medical follow-ups. This is necessary but without exaggeration. However, besides the health aspects, they should not lose sight of the other dimension, which is to perform the recommended Islāmic actions and etiquette for the pregnancy period.

There are some who, as soon as they hear the news of pregnancy, become engrossed in thinking about this child who will take many years of their life. They pray a two-unit prayer and ask God ﷻ, as He knows their child better than them and knows better how their child will turn out. If the child turns out to be an enemy of God ﷻ, then they do not need them, but if the child is one of God's servants and He loves them, they ask God ﷻ to bless their child.

Increasing supplications and recommended actions during pregnancy, specifically by the mother, will significantly affect a child's righteousness. It would not hurt for expecting parents to commit to performing the Prayer for Children during pregnancy, hoping that God ﷻ will grant them their wishes for a righteous child.

44. The Manifestation of Divine Compassion

A mother manifests God's ﷻ compassion for His servants, and man cannot show this great, giving being what it deserves. How beautiful it is for one to feel the tenderness and affection given by their mother since their conception! She is the one who gives the nutrition and minerals of her body to the embryo through the placenta, causing her to feel fatigue, weakness, and sometimes to suffer illnesses.

When the child comes into this world, they are put on their mother's chest and feel comforted by her heartbeat, which they became familiar with when they were close to her heart, turning in her stomach. Remembering that stage in a man's life, that first stage that took nine months and the years of effort spent in caring and teaching is necessary to achieve a true state of thanksgiving and gratitude for the status of a mother.

45. The Prince of the Body

Shayṭān runs through our daily lives as blood runs through our veins. He has a role in breaking up the marital nest, especially if the husband and wife guide society. This sacred structure is the goal of Shayṭān and his soldiers; destroying it would make him very happy! This is because this couple is an element of guidance for a large segment of society, and by influencing them, Shayṭān would relieve himself from having to tempt many others. This is why the more faith, education, and access to education and knowledge that one has, the more significant Shayṭān's attack on them will be.

Shayṭān's attacks often come as whispering, temptation, and finding hurdles and impediments to continuing a righteous path.

Shayṭān has no authority over the body parts, but he can enter the heart, which is his desired goal. The heart is the prince of the body, and if it is possible for Shayṭān to enter this emirate, he would have reached his goal.

46. Polluting the Inner-Self

There are those whom Shayṭān tempts into looking at the forbidden, justifying that they are immune from sin because they are married. However, the effects of those looks are far more profound than one might think. The eye is not just a device that captures images; some interactions happen in the soul beyond the images.

Excessive looking at forbidden changes a person's mental and psychological composition. This, in turn, reflects on behavior and can cause one to become obsessed with desires. They begin looking at things around them in a way tailored to that obsession and turn away from what is allowed to them as it no longer fits their new standard.

How much does this look, committed without much thought, contribute to the pollution of the inner self? Once the soul is polluted, it is not easy to purify. It is like a pure water tank; if we add black ink, would it easily return to being pure? A small amount of ink can pollute a large tank of water. What a consequence!

A person must be conscientious about his soul's clarity and purity and not contaminate it with their hands!

47. The Influence of Society

No matter how much effort a person puts into raising righteous offspring, such as adhering to the worship and etiquette of the wedding night, the acts encouraged when breastfeeding, and the methods of discipline, the possibility of a child deviating from the righteous path remains. This results from the child being influenced by society outside the family, such as school, media outlets, television, etc. Therefore, it would be wrong for parents to rely only on their efforts in disciplining and raising their children. We do not know precisely what happened to the son of God's ﷻ prophet, Nūḥ ﷺ. He is one of God's ﷻ great prophets. Indeed, he did not neglect or fall short of raising and disciplining his son, yet he was still worried about guiding and saving his son even as he was drowning, as mentioned in the Noble Qur'ān:

﴿وَنَادَىٰ نُوحٌ ٱبْنَهُۥ وَكَانَ فِي مَعْزِلٍ يَٰبُنَيَّ ٱرْكَب مَّعَنَا وَلَا تَكُن مَّعَ ٱلْكَٰفِرِينَ﴾

﴿wa-nādā nūḥun-i bnahū wa-kāna fī ma'zilin yā-bunayya rkab ma'anā wa-lā takun ma'a l-kāfirīna﴾

﴿Noah called out to his son, who stood aloof, 'O my son! 'Board with us, and do not be with the faithless!'﴾[35]

Those bad friends were the reason that led him to deviate from his father's righteous path!

[35] Sūrat Hūd, Verse 42.

48. Bringing Joy to the Imām ؑ

Our Imāms ؑ used to send gifts and keep ties with their cousins who opposed their views. Their companions also did the same. Dāwūd al-Raqqi said:

> "I was sitting in the company of Imām Ja'far al-Ṣādiq ؑ when the Imām started speaking and said:
>
> > "O Dāwūd, on Thursday, the report of your deeds was presented to me, and I saw among your deeds the action you have done for your cousin; I was very pleased. However, I know that your action to try to maintain ties with him will cause his early death (because he insists on severing those ties)."[36]

Dāwūd's simple action, sending money to his destitute cousin who used to bear enmity towards him, brought joy and pleasure to the heart of Imām Ṣādiq ؑ. Let us also bring joy and happiness to the heart of our Awaited Imām ؑ with whatever kind of speech or action we can towards relatives and strangers.

49. Cultural Compatibility

When choosing a wife, a man should consider her cultural and religious compatibility. Suppose a man wishes to achieve a distinct level of closeness to God ﷻ, increase his knowledge and certainty, and does not want to limit himself to superficial worship. In that case, he must choose a wife who suits his religious orientation and culture.

---

[36] Majlisī, 'Allamah Muḥammad Bāqir, *Biḥār al-Anwār*, Vol. 71, p. 93, ḥadīth 20.

A wife is a life partner and a helper on the path of guidance and piety. A man could be afflicted with a wife who mocks his worship and knowledge-seeking and invites him to participate with her in some falsehoods broadcast these days on various media outlets. It would be enough for the woman to want perfection and closeness to God ﷻ, even if she has not attained perfection. With God's ﷻ blessings and her husband's effort, this wife can ascend to high knowledge and practical perfection.

50. Appreciativeness

The Lord of the Worlds ﷻ is appreciative and a reward for good deeds. He wanted you to be a human being on the face of the earth and gave you two parents who put up with so much from you. So, you must treat them well, despite their ignorance, lack of awareness, and knowledge of the rules and methods of discipline and education, etc. It is enough that they are your parents!

It is not a source of pride to be good to parents distinguished in knowledge and faith because being of service to them is in response to their faithfulness. However, the utmost perfection is to strip your parents of all qualities and give them one simple attribute: being your parents! After committing to this truth, you can recognize their attributes, such as faith, knowledge, love of Ahl al-Bayt ؑ, and the other attributes of perfection.

51. Mental Images

One usually interacts with others based on the mental image they create for each person. This image can be either positive or negative and, in most cases, does not match reality. For each person we deal with, we create a mental file of judgments and perceptions that becomes the basis of how we interact with them. Often, a person is not consciously aware of this file, but their actions are automatically issued according to it.

A believer should be able to look at things with an eye that is as close to reality as possible. They ask God ﷻ to show them what matters to Him. They ask for the blurriness to be removed from their sight so they can see the reality of the people they interact with daily, such as their spouse, children, parents, brothers and sisters, relatives, and neighbors. A believer should persist in asking: "My God, show me things as they are."

52. Marriage: An Easy Target for Shayṭān

One of the weakest links that Shayṭān can exploit is marriage! He tries to manipulate the believer initially, but the believer might notice and begin monitoring Shayṭān's tricks. However, in a marriage, there are two people with their devil. The husband wants to stand up to his devil and his wife's devil. Similarly, the wife wants to face her devil and her husband's devil. While each tries to banish their devil, another one is lingering in the home! For this reason, marriage is usually an aspect of Shayṭān's rotation to lead people astray. It has been narrated in ḥadīth:

> "Had it not been that the devils hover round the hearts of the children of Ādam, they would have seen the glories of the Kingdom of Heaven."[37]

As the devils hover around the heart, they also hover around the marital home. This process makes it easy for them to hunt their prey.

[37] Majlisī, 'Allamah Muḥammad Bāqir, *Biḥār al-Anwār*, Vol. 56, p. 163.

53. Respecting Feelings

When some men get married, they want to own their wife's heart for themselves as if she has no family. He may even be jealous if his wife's relationship with her family is strong!

The husband is indeed the closest person to his wife, but it is illogical for him to compare the strength of her relationship with her family to the strength of her relationship with him. With the passing of days, their relationship will grow naturally, and he will occupy a larger share of her heart.

His jealousy is a big mistake and could lead to more distance between them. Therefore, each spouse should respect the other's feelings towards their families because those feelings, besides being instinctual, are not the result of a few days, and one who does not have loyalty to their origins cannot have loyalty to someone who was once a stranger to them!

54. Weak Emotional Relationship

Among the dangerous phenomena resulting from a family's disintegration is the weakness of the emotional relationship between children and their parents. This can manifest in not feeling personally affected or sympathetic towards each other when one party has psychological, physical, or financial problems. The Holy Prophet ﷺ and his progeny said:

> "The example of the believers in their affection, mercy, and compassion for each other is that of a body. When any limb aches, the whole body reacts with sleeplessness and fever."[38]

If a believer's relationship with other believers is supposed to be like this, how is their relationship to the origin and reason for their existence supposed to be?

In the past, a son may not marry for fear of becoming busy with his spouse and not being there for his parents, preferring to be denied his righteous offspring in hopes of being a righteous offspring to his parents. Where is this intense emotion in the hearts of children these days?

55. Previous Planning

The effort required to be blessed with righteous offspring does not start at ten when the child has already been shaped. It starts at the time of conception and planning for that time. Supplication is a crucial element in this matter. It is suitable for a woman when she gets married to keep repeating this verse:

﴿رَبَّنَا هَبْ لَنَا مِنْ أَزْوَاجِنَا وَذُرِّيَّاتِنَا قُرَّةَ أَعْيُنٍ وَاجْعَلْنَا لِلْمُتَّقِينَ إِمَامًا﴾

﴾*rabbanā hab lanā min 'azwājinā wa-dhurriyyātinā qurrata 'a'yunin wa-j'alnā li-l-muttaqīna 'imāma*ⁿ﴿

[38] Majlisī, 'Allamah Muḥammad Bāqir, *Biḥār al-Anwār*, Vol. 58, p. 150, ḥadīth 29.

﴾'Our Lord! Give us joy and comfort in our spouses and offspring, and make us imāms of the Godwary.'﴿[39]

One who repeats this supplication repeatedly, day and night, in all their actions and bowing or prostration, will likely be granted distinguished offspring. This is an answered supplication with God's ﷻ permission because it is a good request as it consists of a mother asking God ﷻ to give His representative al-Mahdi عجل الله فرجه another supporter and helper. The desire for righteous offspring needs true supplication, and some of our previous scholars were born due to their parents' blessed supplications.

56. Mental Purity

A young man living in a circle of corruption will not enjoy a happy marital life; even if his wife has all the qualities every man desires in a spouse, he cannot continue living with her. This is because when a man fills his mind with many images of various women, he begins measuring his wife against these images and does not see her as a distinguished image in comparison. As a result, disagreements quickly begin to appear between them. He is then quick to separate, not caring about social customs, his obligation for the dowry, and other matters, not even the reproach he gets from his parents.

In contrast, a righteous believer keeps his mind free from all forbidden images and remains deeply attached and committed to his wife. Such emotional images of marital life are rarely seen except with believing men and women.

[39] Sūrat al-Furqān, Verse 74.

57. Lifeboat

A righteous father is careful to make sure his son is similar to him regarding morals and reputation and tries to raise his son's level regarding his relationship with God ﷻ and his relationship with people. It has been narrated that Imām Muḥammad al-Bāqir ؑ said:

> "Among the signs of a man's happiness is that his son may be similar to him in appearance, morals, and behavior."[40]

Some fathers with a distinctive reputation of righteousness and worship are oblivious to their children and urging them towards righteousness. Prophet Nūḥ ؑ, for example, despite knowing what kind of a person his son was, said to him:

﴿يَابُنَيَّ ٱرۡكَب مَّعَنَا وَلَا تَكُن مَّعَ ٱلۡكَٰفِرِينَ﴾

﴿yā-bunayya rkab maʿanā wa-lā takun maʿa l-kāfirīnaª﴾

﴿'O my son! 'Board with us, and do not be with the faithless!'﴾[41]

This is how a believer should be! Therefore, when a father goes to the mosque, he should ask his son to accompany him and ride the proverbial lifeboat.

---

[40] Kulaynī, Shaykh Muḥammad b. Yaʿqūb, *al-Kāfī*, Vol. 6, p. 4, ḥadīth 2.

[41] Sūrat Hūd, Verse 42.

58. Equality

Jealousy is innate in humans. A believer should not do what causes strife between his children and should ensure that he gives to them equally, regardless of whether that giving is moral or material, to avoid planting spite in their hearts. Practicing inequality between one's children is one of the causes of disobedience. One must be very careful as this is one of Shayṭān's traps a person can fall into without realizing it. Our Holy Prophet ﷺ stressed the importance of equality between children. It has been narrated that he said:

> "Observe equality between your children when giving gifts, and if I were to give preference to anyone, I would give preference to the women."[42]

He also said:

> "God the Exalted likes for you to be equal between your children, even when kissing them."[43]

The Prophet ﷺ once saw a man with two children; he kissed one but left the other. The Holy Prophet said,

> "Should you not treat them equally?"[44]

---

[42] al-Shawkānī, Muḥammad b. 'Alī, *Nayl al-Awṭār Sharḥ Muntaqa al-Akhbār*, Vol. 6, p. 110.

[43] Rayshahrī, Āyatullāh Muḥammad, *Mīzān al-Ḥikmah*, Vol. 4, p. 3673.

[44] Ṭabrisī, Shaykh Faḍl b. Ḥasan, *Makārim al-Akhlāq*, p. 220.

59. Building Materials

Children are not only considered a blessing; they are also building materials. Building materials can be used to build a mosque wherein God ﷻ is remembered, or in other cases, can be used to build a nightclub full of sin. Therefore, a believer's children can be like an ongoing charity or as an enemy.

If a child is left as they are without intervention, they will 'cling heavily to the earth' (be lazy and unmotivated) because this is human nature. Working to better and perfect oneself goes against human nature and requires constant hard work. Therefore, children are a trial, a test, and without constant care, they can become an enemy, even if, in this life, they seem to seek their parents' approval and appreciate the effort and money they spend on them. This animosity might not be seen until the Day of Judgement, as God ﷻ said:

﴿ٱلْأَخِلَّآءُ يَوْمَئِذٍۭ بَعْضُهُمْ لِبَعْضٍ عَدُوٌّ إِلَّا ٱلْمُتَّقِينَ﴾

﴿al-ʾakhillāʾu yawmaʾidhin baʿḍuhum li-baʿḍin ʿaduwwun ʾillā l-muttaqīna﴾

﴿On that day, friends will be one another's enemies, except for the Godwary﴾[45]

60. The Kind Word

Some expect to see an immediate effect on others when advising and guiding them to things that are good for them. Kind words are

[45] Sūrat al-Zukhruf, Verse 67.

like a good seed that awaits suitable circumstances to germinate and grow into a beautiful plant. The one receiving the advice is often resistant and too proud to hear it, especially when angry, but will eventually calm down and return to their senses.

The kind word that stems from good intentions and concern for the guidance of others will reach its intended spot in other's souls. God ﷻ blesses some of His servants and gives their words a magical effect on others' souls. God ﷻ bestows this blessing on those who have pure hearts. How beautiful would it be for one's existence, words, and actions to be a blessing wherever they are? This is how some close to God ﷻ can change the darkest souls with a wise look or an internal signal.

61. Entering the Hearts

The best way to influence others is to reach their hearts and gain affection, as lovers are often obedient to those they love! Hence, we have to create an atmosphere of emotional bonding with those we live and interact with, especially those close to us, so it is easier for us to interact with and influence them. Otherwise, matters remain in a circle of pretense and obligation, wherein we deal with each other based on either fear or greed.

Reflect on this narration to see how much respect the Imām's ؑ servant has for him:

The Imām ؑ called his servant twice and did not get an answer, but when he answered the third time, he said:

> "My son, did you not hear my voice?

The servant answered:

> "Yes, I did".

The Imām asked:

> "Why did you not answer me?"

He replied:

> "Because I am safe from your punishment!"

The Imām said:

> "Praise belongs to God, who made my servant feel safe with me!"[46]

62. The Exemplary Wife

Among the outstanding qualities of al-Zahrā' ﷺ was her keenness to be the perfect wife to Imām 'Alī ﷺ despite all of the hardships and difficulties that can come with marriage. She did not let her relationship with the Prophet ﷺ, Imām 'Alī ﷺ or Imāms al-Ḥasan and al-Ḥusayn ﷺ become an excuse for her to shirk her responsibility to be the best wife to her husband. Upon contemplating the following narration, one cannot help but be overwhelmed with tenderness due to what she took upon herself. Imām 'Alī ﷺ said about her:

> "She used to fill the water skin from the well until her back was affected, she milled with the quern-stone until her

[46] *al-Manāqib*, Vol. 4, p. 157.

> hands developed calluses, swept the house until her clothes became dusty, and lit the fire under the cooking pots until her clothes darkened, and she suffered great harm from all of this."[47]

63. Prayer for Someone in their Absence

A believing woman can bring a man back to his senses using prayers and successful teaching methods. A woman who is involved with an unrighteous husband should increase her prayers for him in his absence.

The path of divine intervention is always open, and a person's heart is between two of God's ﷻ fingers, and He is Merciful. This is why we were instructed to recite the duʿāʾ:

> "O' God, O' Turner of the hearts, make our hearts firm upon your religion."

Note how the duʿāʾ uses the plural "hearts," which tells us that all hearts can be turned, even sinful ones. God ﷻ filled the Pharaoh's heart with kindness towards Mūsā ؑ when he was young. He ﷻ also brought together the hearts of a woman and her husband and increased their love for each other after she complained to the Messenger of God ﷺ about her husband.

[47] Majlisī, ʿAllamah Muḥammad Bāqir, *Biḥār al-Anwār*, Vol. 82, p. 329, ḥadīth 7.

64. Necessity of Separation

When we review history, we see that Fāṭimah al-Zahrāʾ ☖ used to stress the necessity of maintaining an emotional and physical separation between women and men through actions and speech. This could be understood from her saying:

> "Women should not see [foreign] men, and to not be seen by men."[48]

She is also known to have observed the ḥijāb in the presence of a blind man because although he was blind, he still had his sense of smell! She was also delighted that Imām ʿAlī ☖ took it upon himself to care for all household matters outside the home so she would not have to mingle with men. All these actions were her way of teaching us the ills and lapses that can come from the mingling of men and women.

Sayyidah Fāṭimah al-Zahrāʾ ☖ was above being affected by these matters, for she was concerned with what turned her away from this life and that which is in it; she was the best example for the words Imām ʿAlī ☖ used to describe God-conscious people:

> "They accompanied this world with their bodies, while their souls are attached to the heavens."[49]

---

[48] al-Mīrzā al-Nūrī, *Mustadrak al-Wasāʾil wa-Mustanbaṭ al-Masāʾil*, Vol. 14, p. 289, ḥadīth 16741.

[49] Majlisī, ʿAllamah Muḥammad Bāqir, *Biḥār al-Anwār*, Vol. 30, p. 81.

65. The Fruits of Marriage

The most important fruit of marriage is to be blessed with righteous progeny, as it is an eternal blessing. On the other hand, the enjoyment and preoccupation with beauty and companionship in marital life as we know it has a limit, like other things in this life, which ends at the time of the grave and the intermediary world (Barzakh). What remains with a person in Barzakh and on the day of judgment is that which relates to their progeny, as it was narrated:

> "When a human being dies, his deeds come to an end except for three: an ongoing charity, beneficial knowledge, and a righteous child who prays for them."[50]

Hence, working hard to bring up a righteous, disciplined child who will pray for you after your death is one of the best investments. This child could also begin a chain of children and grandchildren until the day of judgment and whose righteousness stems from that first grandchild.

66. Inheritance of Moral Qualities

Though not proven by science as with physical traits, the inheritance of moral qualities is clear through experience and observation. In some families, the emergence of specific traits in all its members is noticeable. For example, some families are known to be sharp, others to be kind, while others are still known for their courage and bravery.

---

[50] *al-Mu'tabar*, Vol. 1, p. 1341.

When Imām ʿAlī ﷺ asked his brother ʿAqīl to find him a wife, he requested that she be born into a family known for their bravery so that she would give him a brave, courageous son who would be there to support his other son, the Master of the Martyrs, Imām al-Ḥusayn ﷺ. This request was also made to show us that these moral traits are hereditary. Therefore, when choosing a wife, a man should seek a woman who will give him righteous offspring and not look only at her physical beauty.

67. Inferior View

Among the causes of disobedience towards one's parents is having an inferior view of them. When one has a mental image of a perfect parent whose characteristics include the highest degrees of piety, righteousness, knowledge, and worship, they can develop negative emotions towards their parents, who may lack those qualities. While we may try to internalize those feelings, they can eventually reflect externally on our behavior, leading us not to give our parents the kindness and respect they deserve.

When God ﷻ says in this verse:

﴿وَإِن جَٰهَدَاكَ عَلَىٰٓ أَن تُشۡرِكَ بِي مَا لَيۡسَ لَكَ بِهِۦ عِلۡمٞ فَلَا تُطِعۡهُمَاۖ وَصَاحِبۡهُمَا فِي ٱلدُّنۡيَا مَعۡرُوفٗاۖ وَٱتَّبِعۡ سَبِيلَ مَنۡ أَنَابَ إِلَيَّۚ ثُمَّ إِلَيَّ مَرۡجِعُكُمۡ فَأُنَبِّئُكُم بِمَا كُنتُمۡ تَعۡمَلُونَ﴾

﴾wa-ʾin jāhadāka ʿalā ʾan tushrika bī mā laysa laka bihī ʿilmun fa-lā tuṭiʿhumā wa-ṣāḥibhumā fī d-dunyā maʿrūfan wa-ttabiʿ sabīla man ʾanāba ʾilayya thumma ʾilayya marjiʿukum fa-ʾunabbiʾukum bi-mā kuntum taʿmalūna[a]﴿

﴿But if they urge you to ascribe to Me as partner that of which you have no knowledge, then do not obey them. Keep their company honourably in this world and follow the way of those who turn to Me penitently. Then to Me will be your return, whereat I will inform you concerning what you used to do﴾[51]

He refers to the necessity of giving our parents their right to respect and kindness based on being your parents alone, not based on their faith and worship and not based on any mistakes they made while raising you, it is enough that they are your parents!

68. The Philosophy of Life

Not understanding the philosophy of life can lead to the demolition of marriage, specifically not understanding that this life is a farm for the hereafter and that a believer sows in this life what they wish to reap in the hereafter.

These days, a materialistic view of enjoying and delighting in the pleasures of life prevails. On this basis, we transform every relationship, whether with people, nature, or the environment, into a thing and an element of pleasure. Some fish migrate in the seas from one area to another, and as soon as they lay their eggs, they die, and their responsibility ends. Those eggs then hatch, and small fish emerge to continue the cycle of life. This is not how it is supposed to be with the children of Ādam! A father's role is not supposed to be relegated to contributing to the birth of his children and then becoming a source for the family's material and financial needs!

---

[51] Sūrat Luqmān, Verse 15.

69. Good Manners

It would be a great loss for a man to live with a woman for a long time in a life closer to individuality than marriage—a life where both are only concerned with themselves. After years together, the man is surprised that his wife left him and went on to marry a righteous man!

In the narrations of Ahl al-Bayt, if a woman marries more than one man throughout her life, then in the hereafter, she is united with the one who was the best to her and had the best manners. So, while her first husband could be serving his punishment in Hell, she could live in complete bliss with her righteous husband in Heaven!

It was narrated that Umm Ḥabībah, the Prophet's wife, asked:

> "O Messenger of God, a woman who had two husbands in this life, then they all die and are gathered in Heaven, which of the husbands would she be married to, the first or the last?..."

The Prophet replied:

> "To the who had better manners with her, Umm Ḥabībah, a person who has good manners attains the goodness of this world and the hereafter."[52]

---

[52] ʿAlī al-Haythamī, *Majmaʿ al-Zawāʾid* Vol. 8, p. 24.

70. Applying Capabilities

Among the guarantees of a happy marital life, in addition to the dimension of faith, is holding dialogue sessions to discuss family matters. Unfortunately, only some pay attention to this aspect.

The husband could be the manager of a big company and hold daily meetings to discuss obstacles and aspirations relating to that company. However, he has yet to meet his wife to discuss and plan how to deal with their children according to their stages of development from childhood, adolescence, and youth! The husband and wife could be highly educated and enjoy great mental capability, yet, unfortunately, they need to apply those skills to build a family.

71. Gracious Separation

A very negative phenomenon that can happen when disagreements arise between spouses, especially when the conflict intensifies to the level of divorce, is the intentional exposure of each other's flaws and the disclosure of marital secrets to outside parties. With their attempts to expose the other spouse, they expose themselves to their community. This is such bad behavior that is not befitting of a believer.

A couple should either stay together in a good manner or separate graciously! Blessed is the couple that has no choice but to divorce, yet the husband extends a valuable gift to his wife and promises not to mention her negatively, and she promises him the same. Each of them absolves the other of any rights lost and ignored during their marriage, and they pray for each other.

72. The Challenge

One of the results of disagreements between spouses is the desire to challenge the other to hurt and irritate them, regardless of whether it was done in sin or not. The husband might prevent a mother from seeing her children, despite knowing that it is her right and that the Noble Qur'ān forbids such action as God ﷻ says:

﴿لَا تُضَآرَّ وَٰلِدَةُۢ بِوَلَدِهَا وَلَا مَوْلُودٌ لَّهُۥ بِوَلَدِهِۦ﴾

﴿lā tuḍārra wālidatun bi-waladihā wa-lā mawlūdun lahū bi-waladihī﴾

﴿neither the mother shall be made to suffer harm on her child's account, nor the father on account of his child﴾[53]

Yet the husband insists on doing this only to break the mother's heart. Similarly, the wife, knowing her husband's sensitivity and jealousy, uses her ḥijāb to instigate him.

It is such a disaster when one uses the religion card, disobeys God ﷻ, and buys their way into the Hellfire to irritate and get back at another person! Humans commit the worst actions when the brain stops working, even if they lead to their demise.

73. Meaningful Dialogue

Meaningful dialogue is an essential element in raising and guiding a teenager. We notice that youth in this age range have a broad knowledge and analytical ability in politics, economy, and culture.

[53] Sūrat al-Baqarah, Verse 233.

As today's arena is full of imported ideas, cultural distortions, and misused mercurial concepts, it is necessary to extend a hand to the youth who live in a small amount of intellectual confusion that comes with their intellectual freedom.

Helping our youth is done by having patient, open-minded discussions. Confrontation and accusations of deviation or disbelief will only lead to stubbornness and blind adherence to those concepts as a means of challenge and provocation. A narration that demonstrates this is:

> "Do not raise your children the way you were raised, as they were created for a different time."[54]

74. Strongholds of Steadfastness

It is no secret that everything around us has become ground for deviation and corruption, as God ﷻ says:

﴿ظَهَرَ ٱلْفَسَادُ فِي ٱلْبَرِّ وَٱلْبَحْرِ بِمَا كَسَبَتْ أَيْدِي ٱلنَّاسِ لِيُذِيقَهُم بَعْضَ ٱلَّذِي عَمِلُوا۟ لَعَلَّهُمْ يَرْجِعُونَ﴾

﴿ẓahara l-fasādu fī l-barri wa-l-baḥri bi-mā kasabat ʾaydī n-nāsi li-yudhīqahum baʿḍa lladhī ʿamilū laʿallahum yarjiʿūn﴾

﴿Corruption has appeared in land and sea because of the doings of the people's hands, that He may make them taste something of what they have done, so that they may come back﴾[55]

[54] Ibn Abi l-Ḥadīd, *Sharḥ Nahj al-Balāgha*, Vol. 20, p. 267, wisdom 102.

[55] Sūrat al-Rūm, Verse 41.

This is the current state of our schools with their curricula and atmosphere, and the state of our streets and markets, not to mention the satellite channels and the internet. The only thing that remains is the family fortress, and if its members surrendered to the encompassing cultural invasion, it would be the fall of the last stronghold of steadfastness. Is it logical for the fortresses' guardian to buy the means of association with the outside world without censoring the corruption it brings, only to carry the burden of its consequences in this world before the hereafter?

75. Rules of Interaction

One should take courses through books or other means and educate themselves on how to best deal with their spouse and children. With this knowledge, one can find a suitable method for each person at different stages in life.

Sticking to one approach when dealing with everyone will not net the desired results; what works with a child will not work for an adolescent, and what works with a teenager will not work with someone in their twenties and beyond. The same is true when dealing with one's wife; interacting with her during the engagement period differs from interacting with her after marriage, and interactions during pregnancy differ from after delivery. Different approaches are needed in one month based on a woman's needs. Therefore, knowledge of the appropriate rules and methods in interactions and education is necessary to ensure the continuity of a happy marital life.

76. The Mind

A woman's university major is not one of the requirements needed to have a successful and happy marriage. What is required, though, is intellect. It has been reported in the narrations:

> "The mind is what the Merciful is worshiped with, and the heavens are acquired."[56]

A sensible, wise woman is one who, when directed to a mistake she is not aware of, is not arrogant and takes the advice she is given. When it is said to her: this is unlawful backbiting, or this is unlawful food, or this dress does not fit the Islāmic description for ḥijāb, or that it is not allowed for you to hit your child, she listens with an open mind and corrects her position. This is the wise woman, even if she holds educational degrees, while the woman careless about acting according to the Islāmic rules is of no weight even if she holds the highest levels of specialization and degrees!

77. The Gift

When the Noble Qur'ān refers to the request of the prophets and others for good offspring, the word "gift" is often used. This means that the person does not ask God ﷻ for this because they are entitled to it but because they want God ﷻ to bestow it upon them out of His generosity.

No matter how hard one works to get their wishes, sometimes things we hope for are out of our hands! How great was the gift

[56] al-Ḥurr al-ʿĀmilī, Shaykh Muḥammad b. al-Ḥasan, *Wasāʾil al-Shīʿa*, Vol. 15, p. 205,

bestowed upon Ibrāhīm when given Ismāʿīl, Zakariya when given Yahya, and Maryam with a son like ʿĪsā 🖿? How appropriate it is then for us to insist on asking to be given a child who will help reform Muslims in the future, for the helpers are few for this religion that has returned to being as foreign as it was when it began!

78. Different Methods of Upbringing

One of the causes of corruption in children is a disagreement between their parents about methods of discipline and upbringing. It is a grave mistake for one parent to play the role of the compassionate, merciful parent who spoils the children while the other takes on the unpleasant, strict role. A child will naturally feel closer to the first parent and, as a result, will develop a distance and an aversion to the second parent from a young age.

It is important to adopt a method that falls between the two roles, between spoiling the child and being harsh and strict, as each method has pros and cons. It is also important to note that a child's needs differ at each life stage, and the methods used must reflect that.

Another thing to be mindful of is distinguishing between mistakes that will not necessarily lead to the child doing something ḥarām and mistakes that will eventually lead to ḥarām. When dealing with the first type of mistake, it is sufficient to advise and guide a child gently, while parents need to stand firmly and forcefully when dealing with the second type; otherwise, the child might not realize the gravity of committing ḥarām and the small mistakes they make as a child could lead to a disaster of a mistake when they are older.

79. Weak Excuses

Some women reject marriage proposals they receive, despite the man being a good believer, for no good reason. They justify it with the excuse that they did not like him based on the first impression. The first impression is not a scale to judge someone; maybe the young man did not show the necessary friendliness, or maybe she was going through a hard time that affected her emotional state and led her to see things in a negative light.

Rejecting a believer for no good reason could harm one's life. It could mean a delay in getting married, or even being deprived of that blessing, and feeling regretful whenever she remembers the believers she has turned away. What a loss! She may have lost the chance to marry a religious believer when they were very few.

80. Globalization

The deviant behavior seen in today's youth, which includes running away from home and complaining about their parents to the courts, is a natural result of cultural globalization and the poisoning of thoughts with deviant cultures.

Just as spiritual perfection is a gradual ascension of the soul to a level where man transcends the level of angels, deviancy is its descent into an abyss where man becomes on a level lower than beasts. This issue does not remain confined to the family but goes beyond and affects the community where the parents' reputation is lost, causing them to lose the respect they once had. This is especially true if the parents had an educational and missionary role in the community because it may be said that if they could educate, their children would not be so bad!

81. Extending the Sight

One of the leading causes of problems between married couples is coveting what others have. For example, a wife who is not content with what she has asks her husband to provide her with what others have, and if he cannot fulfill her wishes, a disagreement starts between them, eventually leading to bigger problems. All things that appeal to a person lose their sparkle after a short time, no matter how much effort one puts into acquiring them; all bliss outside of heaven will become boring!

Some seek to marry a woman and spend years waiting for this dream to come true, only to be surprised after a few nights that this life is not what they imagined: a colorful life filled with all kinds of pleasures! Hence, the lack of attachment to the pleasures of this world is the solution that saves one from all these problems!

82. Transcending One's Self

The intention has a significant impact on a person's behavior. One who serves another person to receive a reward from him will undoubtedly be hurt if they do not get the reward they expect, thus tiring themselves and others. This contradicts the person who does well-seeking nearness to God ﷻ. For example, a mother who views her son as a slave she owns because she spent energy raising him for many years will, without a doubt, create problems over the slightest things with her son's wife and interfere in everything, no matter how small or big, turning her son's life into an unbearable misery. On the other hand, a mother who cares about her son's happiness transcends herself and her ego and does not care even if her son's wife wronged her, as she does not want to burden her son with more worries. If her son is happy with his wife, then she is happy. How beautiful is this perspective, and how many problems does it solve that a person will transcend and go beyond themselves and bear the wrongs of others in the interest of those they love?

83. Respect

The first foundation of a child's upbringing is for the child to live in a state of respect towards their parents. Whoever wants to be able to influence a person, including their child, must first win over their hearts. It is okay for one to explore their child's feelings towards them, and if they find that they hold a special place in that child's heart, then they should prostrate to God ﷻ, thanking Him for this blessing.

A parent, their children, and love will not need to raise their voices or other punishments when they see their child make a mistake or commit a sin. A simple signal will suffice, such as showing the child the heartbreak and the pain their actions caused their parents. Children who love their parents and see the hurt they caused them will boycott these actions for the rest of their lives! This was the way of the Prophet ﷺ when he saw an action he disliked from his companions. He used to turn his face away to let them understand that he did not like that action. This is how Prophet Muḥammad ﷺ taught his companions; we should follow his method when teaching our children.

84. Erosion

A wife is sought for many things: sexual pleasure, reproduction, housekeeping, and companionship. We know that these things encourage the stability of family life. However, they are all susceptible to the influence of the passage of time, just as solid mountains are carved by erosion.

The need for sexual pleasure naturally decreases as time passes and a person ages! As for the need for housekeeping, we can rely on the help of maids! The need to reproduce will also lose its luster as one reaches its fill with the number of children they have!

The companionship of a beautiful woman will no longer be exciting as her beauty will become not only familiar but boring as well! Therefore, finding a solid element that will not weather away with time is necessary, and viewing your wife as someone God ﷻ entrusted you with is necessary.

85. Prerequisites

Sexual pleasure and housekeeping are not fundamental matters in marital life because they are fleeting, and a reasonable person does not hang his hopes on fleeting things. The remaining fruit of marriage is righteous offspring, which might not be truly appreciated during a child's youth as an opportunity to engage may not arise. However, when a young boy grows to be a man, one might be able to depend on his help in their old age.

How beautiful would it be to find companionship and solace in their offspring and their spouse, a companionship and solace that would remain unaffected with time? Therefore, one who wants to be blessed with righteous offspring should consider attaining the prerequisites: choosing a righteous spouse, committing to and repeating the recommended supplications, and continuous care for children.

86. The Greatness of Parental Rights

Being the cause of a child's existence is enough reason to earn a parent's right over their children. But what should a child who grew up away from their father and never felt his affection and care and whose father did not even provide for him financially do? How can such a father be proud of his son when he sees him, and what should he do as he awaits the day he gets married? Some feel like a stranger on that day, and some do not even attend the wedding as they do not feel the deep connections and belonging a biological father feels towards a son he raised. Who is the misfortunate person in this scenario? Is it the son who lived as an orphan while his father was still alive, or is it the father who lived the life of someone deprived of life's greatest pleasure, as if he was not a father when, indeed, he was given that blessing?

87. Unconscious Measuring

A man who frequently looks at women other than his wife, even without lust, and a woman who frequently talks, jokes, and deals with men other than her husband, even without it being suspicious or unconscious, begin to measure their spouse against other people. For example, when a man starts mentally comparing his wife to other women and deems the other women more beautiful, attractive, and educated, he will naturally feel an aversion to his wife upon entering his home! Similarly, a wife who deals with all kinds of men from morning to night will begin to see her husband as just another man and will not see him having that distinctive presence anymore!

88. Threats

Islāmic law dictates that men stay away from places of threat. A lustful look can be a pit, and as the narrations express, a look is one of Shayṭān's arrows, and shaking hands with a woman other than one's wife is a pit! One who falls into this pit must deal with emotional attachments, lustful thinking, and forbidden relationships. Therefore, one must not look at, shake hands with, or be alone with a woman other than his wife, and he must remember the limits of his interactions, as God ﷻ said:

﴿وَإِذَا سَأَلْتُمُوهُنَّ مَتَاعًا فَسْـَٔلُوهُنَّ مِن وَرَآءِ حِجَابٍ﴾

﴾*wa-'idhā sa'altumūhunna matā'an fa-s'alūhunna min warā'i ḥijābin*﴿

﴾*When you ask [his] womenfolk for something, do so from behind a curtain*﴿[57]

﴿إِنِ ٱتَّقَيْتُنَّ فَلَا تَخْضَعْنَ بِٱلْقَوْلِ فَيَطْمَعَ ٱلَّذِي فِي قَلْبِهِۦ مَرَضٌ وَقُلْنَ قَوْلًا مَّعْرُوفًا﴾

﴾*'ini ttaqaytunna fa-lā takhḍa'na bi-l-qawli fa-yaṭma'a lladhī fī qalbihī maraḍun wa-qulna qawlan ma'rūfan*﴿

﴾*if you are wary [of God], do not be complaisant in your speech, lest he in whose heart is a sickness should aspire; speak honourable words*﴿[58]

---

[57] Sūrat al-Aḥzāb, Verse 53.

[58] Sūrat al-Aḥzāb, Verse 32.

One should also refrain from sitting where a woman recently sat, and her body heat can still be felt; though it is not ḥarām , it is one of the precautionary measures!

89. Sayyidah Preference

One looking to choose a wife needs to note a few elements, including their appearance, morals, and hereditary characteristics. With this in mind, if a person is in a position wherein they had to choose between marrying someone who is a descendant of the Prophet ﷺ and someone who is not, there is no doubt that the progeny of Sayyidah Fāṭimah al-Zahrāʾ (عليها السلام) should be given priority, as genes will be inherited from those purified beings through the generations.

Though it is not obligatory to marry a descendant of the Prophet ﷺ, it is preferred if one is given a choice between two equal women in all other aspects. Gaining a relationship with the Prophet ﷺ through marriage is a distinguishing trait. On the day of judgment, a believer could find himself related to Sayyidah al-Zahrāʾ (عليها السلام) as she would be considered a mother to his wife. He could live in the Prophet's household (Ahl al-Bayt (عليهم السلام)).

90. A Blessing and a Test

Children are a blessing from God ﷻ on the one hand and a test on the other. The Noble Qurʾān says:

﴿وَٱعۡلَمُوٓاْ أَنَّمَآ أَمۡوَٰلُكُمۡ وَأَوۡلَٰدُكُمۡ فِتۡنَةٞ وَأَنَّ ٱللَّهَ عِندَهُۥٓ أَجۡرٌ عَظِيمٞ﴾

﴾*wa-ʿlamū ʾannamā ʾamwālukum wa-ʾawlādukum fitnatun wa-ʾanna llāha ʿindahū ʾajrun ʿaẓīm*﴿

﴾Know that your possessions and children are only a test, and that God—with Him is a great reward﴿[59]

A child could become an "ongoing charity" or an enemy. As God ﷻ says:

﴿يَٰٓأَيُّهَا ٱلَّذِينَ ءَامَنُوٓاْ إِنَّ مِنۡ أَزۡوَٰجِكُمۡ وَأَوۡلَٰدِكُمۡ عَدُوّٗا لَّكُمۡ فَٱحۡذَرُوهُمۡۚ﴾

﴾yā-'ayyuhā lladhīna 'āmanū 'inna min 'azwājikum wa-'awlādikum 'aduwwan lakum fa-ḥdharūhum﴿

﴾O you who have faith! Indeed, you have enemies among your spouses and children; so beware of them﴿[60]

And in another verse:

﴿يَٰٓأَيُّهَا ٱلَّذِينَ ءَامَنُواْ لَا تُلۡهِكُمۡ أَمۡوَٰلُكُمۡ وَلَآ أَوۡلَٰدُكُمۡ عَن ذِكۡرِ ٱللَّهِۚ وَمَن يَفۡعَلۡ ذَٰلِكَ فَأُوْلَٰٓئِكَ هُمُ ٱلۡخَٰسِرُونَ﴾

﴾yā-'ayyuhā lladhīna 'āmanū lā tulhikum 'amwālukum wa-lā 'awlādukum 'an dhikri llāhi wa-man yaf'al dhālika fa-'ulā'ika humu l-khāsirūn﴿

﴾O you who have faith! Do not let your possessions and children distract you from the remembrance of God, and whoever does that—it is they who are the losers﴿[61]

---

[59] Sūrat al-Anfāl, Verse 28.

[60] Sūrat al-Taghābun, Verse 14.

[61] Sūrat al-Munāfiqūn, Verse 9.

Therefore, children can become an enemy of the believer who loves and cares for them if they distract their parents from doing good deeds or pressure them to disobey God ﷻ or when the parent obeys their child and helps them sin, as is the case when a parent gives their child money while being fully aware that it will be spent on a sinful activity, or sends a child to a western country to study while knowing that their child will not be able to resist the corruption and deviation.

91. Not Relying on Efforts

Many factors that trigger children's deviation are outside the family sphere of influence, and there are many these days! Therefore, righteous parents should not rely on their efforts alone when raising a child but should also pray for them and take them to places with an atmosphere of worship and the mosque. Moreover, they should keep their children away from corrupt atmospheres, not throw them into the sea with their hands tied with the idea that they can swim and rescue themselves!

The very nature of being submerged in the whirlpool of the sea will lead to drowning. After some youth graduate from high school, their parents send them to drown in the West, thinking that they have raised their children well and do not worry about them, only to have their child lose much of that upbringing and righteousness within the first week of their departure!

92. Love and Mercy

God ﷻ created love and mercy between spouses; love refers to the infatuation and affection they feel at the beginning of their marriage, while mercy refers to the compassion and kindness that remains with them until old age.

A couple in their sixties and seventies may not have the love and affection they had in their youth in the sense of their instinctive desire to have physical relations, but the compassion between them remains intact and increases with age due to the purity of that compassion; compassion not polluted by instinctive tendencies that only benefit one's self and ego.

The heart of the prophet of mercy ﷺ would soften when he remembered Sayyidah Khadījah عليها السلام; he would even honor some women in the city because they were acquainted with her.

93. Lustful Existence

Can one who excessively looks at what is prohibited pay attention to the grave state that they are in, a state wherein their existence turns into a lustful one?

It is known that the brain has special cells responsible for coloring things to suit dominant concerns; a politician, an athlete, and a military person all see things from their point of view and interests. The same is true for the one whose predominant interest is the opposite sex; they start to see the world with a sexual view. If one's existence becomes dominated by the love of women, such a person will have no life or hereafter. His mind will always be busy, leading him to the world of pleasures, whether permissible or prohibited. He will no longer be able to concentrate during his prayers nor have a reaction when the tragedies of Ahl al-Bayt عليهم السلام are mentioned.

94. Accepting what is Available

If a believer marries a woman, then discovers that she is not what he wanted, or that she is incompatible with him, or is not righteous, he should strive to settle and accept what he has, especially if separation is not a good idea because they already have children together. The same is also true for women. If they can learn to accept one another, these feelings will be externalized as oppression against each other!

Such a couple can coexist by bypassing self-inclinations and activating the suitable weapon to change for the better; a man's weapon is his mind, and a woman's weapon is her emotions! Therefore, just as a man can contain his wife through his mind, a woman can contain her husband through her emotions and, in turn, avoid confrontation.

95. Violations

A man and a woman who want to get married will remain strangers to each other as long as the marriage contract between them has not been finalized. Therefore, it is not suitable for a believer to picture a woman in his mind as a wife because she is not his wife yet, and there is no guarantee that she will become his wife. One may die before completing their marriage contract, or disagreement could happen over the dowry, and things do not work out, leading to them going their separate ways.

Unfortunately, some parents unfamiliar with religious rulings encourage their daughters to contact the man who proposed to her and go out alone with him! This action has no religious justification and is among the causes of the destruction of marriage, as many marital disagreements go back to the violations committed before the marriage contract was completed!

96. The Foundation of a Building

Marital life is built on tranquility, affection, and mercy. Unfortunately, some homes contain all kinds of material goods but lack those three moral elements. With the cultural degradation, family disintegration is at its peak.

In the past, when a divorce happened, news of it would shake society. These days, no one is surprised to hear of a divorce as it has become routine and happens frequently. When reviewing court records, you will find divorce statistics astonishing! Not to mention what happens after the divorce, calamities that only God ﷻ knows and that come as a result of this disintegration and could include the corruption of children, the wife, and the husband. A building that's been torn down is hard to restore!

97. Seeking the Cause (of All Causes)

A young man who worships God ﷻ and avoids being preoccupied with falsehoods and moral deviation may ask Him for righteous offspring using this prayer:

﴿رَبِّ هَبْ لِي مِن لَّدُنكَ ذُرِّيَّةً طَيِّبَةً إِنَّكَ سَمِيعُ الدُّعَاءِ﴾

﴾rabbi hab lī min ladunka dhurriyyatan ṭayyibatan ʾinnaka samīʿu d-duʿāʾ﴿

﴾*'My Lord! Grant me a good offspring from You! Indeed You hear all supplications.'*﴿[62]

This invocation will indeed be answered, and the young man's request granted as he is at an age when desires peak in a person! Of course, requesting righteous offspring also includes requesting a righteous wife, as one who seeks the effect will also seek the effector. For this request, it is also recommended to repeat this verse during prayers and in prostration frequently:

﴾وَزَكَرِيَّآ إِذْ نَادَىٰ رَبَّهُۥ رَبِّ لَا تَذَرْنِي فَرْدًا وَأَنتَ خَيْرُ ٱلْوَٰرِثِينَ﴿

﴾*rabbi lā tadharnī fardan wa-'anta khayru l-wārithīn*[a]﴿

﴾*'My Lord! Do not leave me without an heir, and You are the best of inheritors.'*﴿[63]

It is also recommended to perform a prayer called The Prayer of Ja'far al-Ṭayyār ﵇, as it has been tried and shown to work to solve this issue.

98. Wrong Perception

Some people carry the wrong perception of religion and religiosity. They imagine that a religious person abides by the physical acts of worship and that it is enough for one to pray, fast, and perform the pilgrimage! The reality is that religion is more encompassing than this; a big part of religion is also about dealings and interactions!

---

[62] Sūrat Āl 'Imrān, Verse 38.

[63] Sūrat al-Anbiyā', Verse 89.

Worship that includes prayers, fasting, and pilgrimage is within the framework of physical discipline and growing one's relationship with God ﷻ. One who only adheres to the physical dimension of religion and neglects the other dimension, which is the good treatment of others, is not adhering to the whole religion as was asked of him! Therefore, what is meant by trust in this narration:

> "When someone with whose religion and trust you are pleased comes to you (for marriage), conclude the marriage."[64]

It is the good treatment of one's wife and viewing her as a divine trust you are responsible for, not as a slave.

99. Mercy

Moderation in fulfilling children's emotional and mental needs is required because excessive pampering and tenderness could lead to their corruption. This is not to say that a believer should be emotionally dry, as showing affection towards one's children and kissing them brings natural mercy to the soul.

It has been narrated that:

> "The Messenger of God ﷺ kissed his grandsons al-Ḥasan and al-Ḥusayn عليهما السلام, and a man named al-Aqraʿ b. Ḥābis said: I have ten children and never kissed any of them... The

[64] al-Mīrzā al-Nūrī, *Mustadrak al-Wasā'il wa-Mustanbaṭ al-Masā'il*, Vol. 14, p. 188.

> messenger ﷺ said: What can I do when God ﷻ has removed the mercy from your heart."[65]

It has also been narrated that he, ﷺ, said:

> "One who kisses his child does a pious deed, and one who makes his child happy will be made happy by God ﷻ on Judgement Day, and one who teaches his child the Qur'ān the parents will be called on the Day of Judgement and will be clothed with two sets of clothing that light up the faces of the people of heaven."[66]

100. The Parent's Competition

If parents have any competition, it comes from a child's friends! The closeness in age, common interests, shared motivation based on instinct, and the provocation of corrupt media outlets are all factors that can drive a child to lean towards corrupt friends. All those years of discipline and education are suddenly gone with the wind!

It is extraordinary how some parents are careful to protect their children from anything that could cause physical harm; some even worry excessively about the child's skin, for example, yet they leave their children open to the influence of bad friends and the corruption and deviation in the street where a child's soul can be inscribed with all the expressions of corruption!

---

[65] Majlisī, ʻAllamah Muḥammad Bāqir, *Biḥār al-Anwār*, Vol. 101, p. 93, ḥadīth 17.

[66] al-Ḥurr al-ʻĀmilī, Shaykh Muḥammad b. al-Ḥasan, *Wasāʾil al-Shīʿa*, Vol. 21, p. 475, ḥadīth 27623.

If the veil were lifted and the truth made apparent, many parents would wish they were deprived of the offspring that would cause misery in this life and distress in the hereafter!

101. The Reward for Patience

A believer who experiences an increase in righteousness may sometimes face hurt from other people. If that believer can retain patience and justice in the face of that hurt, God ﷻ will increase their reward. If such a person finds it difficult to endure such harm, they should remember that God ﷻ will not let the deeds of people, male or female, go to waste and will grant such a person a great reward for what they have endured. It has been narrated from the Holy Prophet ﷺ:

> "Whoever remains patient with regards to the misbehavior of his wife, every time he is patient, God ﷻ will give him a reward as great as Ayub's for his affliction."[67]

He ﷺ also said:

> "If a woman keeps patient regarding her husband's misbehavior, God ﷻ will reward her as great as Āsiya b. Muzāḥim (the pharaoh's wife)."[68]

---

[67] al-Ḥurr al-ʿĀmilī, Shaykh Muḥammad b. al-Ḥasan, *Wasāʾil al-Shīʿa*, Vol. 20, p. 164.

[68] Ṭabrisī, Shaykh Faḍl b. Ḥasan, *Makārim al-Akhlāq*, p. 214.

102. The Fulfillment of Wishes

A believer in his youth finds joy in life and work, but as he grows old and tired and his hair turns grey, those things do not give him the same pleasure. Instead, his preoccupation with his righteous children and seeing them worship God ﷻ gives him joy and vitality in his old age.

Some parents find that their wishes were fulfilled through their children. For example, a parent who felt deprived of the blessings gained from building a masjid may one day be able to pray in a masjid their child built; another parent may have wished for a religious education but was not able to do but sent their son to seminary where he became a great scholar, and they now benefit from the lectures their son gives and eventually receive the religious education they wished for through their child. Is it not the ultimate happiness for a father to benefit from his son's actions and knowledge?

103. Being Realistic

Some go through their thirties and forties without marrying, and although a mother wishes to see her son married, he never does so because he sets impossible conditions for the woman he is willing to marry. She must have the beauty of a queen and the mind of the best woman. However, it is known that this life is a limited world, and there is a shortage in return for each privilege. Therefore, we see people in their late age settle for the lowest standards! We need to be realistic in our lives; as long as one is not perfect and has their fair share of shortcomings and mistakes, they should not expect perfection from others; they should be tolerant of others' mistakes and attempt to reconcile them without tension and impatience.

When God ﷻ wishes, He will perfect this wife for him, and she will become even better than he ever wished her to be!

104. The Correct View

The inclusive solution for all aspects of psychological and social problems begins by adopting a correct and conscious view of the philosophy of this life, as it is known that intellectual reform leads to behavioral reform. Therefore, viewing others, including family members, as divine trusts who have rights which we will all be carefully asked about on the Day of Judgement, ensures that we will not neglect nor compromise the rights of any person with whom we have a relationship, no matter how superficial and insignificant the relationship is!

Let us reflect on God's ﷻ words:

﴿وَاتَّقُوا اللَّهَ الَّذِي تَسَاءَلُونَ بِهِۦ وَالْأَرْحَامَ إِنَّ اللَّهَ كَانَ عَلَيْكُمْ رَقِيبًا﴾

﴿*wa-ttaqū llāha lladhī tasā'alūna bihī wa-l-'arḥāma 'inna llāha kāna 'alaykum raqība*^{n}﴾

﴿*Be wary of God, in whose Name you adjure one another and [of severing ties with] blood relations. Indeed God is watchful over you*﴾[69]

These words should become the starting point for establishing relationships built on divine fear and human companionship.

[69] Sūrat al-Nisā', Verse 1.

105. Educational Courses

Combining theoretical knowledge and heartfelt love is essential in dealing with children and raising blessed offspring. The knowledge of the correct parenting methods suitable for each stage of life is of great importance for parents to have an active role in raising and educating their children.

Acquiring this knowledge deserves more time than that spent on trivial things. Therefore, Attending educational courses on marital life, listening to family programs in the media, or acquiring educational books discussing parenting is vital. These days, search engines make it easy to obtain useful articles in different fields of knowledge on the foundations of successful and correct parenting.

106. Logical Thinking

The heads of the household should remind themselves that their money and the fruit of their labor for many years will eventually be passed on to their children. This is especially true if that money resulted from the parent spending their youth working hard to support their family.

Shouldn't one stop to think logically about who will receive the fruits of all those years of labor, especially when it happens one night, the night a parent dies and moves to a lonely and unknown world? Meanwhile, the child that inherits the fruits of that labor will move from one of life's pleasures to another, forgetting their poor parent who is screaming and begging them for the reward of one good deed gained from the money they worked hard for to save them from painful torment!

107. Instinct

Instinct is tied to glands in the brain, so when one is continuously exposed to external stimuli, such as looking at certain pictures, those glands pour their secretions into the bloodstream, causing a person, regardless of their marital status or age, to become sexually obsessed.

On certain days in a woman's cycle, her sexual desire increases due to increased levels of certain hormones in her body. It is a similar matter for the man as well. One of the ways that God ﷻ forsakes one addicted to ḥarām is by changing their hormonal makeup to the degree that if that person wanted to seek righteousness after their deviation, they would find themselves with a compulsive tendency to lean towards ḥarām. This is a result of the physiological changes caused by engaging in the ḥarām act in the first place. It has been said that disposing of a choice by choice does not negate having a choice.

108. Shayṭān's Exploitation

It is no secret that Shayṭān pays heed to the believing person; whenever one's faith increases, Shayṭān becomes greedier in tempting them. This is because Shayṭān has been banished from God's ﷻ mercy and intends to seek revenge. Since he missed his opportunity for revenge by manipulating prophets, messengers, and righteous servants, he now intensifies his efforts with the remaining followers.

One of the most apparent manifestations of Shayṭān's control over humans is his entering and meddling in marital life. He often exploits a woman's emotional nature to manipulate and create an atmosphere of feuding and tension between a couple. Among matters that give Shayṭān extreme pleasure to the point where he rises and boasts to his helpers, as is mentioned in ḥadīth narrations, is successfully separating a believing man from a believing woman.

109. Family Tension

Family tension creates disruption and a sense of confusion in the community. A community is a group of families, and a family is a group of individuals, so when stress is put on one of the community's points, it is like a stone is cast into a quiet basin, making waves and ripples expand in all directions! Therefore, when a man has tension with his wife, he stresses the children, his wife's parents, parents, and a whole group of people. Problems then begin between different sections of society! Suddenly, the Day of Judgement arrives, and he carries a burden as big as a mountain. A burden that includes backbiting, lying, false accusations, and beatings. Then he is told: you are the cause for all of that, and you could have eradicated the root of that discord, and things would not have reached such a level!

110. The Scope of Pleasure

When one's philosophy revolves around joy and pleasure, one will begin to view everything within this scope. A wife who views her husband as a financial supporter to fulfill her desires in life will turn away from him when he becomes bankrupt. He will lose the spark surrounding him as a bright halo in her eyes. Similarly, a husband who views his wife as a tool for pleasure will view her differently when she gets older and loses her charm. He will then see her role in his life as having ended and will only see her as a nanny to their children, no different than any other nanny hired to do the job!

111. Determining Destiny

A believing woman's responsibility to her offspring begins before pregnancy, as she is advised to recite the following supplication frequently:

﴿رَبَّنَا هَبْ لَنَا مِنْ أَزْوَاجِنَا وَذُرِّيَّاتِنَا قُرَّةَ أَعْيُنٍ وَاجْعَلْنَا لِلْمُتَّقِينَ إِمَامًا﴾

﴿*rabbanā hab lanā min ʾazwājinā wa-dhurriyyātinā qurrata ʾaʿyunin wa-jʿalnā li-l-muttaqīna ʾimāman*﴾

﴿*'Our Lord! Give us joy and comfort in our spouses and offspring, and make us imāms of the Godwary.'*﴾[70]

During pregnancy, she is advised to monitor her behavior and the lawfulness of her food, to increase her supplications, and to abide by other religious etiquettes. A believing woman will take such advice seriously because she knows that these nine months determine the destiny of her child's life in this world and their eternal life. After all, it is in the mother's womb that the soul is blown into the child, and their body is made using the materials of her body, and the chains begin forming: neurologic, spiritual, genetic, and the like. The mother's role in the child's development is more than the father's, so her right is greater!

---

[70] Sūrat al-Furqān, Verse 74.

112. Dealing with the Opposite Sex

We have to be careful in our interactions with the opposite gender and make certain that we maintain our protection. Imām ʿAlī عليه السلام disliked greeting young women and guarded himself despite being at the highest level of piety and fully aware of God's ﷻ Beauty and Majesty. We can also learn from Prophet Mūsā's عليه السلام interactions with the daughters of Shuʿayb عليه السلام. Mūsā عليه السلام insisted on walking before them when they guided him to see their father. Therefore, to be among their followers, supporters, and those striving to follow their path, we must also live with this level of caution!

Some people become obsessed with the rules of purity and impurity, yet they do not have the same obsession with these rules of interaction. It is because Shayṭān desires people to live in an atmosphere of carelessness in this area!

113. Following the Behavior of the Infallibles عليهم السلام

The believer always ensures that their behavior pleases God ﷻ and that they follow the behavior of the prophets and imāms عليهم السلام, which earns God's ﷻ pleasure in all cases. The Noble Qur'ān mentions the prophets afflicted with bad wives: Prophet Nūḥ and Prophet Lot عليهما السلام. Betrayal was used to describe those wives, but not in the sense of marital betrayal or infidelity, as this would signify weakness and is disrespectful to the prophets عليهم السلام.

Some imāms also suffered the same affliction: Imām al-Ḥasan al-Mujtaba and Imām Muḥammad al-Bāqir عليهما السلام. The wisdom of that affliction is to provide us with a model of patience and endurance, especially for those suffering from an unrighteous spouse.

114. Ḥijāb

When a woman wears the ḥijāb out of fear of going against customs and social norms instead of out of the desire to please God ﷻ, it is not surprising that she does not adhere to the legal specification of the ḥijāb! She covers her hair and body with what attracts attention and is closer to being an adornment than a ḥijāb. This is because she views the ḥijāb as a mandatory constraint imposed on her. Hence, such a woman is quick to take it off at the first chance she gets when going to a Western country, sometimes even while on the plane before leaving her country.

God ﷻ created beauty in women not to be cheapened but for her to enjoy with her husbands to fulfill the goal of procreation and reproduction. Unfortunately, the scales are turned upside down, and everyone is enjoying the woman's beauty except for her husband, who remains deprived.

115. The Treachery of The Eyes

One who keeps their eyes averted from that which is forbidden may still steal glances without being caught. For example, a man out in public with his wife may see something he is forbidden from looking at, so he pretends to look in a different direction while still stealthily looking at what he wants because he is afraid of his wife's watchful eyes.

Imām Ja'far al-Ṣādiq ؑ was asked about God ﷻ, saying:

﴿يَعْلَمُ خَائِنَةَ ٱلْأَعْيُنِ وَمَا تُخْفِي ٱلصُّدُورُ﴾

﴾ya'lamu khā'inata l-'a'yuni wa-mā tukhfi ṣ-ṣudūru﴿

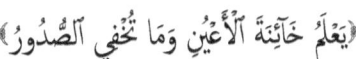

﴾*He knows the treachery of the eyes, and what the breasts hide*﴿[71]

So the Imām ﷺ replied:

> "Haven't you seen a man who looks at something, as if he is not looking at it, that is the treachery of the eyes."[72]

Even if his wife is unaware of those treacherous glances, God ﷻ is Watchful. He is the Witness over everything, and a believer should fear his Lord instead of his wife!

116. Resorting to God ﷻ

A believer should resort to God ﷻ before talking to others about issues that require strategy. This can be done by performing a two-unit (raka'āt) prayer, asking for God's guidance in doing and saying the right thing.

If a believer sees the early signs of deviation in one of his family members and wants to advise that person but worries that their words will not be eloquent and influential, they should seek assistance from the Unseen first.

Despite being Kalīm Allāh (the one who speaks to God), Mūsā ﷺ resorted to God ﷻ for the success of his mission. He elaborated on his request like this:

﴿قَالَ رَبِّ ٱشْرَحْ لِي صَدْرِي﴾

---

[71] Sūrat Ghāfir, Verse 19.

[72] Ṣadūq, Shaykh Muḥammad b. 'Alī, *Ma'ānī al-'Akhbār*, p. 147, ḥadīth 1.

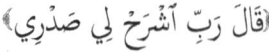

﴿*qāla rabbi shraḥ lī ṣadrī*﴾

﴿وَيَسِّرْ لِيٓ أَمْرِي﴾

﴿*wa-yassir lī 'amrī*﴾

﴿وَٱحْلُلْ عُقْدَةً مِّن لِّسَانِي﴾

﴿*wa-ḥlul 'uqdatan min lisānī*﴾

﴿يَفْقَهُوا۟ قَوْلِي﴾

﴿*yafqahū qawlī*﴾

﴿*He said, 'My Lord! Open my breast for me. Make my task easy for me. Remove the hitch from my tongue, [so that] they may understand my speech*﴾[73]

A believer also needs this support so that his speech becomes influential in the hearts of others.

117. Investment Viewpoint

Man's life is limited. However, one's offspring is an extension and a continuation of one's life. It is like a tree that blooms, dries out, and is uprooted. Its fruit grows into other trees and becomes extensions of the mother tree.

---

[73] Sūrat Ṭā Ḥā, Verses 25-28.

Thousands of years ago, Prophet Ibrāhīm ﷺ asked God ﷻ to grant him righteous offspring. When he attained the position of Imāmate, he again requested the same from God ﷻ. Ibrāhīm's ﷺ supplication was answered through Prophet Muḥammad ﷺ and his progeny ﷺ, and today, we are given our subsistence through the blessings of his son, Imām Mahdi ﷺ.

We are followers of the viewpoint of investment, not of immediate benefit or a recreational viewpoint. Thus, we want our children to be a guaranteed investment for us that continues after our death.

118. Consulting One's Wife

Making one's wife his advisor does not contradict a man's right to manage his family's affairs. A man needs a woman's evaluation of some things, especially since she can be more accurate and observant than him regarding details. At the same time, he is more aware and understanding of things on a macro level. Additionally, she is more experienced and knowledgeable regarding children's issues, as she is likely the one with them from morning to night. Therefore, she can evaluate each child's mood and nature and whether leniency or firmness would work better.

Despite his connection to the heavens, God ﷻ commanded our Noble Prophet ﷺ to practice consultation, and He ﷻ says:

﴿وَشَاوِرْهُمْ فِي ٱلْأَمْرِ فَإِذَا عَزَمْتَ فَتَوَكَّلْ عَلَى ٱللَّهِ﴾

﴾wa-shāwirhum fī l-'amri fa-'idhā 'azamta fa-tawakkal 'alā llāhi﴿

and consult them in the affairs, and once you are resolved, put your trust in God[74]

119. Differentiating between Divine and Personal Commands

A husband who imposes his ideas on his wife and presents them as divine decisions without evidence will undoubtedly be challenged by her. A husband should differentiate between the imposition of divine commands and personal ones.

If the root of a disagreement between spouses is a wife's objection to a religious ruling, here the husband can explain to her that it is a religious ruling and that going against it is ḥarām and that despite the absence of evidence for the philosophy of the ruling, they should both abide by it.

Suppose the source of the disagreement is personal, such as him wanting the house to be arranged in a certain way or wanting her to dress a certain way or other issues within the circle of personal freedom. In that case, the husband must present proof and evidence to convince her!

120. Patience and Abstinence

A young man or woman who is not able to marry or has not found a suitable spouse should remain patient and abstinent and practice the advice given by Imām ʿAlī :

---

[74] Sūrat Āl ʿImrān, Verse 159.

> "If one does not have a wife, let him offer a two-unit prayer, and thank God very much, and ask that God ﷻ sends His peace and blessings to the prophet and his progeny, then let him ask God to give him out of His Generosity, as surely God will bless him with what makes him feel rich."[75]

God ﷻ has His methods for enriching His servants. He could give him a righteous wife, or maybe He will give him more faith that will make it easy for him to be single until it is destined for him to have a righteous marriage, removing any inclination from his mind, even if for only a temporary period, and what a gift and blessing that would be!

121. Looking Beneath the Surface

The same beauty that can steal the hearts of men is no more than a mask of skin that extends inch by inch, with hair to cover what is underneath: the skull. That same skull is used as a sign to indicate danger due to its frightening appearance!

The Lord of the Worlds clothed this skull with beautiful skin so that procreation can be achieved. What is more important than that is to look beneath the surface, past a woman's exterior! Our Holy Messenger ﷺ warned against "the beautiful plant growing in waste," referring to a beautiful woman who grew up in a corrupt environment, as what would appear to you is the beauty of that plant while it lives in waste.

---

[75] Ṣadūq, Shaykh Muḥammad b. ʿAlī, *al-Khiṣāl*, Vol. 2, p. 636.

122. Feeling of Distinction

When some women rise to a certain degree of faith in knowledge in their worship, they begin to see themselves as distinct from their husbands. A woman's husband, who struggles with work from morning until night, does not have the opportunity to improve himself as she does. As a result of this view the wife has of herself, she begins arguing with her husband, and the disagreements escalate until she asks for a divorce, loses her husband and children, and falls into financial trouble. She may even lose the faith she claims to have and possibly stop praying because of the escalating psychological conditions that resulted from making that first irrational decision. What a consequence! She goes from being a woman who claims Gnosticism and wayfaring towards God ﷻ and being the incubator of a family engulfed by divine compassion to abandoning her obligatory prayers!

123. Remediation/Rectification

If a person is unsuccessful in choosing their life partner and their marriage fails, they should rectify the situation by building up the other person. If they discover that their new partner is not suitable for them shortly after the marriage contract is completed or during the engagement period, they could dissolve the contract if they do not fear that doing so would cause other problems.

However, sometimes, after years of marriage and raising children together, dissolving a marriage contract and moving on may not be appropriate, making it necessary for a couple to invest in their existing situation. There are those who, unfortunately, destroy their marital nest after a long time together and end up losing their wife and children, only to start thinking about building a new nest without knowing where this nest will end either!

124. Mutual Respect

One of the most essential foundations of a happy marriage is mutual respect between spouses and avoiding insults in front of others, especially in front of the children.

Children have love towards both parents, but when they see the lack of respect and the hurt caused by one parent to the other, it is natural for them to develop an aversion towards the one causing harm and bias towards the one being harmed.

It is only natural then that a father can lose all the effort he spent raising those children due to this conflicted environment and the war between him and his wife! Surely, the divine blessing cannot be seen in such a home!

125. Friends

Some parents need to learn who their children's friends are and their attitudes and tendencies. Those friends are the ones who shape the behavior of their children without them being aware!

There are many examples of parents that exerted maximum effort, both psychologically and intellectually, in raising a righteous child to eighteen, only to lose them in just one night, one trip to a suspicious place, or their child's association with just one perverted person. Therefore, it is essential to monitor children carefully and thoroughly by observing who they befriend and where they go and using suitable educational methods to protect them from corruption.

126. Unlawful Practices

When a man resorts to ḥarām acts, from looking at ḥarām images to engaging in ḥarām acts, his actions will destroy his marriage.

On the one hand, one who develops a taste for the varied ḥarām will no longer be satisfied with what is permissible (ḥalāl) for him, especially when he compares varied accessible ḥarām and his unchangeable ḥalāl. On the other hand, his wife will lose the respect for him that she once had as she will instinctively reject infidelity. How could he even expect respect from her after that? Moreover, God ﷻ, who deposits friendliness into the hearts of the obedient, can remove that friendliness from the hearts of sinners, and this is the secret behind people being repelled by sinners, even without knowing what sins they have committed.

127. Rushing to Prayer

When a believer falls into a problem relating to himself or his family, he rushes to prayer, seeking help from God ﷻ. This was also the action of the Prophets and Imāms عليهم السلام and of Sayyidah Zaynab عليها السلام, who spent the eve of the 11th of al-Muḥarram, amid the casualties, expressing her sadness to God ﷻ.

A believer speaks to God ﷻ the way a servant speaks to his master, or a lover to his beloved, or one who is afflicted to a generous helper, as God ﷻ says when relating the words of His Prophet Ayyūb عليه السلام:

﴿أَنِّي مَسَّنِيَ ٱلضُّرُّ وَأَنتَ أَرۡحَمُ ٱلرَّٰحِمِينَ﴾

﴿'annī massaniya ḍ-ḍurru wa-'anta 'arḥamu r-rāḥimīna﴾

﴿'Indeed distress has befallen me, and You are the most merciful of the merciful.'﴾[76]

God ﷻ is Hearing and Seeing; he does not need the details of one's issues but wants His servants to pray to Him and ask Him for help.

128. Appreciation

A man should appreciate his wife's efforts and service to him and the children she has given him, children that will carry his name, help him in life, be a source of pride in front of his peers, and do good deeds for him after he dies. His wife has earned a great right, especially as he ages, and begins seeing the signs of goodness in his offspring! So even if his wife reaches a high degree of evil, he must tolerate her to show appreciation for giving him such offspring. Such action is also among the points of loyalty that God ﷻ loves. So, let the husband thank his wife with his tongue and heart and tolerate what he dislikes about her in exchange for this blessing, especially when his children grow up and become his source of emotional and material gifts!

129. Superficial View

Some women have an irrational, superficial view regarding life partners. According to them, some of the specifications required for a life partner are: he must be good-looking, interested in

---

[76] Sūrat al-Anbiyā', Verse 83.

modern tools and technology, or brilliant and educated in things that are often useless. Thus, when someone proposes to a woman like that and does not match her criteria, she rejects him despite him being a believer, a man of good morals and loyalty, and one with the means to start and support a family.

It is no secret that this is one of the tricks of Shayṭān, who hates for this holy structure to be established, and it is important to him that one remains unmarried so that it is easier for them to fall into his traps. We should be cautious of the divine punishments that result from rejecting a qualified believer.

130. Compassion and Kindness

The following narration is one of the masterpieces of Ahl al-Bayt ﷺ, which reflects the state of compassion and kindness they held for children, especially females. It also reflects the depth of their connection towards their grandmother, Sayyidah al-Zahrā' ﷺ.

In the narration, a man named al-Sakūnī said:

> "I went to Imām ﷺ while I was sad and upset, and he told me,
>
> > "O Sakūnī, why are you sad?"
>
> I said:
>
> > "A daughter has been born to me."
>
> He ﷺ said:

> "O Sakūnī, her weight is on the earth, and her sustenance is from God ﷻ. She lives outside your lifetime and eats other than your sustenance."

By God, he relieved me, and then he said:

> "What did you name her?"

I said:

> "Fāṭimah."

He ﷺ said:

> "My, my! Excellent!"

Then he put his hand on his forehead until he said:

> "Be Careful! Since you named her Fāṭimah, you should not insult, curse, or beat her."[77]

131. The Challenge of Adolescence

The practice of masturbation has become a dominant problem in adolescence. It must be studied from the standpoint that there is no room for shame in [learning or asking about] religion. Imām al-Ṣādiq ﷺ was asked about masturbation, and he said:

[77] al-Ḥurr al-ʿĀmilī, Shaykh Muḥammad b. al-Ḥasan, *Wasāʾil al-Shīʿa*, Vol. 21, p. 482, ḥadīth 27647.

> "It is a great sin; God has forbidden it in His Book; he who does it is like one who fornicates with himself, and if I know of one who does it, I will not eat with him."[78]

How ugly it is for a person to leave the serious concerns of life, whether relating to this world or the hereafter, only to focus his attention on such a reprehensible matter: he must conceal it; it is ugly for him to mention it, besides the known psychological and physical harm that it causes!

132. Politeness, Guidance, and Overlooking Others' Shortcomings

It is well known that, in many cases, people's natures and personalities differ greatly. If you are ever in a situation where you would need to interact closely with one incompatible with your nature, the solution is not t to force the other person to adapt to your mood. Instead, you should be able to tolerate the other person. Sometimes, it takes politeness; other times, you should offer guidance, and sometimes, you should overlook their shortcomings.

Confrontation is not the answer and only complicates the matter. The problem reaches its peak when one finds within oneself an aversion to the other person and can no longer be with them under one roof. Thus, dealing with these matters takes strategy, as it is only sometimes possible to cut ties with people like our children's mothers or parents and siblings.

---

[78] Majlisī, 'Allamah Muḥammad Bāqir, *Biḥār al-Anwār,* Vol. 101, p. 30, ḥadīth 1.

133. Constant Pride

When one finds himself in a dispute with his brother, the first thing that comes to his mind is confrontation and clashing along with the following demolition instead of using a policy of containment and the reconstruction that follows.

One of the major mistakes people make in this regard is following the suggestions of the devil that they should seek revenge as they cannot bear the humiliation. However, there is no problem in pretending to bear the humiliation at certain times to attain constant pride for the rest of the time. Consider this text that shows us the position of the Imām ﷺ when one of his relatives stood by him and began cursing him, the Imām ﷺ replied by saying:

> "If what you said is true about me, then I ask God to forgive me... and if what you said about me is not true, then I ask God to forgive you."[79]

134. Internal Grounds of Evil

If we want to remove evil from its roots, we must eliminate all the internal grounds for it. This can be done by arousing the conscience, engaging the intellect, and contemplating the consequences of evil.

Our Holy Prophet ﷺ replied to a man who requested permission to commit adultery by asking him if he would accept it if someone

[79] Mufīd, Shaykh Muḥammad, *Kitāb al-Irshād*, Vol. 2, p. 146.

committed adultery with one of his family members, his sister, for example.

Imām Sajjād (Imām Zayn al-ʿĀbidīn) ﷺ was once walking in Madīnah when he came across a man who used to spend his time performing jokes to make people laugh. The Imām reminded the man of the Day of Reckoning so that the reminder could serve as an intellectual and emotional shock that would reach his core. He said:

> "There is a day for God when the wrongdoers are at a loss."[80]

135. The Top of the Pyramid

The head of a family's household is considered at the top of the family's education pyramid, whether they want to be. The corruption of the family's heads will lead to the corruption of its base as children do not see any educators aside from their parents during the first years of their lives. Therefore, it is not hypocritical for parents to expose their children to some of their good deeds and acts of worship as a way to encourage them to do the same and to conceal their sins from the children so that they do not lose respect for their parents, especially if the children do not expect their parents to commit such acts. Unfortunately, when such a child grows up and returns to his senses, he feels a deep hatred towards his parents, which can lead him to disobedience towards them. This disobedience comes from his deep contempt towards his parents as he views them as the reason for his corruption!

---

[80] Majlisī, ʿAllamah Muḥammad Bāqir, *Biḥār al-Anwār*, Vol. 46, p. 68, ḥadīth 39.

136. The First Circle

Nowadays, women in some countries entrust all or most matters to their servants, even matters of motherhood and affection towards their children. There are those whose role ends as soon as they give birth when the child is handed off to a stranger, who cares for the child until puberty! When this happens, the father does not see any sacrifice or service from his wife that would make him think of returning that favor with loyalty and appreciation. By saying this, we do not mean to record a juristic mandate for women. However, we want women to take Sayyidah Fāṭimah ﷺ as their role model when it comes to bearing the responsibility of the home and to do so in a way that makes the home her priority in both activity and interest ahead of career and other priorities.

137. Crossing the Limits

We have warned many times against the removal of restrictions between sexes. This is because the presence of instinctive attraction between the sexes is a ground for emotional attachment followed by heartfelt pleasure when approaching one another. These emotions cannot be denied except out of arrogance or pride, especially by the female, who is overcome with modesty.

Love causes the desire to be with one another. If it is impossible to do so lawfully through marriage, the other alternatives are committing ḥarām, emotional suppression, or chronic depression. That emotional turmoil could be a divine punishment for those who cross the divine limits, which some take lightly by forgetting the rule: Do not look at the sin, but look at whom you sinned against.

138. Prohibitions and Rebukes

One of the most common mistakes parents make when raising children is the excessive use of rules and rebukes to the point that a child feels resentment and tends to rebel against the parents' orders.

Parents must provide alternatives for each rule. The youth who live in a spiritual and intellectual vacuum will turn to anything that will fill that vacuum. Therefore, filling their time with things that will improve them is essential!

When the youth seem to spend time with people who negatively influence them, a better company should be suggested. When a child reaches physical and mental maturity and is driven by instinct to commit the ḥarām, then it becomes necessary for parents to help them 'immunize half of their religion' by helping them get married. According to some narrations, if parents fail to provide healthy alternatives to their children, they can be considered partners in their child's sin.

139. Divine Watch

One who strengthens within themselves the belief in the divine watch will monitor their behavior at every moment, regardless of whether they are in public or secluded.

Suppose someone knows someone has set up surveillance devices to monitor their movements. Would they behave in a way that condemns themselves, or would their behavior automatically become proper and disciplined, even in the smallest matters?

For example, if a husband believes the following verse to be true:

﴿أَلَمْ يَعْلَم بِأَنَّ ٱللَّهَ يَرَىٰ﴾

﴾*'a-lam ya'lam bi-'anna llāha yarā*﴿

﴾*does he not know that God sees [him]?*﴿[81]

Would he still try to single out and overpower his wife when they are alone or would he be so careful that he would even try not to disturb his wife with his voice when she is asleep?

It should be enough for him to read God's ﷻ words:

﴿قَدْ سَمِعَ ٱللَّهُ قَوْلَ ٱلَّتِي تُجَٰدِلُكَ فِي زَوْجِهَا وَتَشْتَكِيٓ إِلَى ٱللَّهِ وَٱللَّهُ يَسْمَعُ تَحَاوُرَكُمَآ إِنَّ ٱللَّهَ سَمِيعُۢ بَصِيرٌ﴾

﴾*qad sami'a llāhu qawla llatī tujādiluka fī zawjihā wa-tashtakī 'ilā llāhi wa-llāhu yasma'u taḥāwurakumā 'inna llāha samī'un baṣīr*[un-i]﴿

﴾*God has certainly heard the speech of her who pleads with you about her husband and complains to God. God hears the conversation between the two of you. Indeed God is Hearing, Seeing*﴿[82]

And view them as a deterrent and restraint against oppressing one whom God ﷻ defends! Unfortunately, we often make God ﷻ the least important watcher!

---

[81] Sūrat al-'Alaq, Verse 14.

[82] Sūrat al-Mujādilah, Verse 1.

140. Removing the Mines

Believers concerned with improving themselves and reaching perfection must ensure their life is free from the slightest disturbances and interference. This is because being plagued with distractions causes one to live in a constant state of stupor and to lose the ability to concentrate on the matters of this life and the hereafter. Such a person is in constant internal conflict with others, even when they are not standing in front of them.

A believer should try to gain control of their family situation; for example, if their spouse is quarrelsome, they could try to contain the situation by treating their spouse with extra kindness. After all, one whose life is full of mine must work on defusing them permanently so that they do not live the rest of their life expecting a mine to explode at any moment!

Responding to bad treatment with good treatment is hard and a heavy burden on the soul, but one must bear the bitterness of medicine to treat a more bitter and painful sickness!

141. The Miracle of Milk

Amongst the miracles of God ﷻ is the formation of milk, which has been referred to in the Noble Qurʾān:

﴿وَإِنَّ لَكُمۡ فِي ٱلۡأَنۡعَٰمِ لَعِبۡرَةٗۖ نُّسۡقِيكُم مِّمَّا فِي بُطُونِهِۦ مِنۢ بَيۡنِ فَرۡثٖ وَدَمٖ لَّبَنًا خَالِصٗا
سَآئِغٗا لِّلشَّٰرِبِينَ﴾

﴾*wa-'inna lakum fī l-'an'āmi la-'ibratan nusqīkum mimmā fī buṭūnihī min bayni farthin wa-damin labanan khāliṣan sā'ighan li-sh-shāribīna*﴿

﴾*There is indeed a lesson for you in the cattle: We give you a drink pleasant to those who drink, pure milk, which is in their bellies, between [intestinal] waste and blood*﴿[83]

It is well known that blood carries nutrients to the udders, as it carries it to the other parts of the body. The cells of the udders then extract the materials needed to make milk. The resulting fluid is pure milk, great tasting, free from impurities, and free from the characteristics of unclean blood or excrement.

Glory be to God, who guaranteed to humans their sustenance, like a fetus in the mother's womb and as a tiny newborn who has no power over good or harm to themselves!

142. Loyalty

The believer raised and taught in the school of Ahl al-Bayt is a loyal creature. His love for his wife increases because he appreciates her service, bestowal, and struggles in childbearing and raising, even if only one child.

It suffices to think of the pain a mother suffers during childbirth, a pain that can make her wish she had never become pregnant, as the Noble Qur'ān expresses:

﴿حَمَلَتْهُ أُمُّهُۥ كُرْهًا وَوَضَعَتْهُ كُرْهًا﴾

[83] Sūrat al-Naḥl, Verse 66.

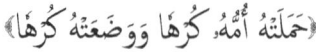

﴾ḥamalathu 'ummuhū kurhan wa-waḍa'athu kurhan﴿

﴾His mother has carried him in travail, and bore him in travail﴿[84]

How much more does she go through when we add the two years of breastfeeding and the years of child-rearing, or rather, what if she spent the years of her life between pregnancy and childcare multiplying her husband's progeny? How ugly would it be then for a divorce to happen after so many years of companionship and after she has given her husband the best years of her youth and given birth to the joys of his eyes, who are his close companions and helpers in this life, and an ongoing charity for him in the hereafter!

143. Affection

Love is a feeling of the heart, and its outward manifestation is affection. It is recommended (mustaḥabb) for a believer to show their love to their fellow believers, especially one's wife, who is the closest person to them. Some men do not express their love for their wives, as if showing emotions contradicts masculinity, and others fear that their wives will become bold and daring if they use romantic words! In reality, though, this person is not acting according to the line of the Prophet ﷺ who says:

> "The words of a man who tells his wife, 'I love you truly', will never leave her heart."[85]

[84] Sūrat al-Aḥqāf, Verse 15.

[85] Kulaynī, Shaykh Muḥammad b. Ya'qūb, *al-Kāfī*, Vol. 5, p. 569, ḥadīth 59.

However, showing love to and spoiling one's wife should not reach a level of exaggeration. Everything should be done with wisdom and should not reach a level where he has to fulfill everything she wishes for, especially if it is not befitting them and could reach a level of extravagance and waste wherein he puts her pleasure ahead of trying to please God ﷻ.

144. Result in Proportion to Effort

One who wishes for righteous offspring should make doing so a personal goal and strive as much as possible to achieve it by working according to the obligations of each stage of his life.

During his bachelor years, he should persist in praying for righteous offspring. When intending to get married, he should look for a wife who comes from a good background. He should remember his wedding night's recommended etiquette, religious rules, prayers, and supplications. He should continue to perform the recommended acts when conception occurs, during pregnancy, and during the two years of breastfeeding. He should then continue to monitor the child and ensure their good upbringing by using educational methods suitable for their age, whether a child, a teenager, or a mature youth, until they reach independence and intellectual maturity.

The effort a person puts into achieving a goal dictates how close they reach their desired result.

145. The Influence of Food

A believer must ensure their food is ḥalāl and be especially strict with the food they purchase for their family. This is important because the energy the body gains from unlawful sources is unlikely to be spent in the obedience of God ﷻ.

The importance of taking extra precautions to ensure ḥalāl food is emphasized for a believing woman during pregnancy, as she carries God's ﷻ trust in her womb. Any food that is ḥarām will influence the life and behavior of the fetus!

These days, ḥarām food is widespread, especially in the West, as alcohol and pig fats are being used in making many things, including bread. Not to mention that some blindly abide by the religious rule that says whatever is sold in Muslim markets is ḥalāl. They no longer care about the permissibility of their food, even when given evidence that the shop owner is negligent in their religious practice, does not tell the truth, and even sells ḥarām merchandise or food!

146. Jostling

Some parents make their children's education their only concern, so they choose the best schools, even if they are the centers of corruption and moral deterioration through prohibited mixing of the sexes and an overall suspicious atmosphere. They put their children in the dragon's mouth only because they wish them to be fluent in foreign languages, for example!

Attention to a child's education is required to attain a level of culture and refinement that will help them as they march through life. However, caution must be practiced when it comes to corrupt environments! Suppose there is ever a jostling between the spiritual world and the educational world. In that case, a parent should not favor this world over religion, as they are not held accountable in the grave for not teaching their child a new language! Instead, they will be held accountable for leaving their children to get lost in the wind!

147. Divine Sustenance

Among the contributors to problems in marital life is a state of anxiety and panic that results from thinking about material matters and living conditions. No matter the degree of submission and trust in God ﷻ a couple reaches, they may still live in a state of confusion and fear of what the future holds.

We must pay attention to this: sustenance from God ﷻ has many blessings compared to the sustenance earned by unsavory means, whether by ḥalāl or ḥarām. Hence, we see some people who, despite living in poverty, enjoy life, are in a state of emotional stability, have righteous offspring, and are successful in performing acts of worship.

148. Salvation Through Amputation

God ﷻ gave believers a way out if they reached a roadblock in their marriage. Despite being the most detested yet permissible act to God ﷻ, divorce may be the only way to salvation from seemingly unending emotional turmoil.

A person may be forced to amputate a body part and would even be willing to pay much money for the operation as it could be the only way to keep that diseased body part from killing them. Divorce, in a way, is like this. A man's wife is a piece of him; if he must separate from her, he will surely live in pain and a state of disability, especially if the couple has children. Life can quickly turn into a state of disarray and panic! Therefore, when considering divorce, one must study matters carefully, compare the advantages and disadvantages, and decide wisely.

149. The Curse

The Lord of the Worlds is Absolute Justice. As one human oppresses another, they distance themselves from the source of their existence, as God ﷻ says:

﴿أَلَا لَعْنَةُ ٱللَّهِ عَلَى ٱلظَّٰلِمِينَ﴾

﴿'a-lā la'natu llāhi 'alā ẓ-ẓālimīna﴾

﴿Behold! The curse of God is upon the wrongdoers﴾[86]

A curse is a prayer or supplication of expulsion and separation from the mercy of God ﷻ. A curse is proportionate to the degree of oppression and injustice a person commits. The more injustice and oppression a person (the pharaoh, for example) commits, the bigger the curse upon that person.

Similarly, one who oppresses his wife will be cursed proportionate to that oppression. Does this not put the believer in a state of panic and fear that they would be expelled from the mercy of God ﷻ? If expelled, who would then reopen the doors for them? We read in the Whispered Prayer of the Repenters:

---

[86] Sūrat Hūd, Verse 18.

> "If You cast me out from Your door, in whom shall I take shelter? If You expel me from Your side, in whom shall I seek refuge?"

150. Double the Attentiveness

A man wishing to marry a woman raised in the West may need to double his attentiveness, unlike if she grew up in a Muslim country. This is because non-believing countries are fertile ground for sin, and a committed believer who lives in such a country is swimming against the current.

He should look at the extent of her religious commitment, especially during puberty and adolescence, because she lacks the maturity and reason to keep her away from ḥarām. It is common in Western countries for girls to be subjected to moral deviation at this age, if not before. Therefore, he should find out if she was afflicted with what the other girls in these communities were afflicted with or if she could protect her well-being and chastity during this critical life stage.

151. Taking Aspects of Religion

Some love to get closer to God ﷻ by increasing their worship. You see them always busy with prayers and supplications and with a high degree of submissiveness accompanied by crying during worship. However, you may see that the same person neglects his wife and does not speak to her, leaving her hanging between marriage and divorce.

God ﷻ says:

﴿فَإِمۡسَاكُۢ بِمَعۡرُوفٍ أَوۡ تَسۡرِيحُۢ بِإِحۡسَٰنٖ﴾

﴿fa-'imsākun bi-ma'rūfin 'aw tasrīḥun bi-'iḥsānin﴾

﴿then [let there be] either an honourable retention, or a kindly release﴾[87]

How can one wish to be closer to God ﷻ when he has taken only the aspect of supplication and worship from religion and left out the other aspect: the good treatment of others, whether they are close to you or not? Such a person is just improving one side of himself without the other, like one who strengthens only one body part. Such a person will be deficient in his growth and perfection and unable to reach his goal.

152. Want What It Is

Some women are afflicted with a husband addicted to committing evil, and there is no hope of reforming him, making her life with him unbearable. If she can, she should be patient with her husband's deviation and accept reality to focus on caring for their children and keeping what remains of their nest for them.

She could assume that her husband died, and she is now a widow, and repeat this slogan: If it is not what you want, then want what it is! However, being hopeless towards her husband does not mean she should not pray for his guidance, as God ﷻ sent down rain after people lost hope, and the servant's heart is between two fingers of

[87] Sūrat al-Baqarah, Verse 229.

The Merciful, and He brings life back to the bones after they have turned into dust.

153. Compliance with God's ﷻ Words

If the divine order to Mūsā and Hārūn عليهما السلام was to speak to the Pharaoh gently, is it not appropriate that our speech with our children, our flock, the joys of our eyes, and our ongoing charity exhibits gentleness and leniency? Won't that be following God's Words:

﴿ٱدْعُ إِلَىٰ سَبِيلِ رَبِّكَ بِٱلْحِكْمَةِ وَٱلْمَوْعِظَةِ ٱلْحَسَنَةِ ۖ وَجَٰدِلْهُم بِٱلَّتِي هِيَ أَحْسَنُ ۚ إِنَّ رَبَّكَ هُوَ أَعْلَمُ بِمَن ضَلَّ عَن سَبِيلِهِۦ ۖ وَهُوَ أَعْلَمُ بِٱلْمُهْتَدِينَ﴾

﴿ud'u 'ilā sabīli rabbika bi-l-ḥikmati wa-l-maw'iẓati l-ḥasanati wa-jādilhum bi-llatī hiya 'aḥsanu﴾

﴿Invite to the way of your Lord with wisdom and good advice and dispute with them in a manner that is best﴾[88]

﴿لَآ إِكْرَاهَ فِي ٱلدِّينِ﴾

﴿lā 'ikrāha fī d-dīni﴾

﴿There is no compulsion in religion﴾[89]

---

[88] Sūrat al-Naḥl, Verse 125.

[89] Sūrat al-Baqarah, Verse 256.

Let us ask for assistance from God ﷻ and supplicate to Him by saying:

﴿رَبَّنَا هَبْ لَنَا مِنْ أَزْوَاجِنَا وَذُرِّيَّتِنَا قُرَّةَ أَعْيُنٍ وَاجْعَلْنَا لِلْمُتَّقِينَ إِمَامًا﴾

﴿*rabbanā hab lanā min ʾazwājinā wa-dhurriyyātinā qurrata ʾaʿyunin wa-jʿalnā li-l-muttaqīna ʾimāman*﴾

﴿*Our Lord! Give us joy and comfort in our spouses and offspring, and make us imāms of the Godwary*﴾[90]

So that our Messenger ﷺ can take pride in our offspring in front of the nations on Judgement Day.

154. Showing Emotion

One of the most important pieces of advice that can be presented to parents is for them to show love, emotion, and pleasure to their children and to stay away from accusations and mistrust!

A child notices when they are treated with suspicion at home, which can cause them to lose self-confidence. Therefore, when a parent sees their child perform a good deed, they should take the opportunity to encourage and praise them and express that by making the child happy and rewarding them for it.

It is well known that reward leads to motivation and encouragement even for mature people; we can extend that concept to encourage righteous acts in our benevolent religion.

[90] Sūrat al-Furqān, Verse 74.

155. Emotional Divorce

Believers should always ask God ﷻ never to remove His blessings from their marital nest. If it was left only to the couple, there is no guarantee that ḥarām would not be committed in that nest, even if only by one of them, and life would deviate from its righteous path.

Another effect of losing Divine blessings in a marriage is a state of emotional detachment between spouses. This is called emotional divorce, and the causes are often unknown! This type of divorce might even be worse than formal divorce because, in an emotional divorce, a person sees another person who constantly brings out their anger and rage before their eyes!

156. Overwhelming Lusts

This era is the worst in the history of mankind in terms of deviation in the interactions between the sexes, temptations, and satanic arrows. These arrows are deadly to both men and women, and those who do not wish to be resistant are the weakest in the face of overwhelming lust!

The issue of lust is not purely ethical, as contemporary uncontrollable lust is classified globally as a state of addiction. One who spends many long hours in front of the television or on the internet is said to be ill and in need of psychological treatment. What if those long hours were spent on something ḥarām?

157. Immunization

Suppose a wife notices a change in her husband's behavior; he becomes distant from her and can no longer tolerate her. In that case, she should not begin monitoring him, asking him about his comings and goings, spying on his matters, searching his pockets, etc.

Such actions will only fuel her husband's rage and anger and increase their distance. Though her good objective is to immunize her husband, the wife must find the preferred approach. She should still do whatever it takes to save her husband and make him immune to deviation, not to lose any gains he acquired in their marriage.

158. Equal Shares

Marriage is like a company where equal shares of efforts are divided between the spouses, and both should appreciate that aspect. It is a mistake for either of them to think they have exerted more effort than the others with their children. It has been proven that the fertilized cell is a mixture of genetic materials that result from the union of the woman's egg cell and the man's sperm cell. That means a formative, psychological, and emotional union results from their equal efforts. Viewing spouses as partners in this company, where their efforts are close to a degree, is a requirement for the stability of a marriage.

159. Poverty

One of the factors that cause worry in a person's life is the fear of hardship in living and the lack of sustenance. It is recommended for a believer to ask God ﷻ to enrich him from His bounty; however, He wishes, whatever He wishes, and wherever He wishes, as He knows His believing servant best and knows what would safeguard his servant's faith. After all, what is the benefit of an abundance of wealth if it distracts you from remembering God ﷻ?

A man once asked the Noble Prophet ﷺ to ask God ﷻ to make him rich, so the prophet did. The man was given money, and the number of sheep he owned increased, compelling him to leave Madīnah for pasture for his new sheep. This led to the deprivation of the blessings he once enjoyed from being near the Prophet ﷺ and the loss of the man's faith! From what is apparent, this man became rich, yet he suffered the worst poverty!

160. The Active Role

We have mentioned Sayyidah Fāṭimah عليها السلام's chastity, moral excellence, and commitment to her marriage and bringing up her children, from which the leaders of the Youth of Paradise عليهما السلام were born. Nevertheless, that commitment did not prevent her from playing an active role in the life of the Ummah.

When she needed to go to the mosque, she delivered a now-famous sermon to defend her faith and support the Imām of her time. She did not hesitate to deliver her infamous sermon, citing the Noble Qur'ān at times and dealing with precise and delicate ideological matters. That sermon is the subject of research and study among scholars today.

161. Attempt to Change

If a man finds himself in a marriage with a woman he does not find suitable for him yet finds it difficult to separate from her because they have children, his only option may be to try to change the things he does not like about her. However, this requires patience, wisdom, and outstanding ability. For example, if someone has a piece of iron and wants to change its shape, they must melt it and mold it into the desired shape. Similarly, a woman lacking faith can be changed through the same process. However, this process requires divine aid to succeed, and careful planning is needed to contain and embrace a woman in this state.

162. Extra Caution

Extra caution should be taken about the youth, who often acquire corrupt traits when traveling to corrupt countries. It is unfortunate for the guardian, the shepherd of his flock, to throw his flesh and blood into a swamp of vices while using God's ﷻ money.

It is also necessary to take extreme caution not to compromise any of the rules God ﷻ set for us, especially about the ḥijāb and the rules of interaction between the sexes. Unfortunately, many people disassociate themselves from these restrictions when they leave their conservative environment as if suddenly out of their Master's sight!

163. Mental Maturity

Humans have both physical maturity and mental maturity.

Physical maturity is usually accompanied by something other than rationality and management skills. Hence, the appropriate age for a girl to marry is when she reaches a state of maturity that enables her to attend to family affairs and manage a household.

A mother should prepare her daughter emotionally and mentally by getting her involved in the home affairs and caring for her siblings. Total dependence on servants weakens this ability in girls, and when they get married, they can suddenly find themselves overwhelmed by the demands of married life.

164. Drinking Alcohol and the World of Creation

Drinking alcohol is not like other forbidden acts. It has been narrated that Imām Jaʿfar al-Ṣādiq ﷺ said:

> "One who marries his well-behaved daughter to a drunkard has broken his family ties (Qaṭʿa al-Raḥm)."[91]

Theft, adultery, usury, etc., are committed externally, but alcohol enters the body and affects the composition of the cell, which means it has a link to the world of creation. Therefore, when a woman is addicted to drinking alcohol, drugs, or smoking, the toxins that enter her body are passed through the cells to the body of the fetus, who then becomes addicted to these things.

165. Clear Boundaries

One of the common mistakes made by parents is not setting clear boundaries between the ḥarām and the undesirable (makruh) and

[91] Ṭabrisī, Shaykh Faḍl b. Ḥasan, *Makārim al-Akhlāq*, p. 238.

between the wājib and the mustaḥabb. Using similar deterrence in all these cases distorts the boundaries between them.

A good educator must teach those under their care that there are red lines that cannot be crossed, and it is necessary to show some firmness in this area while showing some leniency when it comes to things that are not desirable yet do not reach the level of ḥarām. There is no denying that the deterrence and anger which arise in many situations are due to a person's ego and do not stem from a desire for the victory of God's ﷻ religion!

166. The Courage to Retreat

If a man discovered that his choice of a partner was flawed, he should be courageous and daring and retreat from moving forward with that relationship. There is no point in committing to a life they will hate out of fear of the shame they may feel from the community, traditions, etc. As long as they are at the beginning of their engagement, or even after they are married but before they have children, the door is still open for them to retreat.

However, some cheat themselves and go on to marry someone that they hated even before their engagement, and this hate continues after marriage. They insist on continuing the relationship until things become more and more complicated! In cases like this, retreating with the least possible losses would have been the best option for everyone involved!

167. Preaching and Reprimanding

Mistakes made by guardians when taking a stand against an evil act can fuel the fire of dissension. Some of the common mistakes in this matter are using the method of direct preaching while also reprimanding. This can especially cause trouble if the other person sees themselves as more educated and wiser than the preacher. Their automatic response will be to reject the advice out of spite for the one giving it!

Things have reached a dangerous level when a dissenter/rebel cannot separate between the one giving advice and the advice itself. They then challenge the other party by rejecting their words even if they are right! In this case, the responsibility to tread carefully increases for those who belong to the religion, even if they are not scholars, as they can betray the message they carry!

168. Avoiding Dangerous Traps

Women, by their nature, are the center of men's fascination. A woman is like a flower that attracts different kinds of bees. Therefore, the advice that can be offered to women who want to work outside the home or enroll in educational institutes is to protect themselves from falling into dangerous traps! Otherwise, the person will be like one entering a dangerous whirlpool claiming to be learning to swim. It is illogical and unacceptable!

One should not be thrown into the sea, relying only on their basic information about swimming, but should instead have confidence in their ability to resist. Only then will they be able to enter the whirlpool. Otherwise, reason and religion dictate that, as a precaution, one should not enter areas of a suspect nature.

169. Nature of Relationships

A man's temptation to a woman's aesthetic cannot be compared to a woman's temptation to a man! God ﷻ has placed captivating beauty in women. The beauty of their hair and face and even the adornments hidden under the ḥijāb, such as an ankle, can greatly impact those whose hearts are diseased.

Since the relationship between the sexes is tense and ready to explode at any moment, Islām has set substantial limitations regarding their interaction, including those governing looks, touching, and indulgence in unnecessary talk. There is even a prohibition against sitting in a place where a woman recently sat, and her warmth remains because sensing the warmth of a woman's body can make some men indulge in an imaginary world of artificial lust.

170. Optimistic View

Parents should have an optimistic view of their children, not demeaning, and should not underestimate or belittle them. If one child does not show signs of righteousness, the parents should remain optimistic as God ﷻ could change them or bring out the goodness in their offspring or grandchildren!

This eternal view is one of the factors that affect family cohesion. Prophet Muḥammad ﷺ said:

> "Get married and increase in number, for I will pride myself in your number over other nations on the day of judgment."[92]

[92] Sabzawārī, Shaykh Muḥammad, *Jami' al-Akhbār*, p. 101.

And Imām ʿAlī 🕊 refrained from killing some enemies on the battlefield to preserve the future light he saw in their lineage.

171. Influence

Having influence when educating or disciplining others does not happen through mere words from the tongue or through beating, scolding, and threatening the other party. Instead, it is the result of internal interactions that move from the influential educator's side to the side of the person being influenced. For example, suppose a husband feels and truly believes that backbiting is like eating dead meat, and he sees that his wife commits backbiting. In that case, he cannot successfully transfer his feelings to her through external movements, such as scolding her. Instead, he must first create a close, loving relationship with her and then invest in this relationship to rid her of this evil act.

172. Self-Monitoring

Self-monitoring is crucial in any integrative process in life, whether with an individual, family, or the community. It is like the mirrors on a car that helps the driver see danger around him, and it is like the brakes that allow him to stop when needed.

Self-monitoring is necessary, especially when interacting with one's wife, as crossing the lines in that relationship is easy. People may seldom monitor themselves when dealing with a partner at work, their coworkers, or even their parents because encounters with them are less frequent. Spouses, though, are the easiest victims considering the closeness of the relationship, making it easier to cross the lines!

173. Delicate Vases

Some men consider women servants and think they must do whatever they want! However, Islām did not make housework obligatory for women.

Imām 'Alī ﷺ pointed to this when he said:

> "A woman is a flower and not a slave at home."[93]

Therefore, a man's treatment of his wife should be gentle and kind, unlike a servant who is there to perform housework. Another narration says:

> "Be gentle with the delicate vases (women)."[94]

A vase is where roses are held and placed in a safe place where they cannot be scratched, especially if decorated with sapphire and emerald. It was narrated that:

> "God is never more unpleased than to see women and children (being mistreated)."[95]

---

[93] al-Ḥurr al-'Āmilī, Shaykh Muḥammad b. al-Ḥasan, *Wasā'il al-Shī'a*, Vol. 20, p.168, ḥadīth 25327.

[94] Majlisī, 'Allamah Muḥammad Bāqir, *Biḥār al-Anwār*, Vol. 22, p. 263.

[95] al-Ḥurr al-'Āmilī, Shaykh Muḥammad b. al-Ḥasan, *Wasā'il al-Shī'a*, Vol. 21, p. 484, ḥadīth 27652.

174. The Islāmic View

People have different views on children. Some want to have children so they can feel the joy and pleasure of having them around, like an unmarried woman who wishes to become a mother to a beautiful child so she can feel the joy of caring for them and playing with them. Others want children so they can have helpers, and they have many children so they can eventually have workers who do not need to be paid.

However, according to the Islāmic view, having a righteous child is like having stocks for the hereafter; they are man's capital in life beyond this world. They are there when a person is most in need of ongoing charity after death:

> "When the son of Ādam dies, no further reward is recorded for his actions, with three exceptions: a charity whose benefit is continuous, knowledge from which benefit continues to be reaped, or this righteous child who continues to supplicate for him."[96]

175. Moderation

A parent must practice moderation in caring for their children. Some parents exaggerate when caring for their children, not in the religious aspect, but in caring about their children's appearance, education, and entertainment. Some parents even put this goal ahead of themselves and their worship.

---

[96] Shahīd Thānī, Zayn al-Dīn al-'Amilī al-Juba'ī, *Munyat al-Murīd*, p. 103.

It is illogical for someone to miss group prayers to buy their child the sweets they asked for or to take their child on Friday to the amusement park on a day of worship! Imām ʿAlī ؑ taught us a great lesson in this aspect when he said:

> "Do not devote much of your activity to your wife and your children because if your wife and children are lovers of God, then He will not leave His lovers uncared for, and if they are enemies of God, then why should you worry and keep yourself busy with the enemies of God."[97]

176. Emotional Framework

Suppose a dispute arises between spouses in a personal matter, and it becomes necessary for a man to impose his opinion. In that case, he should do so in a friendly manner that does not make his wife conclude that it is an issue of control.

Humans go through fluctuations in their emotions, and women are especially prone to fluctuations. They are prone to favoring something, then disliking it, loving it, and later hating it.

Therefore, a husband should have a sensing device to gauge his wife's emotional state so that he does not argue with her while she is in the midst of a nervous breakdown. He should not argue with her when she is resentful towards him for an incident that recently happened between them. Instead, he should choose the right time and resolve the dispute within that emotional framework.

---

[97] Nayshābūrī, Muḥammad b. Ḥasan al-Fattāl, *Rawḍat al-Wāʿiẓīn wa Baṣīrat al-Muttaʿiẓīn*, Vol. 2, p. 429.

177. Mutual Giving

Marital life requires mutual giving, not self-interest, without caring about the other spouse. Just as the husband tries hard to secure his family's needs and manage their affairs, the wife should take his hand with tenderness and kindness and help him attain what benefits him in the future. This requires one to forget about themselves, which is a requirement for those who feel a sense of responsibility. A responsible father, for example, overcomes and puts his wishes aside to secure what his family needs first. Similarly, a responsible mother ensures her children are fed and happy before she eats and puts their needs before hers.

It is also necessary for each spouse to appreciate the other spouse's efforts: the wife should appreciate her husband's efforts, and the husband should appreciate his wife's efforts. Life will then become very beautiful!

178. Wealth and Poverty

Some people leave this world while being poor in knowledge and finances; they leave no ongoing charity to benefit from after their death. However, they may leave behind a righteous son or a grandson who becomes a distinguished scholar who attains what their dead relatives did not. The deceased then receives the reward for building tens of mosques or for knowledge that is being benefited from, all due to their righteous son or grandson!

Meanwhile, some parents send their sons and daughters to Western countries, fully aware that their children will fall into corruption and deviation, to make their children a source of money for them.

What a big difference between the two: the first is a wealthy poor person, and the other is a poor wealthy person!

179. Attraction

A woman who notices her husband's preference for being outside of the home and his attachment to someone other than her, whether a legitimate attachment or not, should work to over-satisfy him emotionally and physically until he stops.

Through her misbehavior with her husband, a woman may push him to what she fears and increase his distance and attraction towards someone with more beauty and emotion than she has!

Even after years of companionship, some men prefer to leave home and abandon their children to live in a far-away apartment with a woman they love. Therefore, it is necessary for a wife to increase her efforts in attracting her husband towards their marriage, not to push him away. In addition, once he returns, it is not rational to shame him and keep reminding him of the past.

180. Addiction to Looking

One addicted to looking at pornographic images naturally will become a creature whose main obsession is women. In turn, he will become easy prey for the devil, who attaches himself to this person and pushes them to commit sins involuntarily.

This person can suddenly find himself committing such immoral and evil actions that he would not have expected of himself! The introduction to sin is optional, but the result is not! It is like a person who committed suicide; it was their choice to throw themselves from the top of a tall building, but their fall was due to gravity. No one says that they hit the ground because of gravity and are not guilty of killing themselves!

How excruciating it is for a person to endure long torment for a night they spent in sin, ending their night at dawn when the righteous are ending their night of worshipping their Lord, seeking His pleasure!

181. Self-Control

Some husbands do not behave well with their wives because of the large disparity between their thinking and orientation. The husband could remain on this path for years, causing a rift in his family. However, he is the most harmed by this; his actions cause wounds in the hearts of his children, young and old, and he repels them out of sympathy for their mother, not to mention the psychological trauma that affects the whole family. Therefore, even if the father is correct, he should control himself and discuss what bothers him privately with his wife. At the least, he will not lose his place in his children's hearts, especially at the age when they need him the most.

182. The Woman's Role

A believing woman has a significant role in her husband's success and accomplishments in life. As the saying goes: "Behind every great man, there is a woman." For this reason, God ﷻ chose Sayyidah Khadījah ؏ to be Prophet Muḥammad's ﷺ wife during the most challenging time of his life, at the beginning of his message.

During that time, the two suffered long years of adversity and misery, displacement to Abyssinia, and an economic and social boycott in the valley of Abū Ṭālib (Shiʿb Abū Ṭālib). Sayyidah Khadījah ﷺ was the best companion and helper to the Prophet ﷺ and was his source of comfort among the people. Sayyidah Fāṭimah ﷺ was also an important element in the life of Imām ʿAlī ﷺ and used to soothe the pains he lived through.

183. Objective Assessment

The primary solution to preventing tensions in dealing with others lies in clearing the mind of the collections of images and thoughts towards those we deal with. This can be accomplished through objective assessment. To practice objective assessment, we must allow the mind to judge others without emotional whims.

Being fair and equitable is another vital point to consider, as we should always try to be fair when judging and evaluating others by getting past ourselves.

Another critical point is to practice balancing the pros and cons of every situation before going forward. We should also remain cautious of the devil's insinuations because the devil will try to distort the other party's image in a believer's mind and cause him to distrust others. Last but not least, we should also be persistent in asking God ﷻ to grant us the ability to see things as they are.

184. The Meaning of Beauty

Beauty has two meanings: there is purely physical beauty, like that of a rose with its color, smell, and shape, and there is human beauty mixed with spiritual attraction. The second type of beauty is needed in marriage, as a woman can be beautiful according to the measures and standard specifications of beauty yet lack spiritual attraction. Her apparent beauty alone is not enough to achieve a happy marriage. Those who marry such a woman only for her apparent beauty will quickly develop an aversion towards her. God ﷻ designed this world so that every material beauty in this life loses its luster, and everything new has glamor!

185. Favorable Circumstances

Among the blessings that God ﷻ bestowed upon women is freeing them from the obligation of seeking their livelihoods. Therefore, if a woman wants to become closer to God ﷻ, her circumstances are favorable thanks to a life free from the demands levied upon a man. Unfortunately, those who capitalize on this free time to get closer to God ﷻ are very, despite their circumstances being more suitable for them as they are often less busy, alone in their homes more often, and possess deeper emotions. This, combined with the struggles a woman endures during pregnancy, childbirth, and child-rearing, is enough to remove a mountain of sins, so why don't more women take advantage of this blessing?

186. A Realistic Issue

The emphasis on marrying a pious woman (when we say: "Select the religious spouse, so that you may be blessed."[98]) goes back to an issue with no room for idealism. Instead, it is a realistic issue because a pious religious woman is the best helper for a man in his religion and his life and is not one that he should be wary of.

---

[98] al-Ḥurr al-ʿĀmilī, Shaykh Muḥammad b. al-Ḥasan, *Wasāʾil al-Shīʿa*, Vol. 20, p. 50.

A pious religious woman is a woman of morality, chastity, and honesty. She does not overstep her limits and will not ask her husband for something not religiously permitted. All that can be asked of her is to have a minimum amount of beauty, as a woman who is religious and has an acceptable appearance cannot be compared to a woman who has a high degree of beauty, yet no religion to speak of!

187. The Righteous Individual

One of the best blessings of marriage is the ability to fulfill the duty of adding righteous individuals to the nation. If a child dies while in the mother's womb, then that child will stand at the gate of heaven, refusing to enter until their parents enter with them.

It has been narrated that Prophet Muḥammad ﷺ said:

> "Don't you know I shall brag about your numbers to the other nations on Judgment Day? I shall do so till stillborn remains at the gate of Paradise refusing to enter; it will be said to him: "Enter", but he says, 'No, not till my parents enter'. He thus seeks intercession for them, after which they shall all enter Paradise."[99]

If a child is born and dies before his parents, they become a reward for their parents. If a child outlives their parents, they may ask for forgiveness on behalf of their parents. It was also narrated that:

[99] Shahīd Thānī, Zayn al-Dīn al-ʿAmilī al-Jubaʿī, *Musakkin al-Fu'āwid*, p. 23

> "Happy is a man who does not die until he sees his offspring,"[100]

And miserable is the one with no children.

188. The Origin of Corruption

The origin of the corruption that arises from forbidden interactions often begins with a simple look. For this reason, in Sūrat al-Nūr, the Noble Qur'ān calls on believing men and women independently to lower their gazes.

If one returns to their senses, they will see that looking at women 'neither nourishes nor avails against hunger' and that it is pointless and useless. Instead, it makes a person more interested and drawn to the beauty of someone who cannot always be reached. This leads to suffering, grief, and depression. Moreover, the appearance of a man's lawful wife may pale compared to the various images he has stored in his mind.

189. Keeping the Intimate Relationship Confidential

One of the negative phenomena seen these days is couples touting their intimate marital relationship to others. We see this when a person shows respect to their spouse in front of others to show off the extent of their love for each other.

Indeed, kindness, gentleness, and tender words that reflect the affection between a couple are encouraged. However, acting this

---

[100] al-Ḥurr al-ʿĀmilī, Shaykh Muḥammad b. al-Ḥasan, *Wasā'il al-Shīʿa*, Vol. 15, p. 96.

way in front of others or disclosing it to them may cause arousal in some and could lead to envy, jealousy, and heartbreak for those deprived of this blessing. Therefore, it is best to keep this intimate relationship confidential; the wise will hide their love just as they hide their money!

190. Glimpse

It has been narrated that Imām Ja'far al-Ṣādiq ﷺ said: "There is nothing more gainful than lowering one's gaze, for the sight is not lowered from things which God has forbidden unless the witnessing of Majesty and Glory has already come to the heart."[101] When a religious young man lowers his gaze from the fleeting beauty of humankind, God ﷻ will show him His beauty, and what a difference between the Beauty of God ﷻ and the passing beauty of women!

What we see in the beauty of nature and women is nothing but a glimpse of the magnificence of God's ﷻ creation; this captivating human beauty we see was only something that looked like chewed flesh at the beginning of its creation, scary looking, but the Lord of the Worlds shaped it in the womb as He wished.

191. Study and Research

The ability to properly germinate a seed and grow it to its fruition takes scientific knowledge, which can take years; we call it agricultural engineering. The goal of that science is to identify some of the secrets of botany, a feat that pales in comparison to understanding the complexities of the human soul!

---

[101] Majlisī, 'Allamah Muḥammad Bāqir, *Biḥār al-Anwār*, Vol. 101, p. 41, ḥadīth 52.

Doesn't the upbringing and discipline of a child, who is a human being, deserve study and research, even if only on a general level? Why don't we increase our knowledge of the human soul, the most cherished thing in existence, to better understand how to raise our children?

192. Promise of Riches

Many believers read this verse without genuinely believing it:

﴿إِن يَكُونُوا۟ فُقَرَآءَ يُغْنِهِمُ ٱللَّهُ مِن فَضْلِهِۦ ۗ وَٱللَّهُ وَٰسِعٌ عَلِيمٌ﴾

﴾'in yakūnū fuqarā'a yughnihimu llāhu min faḍlihī wa-llāhu wāsi'un 'alīmun﴿

﴾If they are poor, God will enrich them out of His grace, and God is Bounteous, Knowing﴿[102]

It is worth noting that this verse does not refer to people living hand to mouth or people who fear poverty in the future. Instead, it addresses those in the worst condition, those who are truly destitute.

The promise of riches comes from God's ﷻ grace and is not due to a person's potential. This means that even if one is poor and lacks the conditions and qualifications to support themselves and their family financially, God ﷻ promises them richness from His grace, which He gives to whomever He wishes.

[102] Sūrat al-Nūr, Verse 32.

193. The Marital Relationship

Marriage is not like a transaction, where one tries to dominate the other as if they own them, and it is not like temporary contracts where one party tries to get rid of the other whenever they want.

Instead, it is a relationship representing the peak of the intermingling and the pairing of two souls. Just as the spouses' characteristics are mixed into the first fertilized cell, which is the beginning of another human being (their child), they should renounce their subjective impulses in their marital nest. This is how a mother turns her soul into a cradle for the soul of her child, just as her womb was once a cradle for their body.

194. Haram and its Relatives

Looking at what is forbidden is an injustice to one's self. Doing so delays their transcendental journey, as every sin they commit impedes their journey to get closer to God ﷻ.

Avoid sins of all shapes and kinds to keep this injustice at bay. One of our great scholars once said: leave ḥarām and its relatives! A thing might not be forbidden on its own, but it can lead to it in time, such as talking to women for men. While talking to women is allowed, it becomes so if done provocatively or leads to fear and suspicion. It is said that

> "One who circles a fire will almost fall into it."[103]

---

[103] *Kashf al-Lithām*, Vol. 2, p. 145.

195. An Entity

The wife who knows she is a partner in everything her husband achieves does not feel inferior to him or feel that she has deficits. She realizes that she is establishing an entity out of her blessed family and that every good from that entity is eventually attributed to the entity.

This is the customary view when taking countries as an example. A country has branches of government, and only some of its members excel in their work. However, since the country is seen as an entity, any success - even if it were due to a single minister - is attributed to the whole government and not just that one minister. Similarly, the blessings in a family of believers are attributed to the whole entity, which consists of the father, the mother, and the children. It is also similar to how we attribute all goodness and blessings we receive to the Prophet ﷺ and his family عليهم السلام we do not partition the good. Instead, we attribute it to the whole blessed family.

196. The Devil Works in Stages

Every human, man or woman, has great potential in achieving nearness to God ﷻ. However, a woman may be more capable of achieving it faster than a man due to specific characteristics that distinguish her. However, the problem lies in not investing those capabilities and powers, which is one of the traps of the devil who tries to stand between a person and uncover the treasures inside them!

The devil works on a person in stages, the first of which is when he tries to occupy that person with the major sins. If he fails, he gives up and moves on to lesser sins. If that does not work, he tries to occupy a person with what is permissible to prevent them from doing what is recommended. If that person is determined to do the recommended acts, the devil tries to occupy them with doing the least recommended ones. Suppose the devil gives up hope in occupying them with what he wants. In that case, he starts trying to strip the recommended acts from their content and essence by distancing them from the sincerity of their actions and their intention to seek nearness to God ﷻ. However, the devil gives up on one who protects their sincerity and devotion and will no longer have the means to lead them astray.

197. Barriers

One of the remarkable narrations from the Holy Prophet ﷺ discusses the effect of anger on faith; in it, he says:

> "Anger ruins faith, just as vinegar ruins honey."[104]

Vinegar and honey have two jarringly different tastes: honey has a pleasant, sweet taste, while vinegar is an acid with a stinging taste. Some are surprised and wonder why they do not see any distinction in their life; though they have been committed to performing the night prayers for years, they do not miss Ḥajj or 'Umrah and ensure their zakāt (alms-giving) is paid!

It is distressing when we do not see the effects of our actions as expected. However, the reason for this is more than the lack of action required to see the desired effects, as those requirements are plenty in a believer's life. Instead, it is due to a barrier that prevents the effects of action from being seen.

[104] Daylamī, Ḥasan b. Muḥammad, *Irshād al-Qulūb*, Vol. 1, p. 177.

For example, if you put a moist wooden stick on fire, it will not ignite for a while, yet if you let it dry out first, then one matchstick would be enough to ignite it. Therein lies our problem: the moisture that permeates our lives and creates a barrier between us and the desired effects of our actions!

198. Prevention Before Cure

Psychological stability is significant in expediting a person's movement towards attaining nearness to God ﷻ. Hence, a believer should be attentive to the environment they live in. If they suspect the presence of any mines in it, they should try to remove them to prevent an explosion and think of the solutions to a crisis before it befalls them.

If they suspect someone is trying to cause a problem for them, the believer may visit them and offer them a gift before the person has the chance to act on it. With this move, they manage to avert the problem, which is better than falling into the problem and then trying to solve it after the fact.

This is the believer's policy in life: "An ounce of prevention is better than a pound of cure," as a believer strives to have a life where there is never any blurriness and tension around them, whether in their family life or social life. In addition, they always ask God ﷻ to remove any matter that would stand in their way of attaining nearness to Him, as we read in one of the Fifteen Whispered Prayers:

"My Lord! Shield me from every obstacle that distances me from you."[105]

199. The Lack of Distinction

Believers, for the most part, are similar in their level of faith, and it is rare for us to see a distinguished person whose situation does not match their good deeds! We are like those who want to build a home for themselves, so they build a wall during the day, yet when the night comes, and while the wall is still wet, they kick it, destroy the wall they built, and repeat it day after day! If such a person worked on building his home in such a manner for fifty years, would he ever succeed in completing it? The Noble Qur'ān also discusses such a matter using a different example wherein God ﷻ says:

﴿وَلَا تَكُونُوا كَالَّتِي نَقَضَتْ غَزْلَهَا مِنْ بَعْدِ قُوَّةٍ﴾

﴿*wa-lā takūnū ka-llatī naqaḍat ghazlahā min ba'di quwwatin*﴾

﴿*Do not be like her who would undo her yarn, breaking it up after [spinning it to] strength*﴾[106]

The secret behind this is our lack of self-monitoring and our oppression of ourselves and others.

[105] Majlisī, 'Allamah Muḥammad Bāqir, *Biḥār al-Anwār*, Vol. 91, p. 161.

[106] Sūrat al-Naḥl, Verse 92.

200. The Most Dangerous Destroyers

One wishing for a wife other than his own is among the most dangerous things that can destroy a marriage. This calamity becomes greater when he tells his wife about it!

A husband who thinks about another woman could be punished for this deed, even if the woman he wishes for is just an image of perfection, which his wife lacks, as this does not justify this terrible deed.

The correct way to deal with this matter is for him to ask God ﷻ from His bounty and to ask God ﷻ to bless his marriage. A believer is satisfied with what God ﷻ destines for him, and tolerating a bad wife is a good test, as at least she is under his authority instead of being tested by an oppressive ruler.

201. Avoiding the Consequences

Hiring servants has become a widespread phenomenon in some countries. It is no secret that this has consequences, as bad treatment and oppression of those without help except for God ﷻ hastens divine punishment.

In addition, when the servant does not wear the correct ḥijāb and exposes her arms and legs while a man looks at her without a care, he comes on the Day of Judgement carrying the heavyweight of looking at what was not allowed for him. Some homes have also been destroyed due to the temptations that arise when the servant is physically attractive. Therefore, if one could do without a servant to avoid these consequences, it would be better for all involved!

202. Appreciating the Good

A believer's relationship with his wife when he reaches an advanced age is usually stronger than in his youth. The reason is apparent: lust was the strongest motive that moved him toward her in his youth. Now, in their old age, and after years of companionship that united them in good and bad times, and after she has given him righteous offspring - the source of his pride and the ongoing charity that will help him through this life and the hereafter - he sees what he has as blessings that came to him through his wife. Even if she did not bring them up, she gave birth to them, which is enough. Generally, a believer always remembers the good someone does for them, and those who do not appreciate the good should know that something is lacking in their faith.

203. Selfishness

Some women complain about their husband's negligence towards them and how they have changed from how they were during the engagement period. Some add that they long to see their husband yet cannot because he is either busy with work or out with friends.

They exert much effort to serve him and ensure he is comfortable at home, yet he is selfish and does not care about anyone but himself! How beautiful it is when a husband appreciates his wife's giving and service as she tires and spends hours of her life for his comfort! Therefore, he should try to dedicate even an hour to sit with her, to help teach her what she does not know in religious teachings, and to share information he learned from attending the mosque.

We hear many women complain that they do not know about matters that pertain to them, and this goes back to the husband, who did not try to teach them when they were under his care. God ﷻ says in the Noble Qur'ān:

﴿يَٰٓأَيُّهَا ٱلَّذِينَ ءَامَنُوا۟ قُوٓا۟ أَنفُسَكُمْ وَأَهْلِيكُمْ﴾

﴿*yā-'ayyuhā lladhīna 'āmanū qū 'anfusakum wa-'ahlīkum*﴾

﴿*O you who have faith! Save yourselves and your families*﴾[107]

204. Burdened

When some people are granted a taste of the spiritual blessings they gain during a visit to the holy sites, during their worship on the nights of Qadr, or even in gatherings remembering the Prophet's Household عليهم السلام, we find that they begin to feel burdened by interacting with people. They may not act like their usual selves and no longer give their family their rightful attention, with the excuse that they are engrossed in their special state!

Nevertheless, our Holy Prophet ﷺ was the kindest person to his family when he had moments with God ﷻ that not even a close angel or any other messenger could bear. Our Prophet ﷺ spoke with God ﷻ during Mi'rāj, where God ﷻ revealed many things to him. Despite these special spiritual moments, our Holy Prophet ﷺ interacted with people and regularly dealt with their problems. One of his wives once said:

> "The Messenger of God ﷻ used to converse with us and us with him, and when the time for prayer came, then it was as though he did not know us and we did not know him."

[107] Sūrat al-Taḥrīm, Verse 6.

205. Points of Disagreement

From its inception, marriage is no less important than a company that operates according to a set of rules. As such, a set of rules should be established and relied upon by spouses from the onset of their marriage, with the most important rule being that all points of disagreement should be discussed calmly.

Unfortunately, when some men argue with their wives, they push them away from religion and, at times, lead them to disbelief. They do so by supporting all of their orders and points of view with the verse of guardianship and maintenance:

﴿ٱلرِّجَالُ قَوَّٰمُونَ عَلَى ٱلنِّسَآءِ﴾

﴾ar-rijālu qawwāmūna 'alā n-nisā'i﴿

﴾Men are the managers of women﴿[108]

And because they are the man of the house as if manhood is a requirement for having the correct opinion!

The guardianship of the man applies to the management of the family and finances. It does not apply to the realm of thought and the programming of life, where the woman's argument could be stronger and her reasons more convincing! Therefore, calm discussions and respecting the other's point of view make them more open-minded and likely to agree with each other's arguments.

---

[108] Sūrat al-Nisā', Verse 34.

206. Conditional Love

Most of the love that spouses have for each other is conditional, as they see each other as a means to achieve their happiness. It is rare to see true love! To explain this point, think of this: if a wife were asked to choose between her husband dying and him marrying another woman, she would prefer his death! If her love were true, she would have put him ahead of herself and chose to be happy for his happiness, even with another woman. The same is true for the husband; if his love for his wife were true, it would not end even if he no longer felt he was getting what he wanted from her for some reason. True love is the love for the other's self, not love for one's self!

207. Investment Aspect

Placing importance on raising righteous offspring is considered one of the best and most guaranteed investments! One of the most rewarding moments in life is when one sees the fruit of one's existence and the effects of one's upbringing, walking before one's eyes on the face of this earth, building the land, and spreading goodness among the people.

This becomes especially important when one feels they are approaching the end of their life, as they begin to see that their role in this world is about to end and their offspring begin a new role in the movement towards reaching perfection. Their offspring's journey will have effects that reach the parent in the grave, where they await even the smallest amount of good deeds to add to their scale as their deeds have stopped accumulating and their time of reckoning has begun!

208. The Seduction of Women

In Sūrat Yūsuf, the Noble Qur'ān points to the elements of seduction that Zulaykha prepared in the palace of al-Aziz to seduce Prophet Yūsuf ﷺ. She began by propositioning him using a gentle and kind request and then locked the doors to ensure privacy and seclusion. She then verbalized her intention with the order 'Come to me!' to show her strong need for what she desired.

On the other hand, the Qur'ān shows us the elements of remaining steadfast, as was demonstrated by Yūsuf ﷺ. He begins by seeking refuge in God ﷻ as the seduction of women is a difficult test; he then goes on to remember that he is in the hands of God ﷻ, who has showered him with blessings and given him a good life. He recognizes that it would never be to return the Benefactor's kindness and favors by challenging His orders and doing what He has forbidden, especially as we return to Him after this life where temptations cease to exist.

209. The Love for God ﷻ

The Noble Qur'ān threatens those who put the love of their parents, children, brothers, tribes, wealth, dwellings, and business ahead of their love for God ﷻ and His messenger ﷺ by saying:

﴿فَتَرَبَّصُوا۟ حَتَّىٰ يَأْتِيَ ٱللَّهُ بِأَمْرِهِۦ﴾

﴾*fa-tarabbaṣū ḥattā ya'tiya llāhu bi-'amrihī*﴿

﴾*then wait until God issues His edict*﴿[109]

[109] Sūrat al-Tawbah, Verse 24.

Is this threat not enough for us to examine the corners of our hearts to find that the sneaky love that entered His kingdom is not for Him?

We should know that the love for the Creator of love starts as an obligation and then turns into passion and infatuation, making people belittle everything between them and their Lord.

Didn't the truthful Yūsuf ﵇ say:

﴿رَبِّ ٱلسِّجۡنُ أَحَبُّ إِلَيَّ مِمَّا يَدۡعُونَنِيٓ إِلَيۡهِۖ﴾

﴿*rabbi s-sijnu 'aḥabbu 'ilayya mimmā yad'ūnanī 'ilayhi*﴾

﴿*My Lord! The prison is dearer to me than to what they invite me'*﴾[110]

Being in seclusion and alone with his Beloved Lord was dearer to Yūsuf ﵇ than seclusion with any mortal being, even if that mortal was a princess in her palace.

210. Personal and Social Behavior

Luqmān the wise ﵇ once connected two seemingly separate matters that complete each other: one's personal behavior and social behavior. He connects one's behavior with God ﷻ, represented by establishing prayers with all their limits and rules, as everything depends on one's prayers according to our religious texts.

---

[110] Sūrat Yūsuf, Verse 33.

On the other hand, he brings attention to the importance of one's social behavior, represented by monitoring the social environment one lives in and not losing one's sensitivity towards sin, especially when it is committed within one's close circle. If one loses that sensitivity, then the ugliness of sin will lessen in their eyes, making it easier for them to commit that sin someday. This is one of the biggest reasons migration to countries where sin is widespread is discouraged, for fear that the ugliness of sin will become ever more normal.

211. Monitoring and Accountability

The self-monitoring and accountability mentioned in Luqmān's advice is customary for those connected to the heavens. That is because the person who does not monitor themselves is not safe from slipping into sin.

Abundant worship and a long history of devotion cannot intercede on behalf of a person who might slip during one of their tests; they could end up losing their present, corrupting their future, and possibly even nullifying their past.

Some of the disheartening and disappointing examples we see among some believers today result from their negligence in this matter. The time of the occultation of our Imām is filled with relapses and declines, both spiritually and ideologically, especially as we approach the time of his reappearance.

212. Limited Energy

Every human has a limited amount of energy, and the woman who carries the concerns of her children, husband, and job will naturally find her energy dispersed, often resulting in marital problems! Undoubtedly, the less energy and activity a woman spends outside the home, the more she will excel in her role inside the home, raising her children and bettering her relationship with her husband.

A woman was not created to provide her husband's livelihood and sustenance, nor was she created to be an economic component. Therefore, it would suit her better to return to the best role she was created for; as a famous poet once said:

> "The mother is a school, and if you raise her well, then you have raised a great nation."

213. Chastity and Modesty

One of the many practical lessons we can learn from the life of Sayyidah Fāṭimah al-Zahrā' ﷺ is her strong emphasis on the importance of chastity for women in its highest forms!

We learned from the narrations that she was happy when the Prophet ﷺ gave her the responsibility of managing the home affairs, which meant that she would not have to mingle with men. She was also happy when Asmā' b. 'Umays al-Khath'amiya fashioned a coffin so that her body size would not be identified during her funeral, even though she was buried at night in the presence of a small number of Imām 'Alī's ﷺ companions.

This brings us to the question we should all ask ourselves as those who claim to be her followers: where do we stand in our interactions with the opposite sex?

214. Divine Love

Divine love is one of the strongest ties a married couple can have; when its cause is identified, its effect becomes understood and its result predictable. One who feels the essence of divine love in their heart, which is the purpose of existence, will feel that love flows through everything that reminds them of the Beloved God. This will lead their love for all creation to grow, for it depends on God ﷻ, who cares for all His creation.

In a marriage, divine love will lead one to love their spouse uniquely as they will view them as God's dependent and strive to treat and care for them well. If their spouse returns that treatment with denial and in a manner that does not reflect that kindness, they are more able to bear it and remain patient. They will feel glad that they successfully served a dependent of their Beloved God and tolerated the hurt for His sake!

215. Planting the Seed

A believer should never be negligent in the remembrance of God ﷻ. Even on their wedding night, when most are instinctively motivated, a believer remembers to perform the recommended acts of worship for that night. They pray to and beseech God ﷻ and invoke Him to bless their marriage and grant them righteous offspring. On that night, the believer plants the seed, which grows with God's blessings under His care and continues to water and tend throughout his life until he harvests the fruit that will benefit him during the lonely nights in his grave. It was narrated:

> "When the son of Ādam dies, their deeds end except through three: an ongoing charity, a knowledge that is benefited from, or a righteous child who supplicates for him."[111]

216. Admitting Mistakes

Admitting mistakes while raising children or neglecting some of their rights should not be considered a source of humiliation and shame. Doing so has an exceptional impact on children.

Being a believer does not mean one is infallible. Just as we continuously open new pages in our relationship with God ﷻ, we should do the same in our relationship with our children. Let us not forget God's ﷻ involvement in our relationships; he instills love in the hearts of his believers, as He ﷻ tells us:

﴿إِنَّ ٱلَّذِينَ ءَامَنُوا۟ وَعَمِلُوا۟ ٱلصَّـٰلِحَـٰتِ سَيَجْعَلُ لَهُمُ ٱلرَّحْمَـٰنُ وُدًّا﴾

﴿'inna lladhīna 'āmanū wa-'amilū ṣ-ṣāliḥāti sa-yaj'alu lahumu r-raḥmānu wudda^{n}﴾

﴿Indeed those who have faith and do righteous deeds—the Beneficent will endear them [to His creation]﴾[112]

---

[111] *al-Mughnī*, Vol. 2, p. 428.

[112] Sūrat Maryam, Verse 96.

217. Gains

Before deciding to get a divorce, a believer should weigh the positives and negatives and then decide wisely. If they conclude that continuing life with their spouse will only increase sin and anxiety, divorce is the better option, as stopping losses is a form of gain. It was narrated that Imām al-Ṣādiq 🕮 said:

> "Among those whose supplication is not answered is a man whose wife hurts him with everything she can, and he stays that way and asks God, saying:
>
> "O God, save me from her!"
>
> God says to him:
>
> "My servant, didn't I make you responsible for her, so if you wish, leave her, and if you wish, keep her."[113]

218. Sins of Lust

Among the sins involved in destroying marriage are those committed due to lust. Sins of lust are those related to the world of inner arousal, whether by way of sight, hearing, or thought (by imagining forbidden images).

A husband who looks at images that are religiously prohibited may see images of women more beautiful than his wife and will come to learn about pleasures more superior than the permissible pleasures

---

[113] Majlisī, ʿAllamah Muḥammad Bāqir, *Biḥār al-Anwār*, Vol. 100, p. 234, ḥadīth 6.

he finds with his wife! As the days go on, he may begin abstaining from what is lawful and increase his rewards and blessings as the Lord of the Worlds promised. In this way, he abstains from what is lawful and what is recommended and commits what has been forbidden instead!

219. Educational Environment

A teenager's educational environment is one of the most important elements influencing their behavior. These days, school dominates an adolescent's life. Despite that, some parents, often due to financial savings, proximity to the school, and the like, will send their children to a corrupt school or one that is known for having widespread deviation and unlawful mixing of the sexes. They forget that money spent in this aspect is a guaranteed investment in their children, and it is more worthy of their spending than other areas of life!

220. Absence of Pleasures

Despite being distracted by pleasures, busy with their education, or spending time with their friends, some people can remain in a good emotional state and have high morals in their interactions with others. However, as soon as these pleasures are absent, they quickly become temperamental and hard to deal with!

It is like how an infant, calm and happy as long as they are breastfeeding, cries incessantly as soon as their feeding ends, and they are separated from their mother. A spiritually mature person is distinguished in this manner, as when pleasures are taken away from them, they can retain their mental and emotional stability.

221. Ineffectiveness

One of the biggest consequences of anger is losing the ability to develop a sound argument to convince the other side of your position in a tense situation, even if you are right. This could cause a person to miss out on their lawful goals in life.

A tense and angry person loses their effectiveness on those around them, which makes them incapable of removing evil from their environment. Imām ʿAlī ☙ commented on this situation in a beautiful saying when he said:

> "A strong feeling of anger changes how a person speaks, destroys the pillars of logic, and makes a person's comprehension scattered and disturbed."[114]

222. Family Tension

Family tension can drag a person into being harsh when dealing with others. One who has an unstable marriage tends to be provoked by the slightest thing and loses control of themselves, adding complications and tension to their already shaky life!

A wise person must establish their marital nest on a solid foundation of kindness and understanding that the devil cannot infiltrate. One should remember that external tension has internal roots, and if a matter remains undealt, it can lead to disappointment and defeat even in acquiring worldly gains.

---

[114] Karājukī, Muḥammad b. ʿAlī, *Kanz al-Fawāʾid fī Tanwīʿ al-Mawāʾid*, Vol. 1, p. 319.

223. Abhorrence

A harsh person will gradually become abhorred and detested in their circle, causing them to lose positive influence on those around them. Those dealing with such a person may intentionally avoid righteous advice due to their harsh way of interacting. To emphasize the seriousness of such behavior, God ﷻ warned His Prophet ﷺ against abruptness and harshness in dealing with people when He says:

﴿فَبِمَا رَحْمَةٍ مِّنَ ٱللَّهِ لِنتَ لَهُمْ ۖ وَلَوْ كُنتَ فَظًّا غَلِيظَ ٱلْقَلْبِ لَٱنفَضُّوا۟ مِنْ حَوْلِكَ ۖ﴾

﴿fa-bi-mā raḥmatin mina llāhi linta lahum wa-law kunta faẓẓan ghalīẓa l-qalbi la-nfaḍḍū min ḥawlika﴾

﴿It is by God's mercy that you are gentle to them; had you been harsh and hardhearted, they would have surely scattered from around you﴾[115]

This shows us that people will avoid a harsh person, even if they have other good qualities, and it could have happened to even the person with whom no one can compare in terms of their good qualities!

224. The First Anger

Many people complain about being overcome with fury, rage, and a lack of control when confronting others. We sometimes see this in relationships where we do not expect it to happen, such as a child's rage towards their parents or between newlyweds.

---

[115] Sūrat Āl ʿImrān, Verse 159.

Unfortunately, rage can destroy families, even when the root of disagreement is insignificant. Therefore, we always warn family members and those with close interactions with them: be careful of that initial anger as it causes one to lose face! A clay vessel restored after shattering cannot compare to a never-broken vessel!

225. Sincerity

A problem in some marital disagreements is that spouses only address their shortcomings if they see their partner doing the same. We should remember that believers improve themselves for God's ﷻ sake, not to attain anything in return.

God ﷻ does not bless what was not done for Him! We should never forget that all hearts are subject to His Might and Will; If He wishes, He would instantly change a husband's heart, leading him to feel indescribable attachment and love towards his wife, or just the opposite. Those who do things for the sake of other people should also expect their reward!

226. Decency and Decorum

The nature of the close relationship between spouses often leads to the disappearance of decorum between them. Nevertheless, how beautiful it would be if the couple's relationship were similar to that of their relationship with strangers in terms of behavior. When one of them enters the home, the other rushes to greet them with love and affection, and when one stands to leave, the other gets up and walks with them to the door; nothing but the most polite and kind words are used when conversing.

That couple would eventually find that if they did something to anger their spouse, causing them to lose their composure, politeness, and the mutual respect they practice in their daily interactions, it would likely make the angry one restrain their anger and stop uttering inappropriate and obscene words.

227. Spiritual Affection

A marriage in which spouses have affection for each other stems from their faith, and the nature of the relationship that ties them is lovely!

The most beautiful home on the face of the earth holds two spouses who stay up at night in worship. Each takes a separate room to pray in, and God ﷻ and the angels watch both. The husband adds his wife to the list of forty believers he prays for, saying: "Oh God, please forgive my wife." Meanwhile, the wife is in the other room doing the same, saying: "Oh God, please forgive my husband." It is such a breathtaking sight to behold! Can such a family, whose home is filled with worship at night and respect during the day, break apart or separate?

228. The Slogan of Marital Life

God ﷻ says:

﴿وَمِنْ ءَايَـٰتِهِۦٓ أَنْ خَلَقَ لَكُم مِّنْ أَنفُسِكُمْ أَزْوَٰجًا لِّتَسْكُنُوٓا۟ إِلَيْهَا وَجَعَلَ بَيْنَكُم مَّوَدَّةً
وَرَحْمَةً ۚ إِنَّ فِى ذَٰلِكَ لَـَٔايَـٰتٍ لِّقَوْمٍ يَتَفَكَّرُونَ﴾

﴾*wa-min 'āyātihī 'an khalaqa lakum min 'anfusikum 'azwājan li-taskunū 'ilayhā wa-ja'ala baynakum mawaddatan wa-raḥmatan 'inna fī dhālika la-'āyātin li-qawmin yatafakkarūn*[a]﴿

﴾*And of His signs is that He created for you mates from your own selves that you may take comfort in them, and He ordained affection and mercy between you. There are indeed signs in that for a people who reflect*﴿[116]

This verse is the guiding light for marital life; no married person or anyone planning to marry should overlook it, and anyone striving for a happy marriage should contemplate it. Therefore, we need to reflect on its words discussing marriage as a sign, the meaning of a mate or a spouse, the affection and the mercy placed between spouses, and the goal sought out of marriage!

229. The Toughest and the Strongest

Among the things that bring about clemency and the suppression of anger are reminding oneself of the rewards gained in this life before the hereafter.

The Messenger of God ﷺ once passed by a group of people who were throwing rocks; he asked:

> "What is this?"

They answered:

> "We do this to see who is the toughest and the strongest among us."

---

[116] Sūrat al-Rūm, Verse 21.

The Prophet ﷺ then said to them:

> "The toughest of you is the one who controls himself when angry, and the clement amongst you is the one who forgives when able to act out their rage."

The Messenger ﷺ also said:

> "Whoever suppresses their anger, though they can act out their rage, God will fill their hearts with security and faith."[117]

Thus, one who suppresses their anger even when they can levy punishment will feel the sweetness of faith in their hearts. Congratulations to the one who has swallowed their anger and won the pleasure of God ﷻ!

230. Internal Repulsion

One of the effects of repeated anger and transgression caused by physical and emotional abuse is the development of internal repulsion. This is one of the most complicated situations a person can face and may need Divine intervention to be solved.

A husband who abuses his wife and later seeks to repair his relationship with her will find that even if he increases his spending on her and showers her with the most expensive gifts, it will not heal the internal wounds he has created. Regarding this matter, the Holy Prophet ﷺ said:

---

[117] Majlisī, ʿAllamah Muḥammad Bāqir, *Biḥār al-Anwār*, Vol. 68, p. 410.

> "Does one of you beat his wife and then expect to keep hugging her?"[118]

Here, our Holy Prophet ﷺ wanted to bring our attention to the effects of a husband's abuse of his wife, which ultimately leads to a lack of harmony between them and, many times, to the destruction of their marriage!

231. Going Against Natural Disposition

Part of what attracts a woman towards a man is his masculine characteristics. The more strength and wisdom a man displays, the greater he becomes in his wife's eyes. This fulfills an emotional need for her and makes her feel safer as she sees that her husband can compensate for any shortcomings or physical weakness she may have.

On the other hand, a man is attracted to a woman's femininity and her, showing her weakness and need for him. It becomes clear when we look at marriages today that many problems and disagreements stem from going against this natural disposition. A weak man will not have a special place in a woman's heart, and a man will not be attracted to a masculine woman.

232. Marital Status

The word spouse has a profound meaning. Marriage is a union achieved by combining and joining two things, wherein each is called a spouse.

---

[118] al-Ḥurr al-ʿĀmilī, Shaykh Muḥammad b. al-Ḥasan, *Wasāʾil al-Shīʿa*, Vol. 20, p. 167, ḥadīth 25323.

Before marriage, a man and a woman were on their own, and each was a single individual; through marriage, they moved from individuals to marriage. The unit created through their marriage will break should one of them decide to leave it, meaning for each to remain in this unit, they also need the other to be there.

Therefore, a man should not make his wife feel like he did her a favor by marrying her and that she would have remained a single woman if it were not for him. Similarly, a woman should not make her husband feel like her marrying him was a favor, and he owes her for saving him from becoming a corrupted youth and that it was due to her that he managed to safeguard half of his religion. They should both be grateful to God ﷻ, who made and willed this integrative status (marriage) for people to reproduce and build the earth.

233. Choice

Some women who do not wear the ḥijāb and are advised to wear it respond by saying: "if God guides me, I will wear it!" This must be the silliest thing to say!

God ﷻ gave humans a choice in their actions; they are not forced to act a certain way. By attaching a choice to the Will of God ﷻ, it is as if she is saying that ﷻ forced her to commit this sin!

Did she not read that God ﷻ says:

﴿وَقُل لِّلْمُؤْمِنَٰتِ يَغْضُضْنَ مِنْ أَبْصَٰرِهِنَّ وَيَحْفَظْنَ فُرُوجَهُنَّ وَلَا يُبْدِينَ زِينَتَهُنَّ إِلَّا مَا
ظَهَرَ مِنْهَا ۖ وَلْيَضْرِبْنَ بِخُمُرِهِنَّ عَلَىٰ جُيُوبِهِنَّ ۖ﴾

﴿wa-qul li-l-mu'mināti yaghḍuḍna min 'abṣārihinna wa-yaḥfaẓna furūjahunna wa-lā yubdīna zīnatahunna 'illā mā ẓahara minhā wa-l-yaḍribna bi-khumurihinna ʿalā juyūbihinna﴾

﴿And tell the faithful women to cast down their looks and to guard their private parts, and not to display their charms, beyond what is [acceptably] visible, and let them draw their scarfs over their bosoms﴾[119]

Or is she expecting an angel to descend from the seventh heaven to put the ḥijāb on her?

234. Observing Religious Rulings

Observing and remaining mindful of religious rulings undoubtedly affects the ability to be blessed with righteous offspring. A couple whose marriage was built upon sin will have divine care lifted from their lives, and as God ﷻ says:

﴿وَٱلْبَلَدُ ٱلطَّيِّبُ يَخْرُجُ نَبَاتُهُۥ بِإِذْنِ رَبِّهِۦ ۖ وَٱلَّذِي خَبُثَ لَا يَخْرُجُ إِلَّا نَكِدًا ۚ كَذَٰلِكَ
نُصَرِّفُ ٱلْآيَٰتِ لِقَوْمٍ يَشْكُرُونَ﴾

﴿wa-l-baladu ṭ-ṭayyibu yakhruju nabātuhū bi-'idhni rabbihī wa-lladhī khabutha lā yakhruju 'illā nakidan﴾

﴿The good land—its vegetation comes out by the permission of its Lord, and as for that which is bad, it does not come out except sparsely﴾[120]

---

[119] Sūrat al-Nūr, Verse 31.

[120] Sūrat al-Aʿrāf, Verse 58.

A man who has an illicit relationship with a woman and has relations with her as one is meant to have with his wife, then decides to repent and marry her will be like the family that was founded on piety from its first day, even if the man couple repents for their sin. One who has sinned and repented is not like one who never sinned to begin with.

235. Benefits of Breastfeeding

During the two years, a mother breastfeeds her child, feeds them milk, and pours affection and love. Breastfeeding has a profound effect on strengthening the relationship between a mother and child and leaves a significant impact on the child's soul! These effects become apparent when the child matures and approaches their twenties, during which a mother often becomes afraid that her child will fall into sin.

When the mother raises her hands to invoke God ﷻ to protect her child, it will affect him, causing him to resist the temptation to sin more easily. Her invocation reawakens an internal voice he hears, which was formed due to the tremendous effort his mother spent during those two years of breastfeeding.

236. Polluting the Natural Disposition

When a child is born, they enter this world with the natural disposition that God ﷻ created us with to love righteous principles and morals. However, as they start comprehending the world, they suffer a shock. This is because they suddenly see conflicting sides around them.

There is a conflict between an incorrect method of upbringing and what natural disposition compels a person to do or between the great morals that a person learns and what they see people practicing. With time, the healthy natural disposition they were born with becomes polluted, and they, too, end up following the footsteps of those who were polluted before them!

How beautiful it would be for parents to protect their child's innocence, the purity of their natural disposition, and their spiritual health through puberty until their child reaches mental and emotional maturity and gains independence!

237. Acquiring Divine Morals

One who strives to possess even one of God's ﷻ attributes, his mercy, for example, opens themselves up to the possibility that God ﷻ will bestow them with more of His attributes out of His Bounty. Suddenly, this person finds that they have reached a high level of spirituality and has been given a fantastic spiritual gift that never crossed their mind.

It is all due to wanting to imitate one of God's ﷻ attributes: mercy, and what a great attribute to have!

Among its most prominent manifestations is having mercy on one's soul by training it to behave in a manner that gains God's ﷻ pleasure. A person who does not monitor their actions is a person who is oppressing themselves, and among what must be monitored are one's eyes, as most deviation comes from extending one's eyesight towards that which God ﷻ has prohibited.

238. Mindfulness of Divine Watch

Transgression between spouses sometimes stems from a belief that marriage is a closed bubble, and no one knows its secrets except for the religious leaders and arbitrators the couple seeks assistance from when an issue arises.

A husband may mistreat his wife but hide those negatives from others to not harm his reputation and lose respect. Moreover, living together for a long time could lead some men to stop viewing their wives humanely or vice versa, leading them to lose their decorum, decency, and respect for each other. The solution is for believers to remain mindful of the continuous Divine watch and to remember to care for what has been entrusted to them!

239. A Wife and a Friend

A believer should choose a wife who is also a friend to him, one with whom he shares an understanding that will last a lifetime, not a wife who will fulfill just one aspect of life and become monotonous very quickly!

Some women sit with their husbands and tell them everything they have taken care of in their absence to relieve them of the stress of worrying about those matters. What a great life that is!

What if the couple set aside time daily to study a new jurisprudential ruling, the meaning of a verse from the Noble Qur'ān, or even to discuss a ḥadīth from the Household of the Prophet ﷺ? Is it possible for such a couple to run out of things to discuss, as many couples do a few days after their engagement?

240. Combining the Means to an End

A believer combines the hard work of preparing a suitable environment and righteous foundation to raise children with prayer and supplications, as was narrated:

> "Tie your camel with a rope, and then say that you trust God will protect your camel."[121]

On the day of the Battle of Badr, the Messenger of God ﷺ went out with his army and invoked God ﷻ, saying:

> "O' God!... If this group is destroyed, You will not be worshipped on earth."[122]

The Prophet ﷺ could have just stayed in his masjid and asked God ﷻ to punish Quraysh for what they have done, yet this is the way of life: it is necessary to combine material and spiritual means to reach an end.

A believer should not neglect to raise their children and depend only on supplications and prayer, hoping they turn out all right. One harvests as much as the effort they have put in.

241. The Wise One

The spread of evil in all forms is one of the most apparent trials of this era. If a believer finds himself struggling to refrain from visiting corrupt and deviated websites and channels, he should remind

---

[121] Rayshahrī, Āyatullāh Muḥammad, *Mīzān al-Ḥikmah*, Vol. 4, p. 3661.

[122] Ibn Abi l-Ḥadīd, *Sharḥ Nahj al-Balāgha*, Vol. 3, p. 259.

himself that these images are nothing but pulses of light and that the screen is just glass that contains some inscriptions; the wise one would not want to enter the Hellfire because of these inscriptions on a piece of glass! If he even finds himself alone with an ajnabiyyah woman (a woman he can marry but is otherwise unmarried to), he should peel away the layer of beauty and look at what is beneath it, and he will see that nothing is tempting.

242. The Unveiled Woman

When we love someone, we dislike anyone who is hostile towards them and causes them pain. Suppose a man who loves a beautiful woman was told that this beautiful woman hit or disrespected his mother. Would he still desire this woman, or would his whole existence turn into abhorrence and aversion towards her?

An unveiled woman essentially put a religious ruling under her feet. She crossed the limits set by God ﷻ. So how could a believer who feels even the slightest love for God ﷻ find inclination toward this sinner?

A believer cannot help but feel disgusted and intense aversion towards the one who declares open rebellion and defiance of the Creator and Lord and does not find any pleasure or fascination when looking at her!

243. Tolerance

People are different, and spouses are no exception as they are two different human beings, each with a temperament and natural disposition that distinguishes them from others! Therefore, agreements, concessions, and tolerance are needed when a mistake is made, which is likely to happen because humans are not infallible. If a wife makes a mistake once, her husband should remember that he has, or will, make many mistakes.

Taking the initiative to do good and being kind to others to avoid tension before it starts is a sure way to guarantee family happiness. Those who act according to this verse:

﴿وَلَا تَسۡتَوِي ٱلۡحَسَنَةُ وَلَا ٱلسَّيِّئَةُۚ ٱدۡفَعۡ بِٱلَّتِي هِيَ أَحۡسَنُ فَإِذَا ٱلَّذِي بَيۡنَكَ وَبَيۡنَهُۥ عَدَٰوَةٞ كَأَنَّهُۥ وَلِيٌّ حَمِيمٞ﴾

﴿wa-lā tastawī l-ḥasanatu wa-lā s-sayyi'atu dfaʿ bi-llatī hiya 'aḥsanu fa-'idhā lladhī baynaka wa-baynahū ʿadāwatun ka-'annahū waliyyun ḥamīm^un^﴾

﴿Good and evil [conduct] are not equal. Repel [evil] with what is best. [If you do so,] he between whom and you was enmity, will then be as though he were a sympathetic friend﴾[123]

Will be safeguarded from the evils of anyone they fear, and its results are guaranteed.

244. Violations

God ﷻ, the Lord of the Worlds, is the One who made love and mercy between a married couple. Immediately after signing their marriage contract, spouses begin to yearn for each other, as if they have already been together for years. However, violating religious guidelines can cause love and mercy to be lifted from their marriage!

---

[123] Sūrat Fuṣṣilat, Verse 34.

This can be likened to a son who traveled far away, and his father made sure to give him enough money to last him for the duration of his travels. However, the son spent all the money in one night and ended up sorrowful, lamenting, and regretting what he had done! Far be it from God, the Lord of the Worlds, to wrong us, as He is the Most Loving, the Most Kind, Most Generous Lord, but we, with our violations, take away the sweetness of our blessed marriages!

245. Seeking Forgiveness for the Chain of Parents

One of the main fruits of marriage is to leave behind a progeny that will remain as long as this life remains, as humans naturally want to be remembered and for their impact on this life to be eternal. It is beautiful for a believer to ask for forgiveness for everyone who had a role in bringing him into existence during their night prayers, forming a chain of fathers and mothers that go back thousands of years, and to ask God ﷻ to have mercy on those who deserve mercy and to forgive those who have sinned.

In their prayer, the believer says:

> "O God, forgive me, and my parents, and my parents' parents back to Ādam the father of humankind ﷺ."

Whoever remembers their ancestors in their prayers during their life will find that, in the Day of Judgement, those ancestors will thank them.

246. The Scary Father

Some fathers seem to turn into military commanders at home; some even brag about this abhorrent attribute, claiming that they are so respected and revered at home that when they enter, everyone stands quiet and motionless as if they were statues out of utmost respect. Such a father cannot be considered an ideal father, not even close.

A believer is bright and cheerful; he brings happiness and joy to the hearts of others, especially to his wife and children. When such a father is absent from the home, his wife and children miss his presence, and when he travels, his whole family feels the pain of separation and suffers depression! Unfortunately, though, some homes look forward to the day the father travels so that they can enjoy a few peaceful days and nights.

247. A Source of Temptation

Some family visits represent a source of temptation, especially when both sexes mix at the dinner table with adolescents. These days, those who chase their desires exchange words with their eyes, later contacting each other and eventually meeting. And then get in contact with each other and eventually meet!

Strangely enough, if an epidemic becomes widespread in a place, we find that people take precautionary measures and avoid that place at all costs! Nevertheless, some people, aware that certain family visits can lead to weakness in one's religious commitment, do not show the slightest care! On the Day of Judgement, such a person will be surprised by a burden of sins they did not expect!

248. Divine Graciousness

It would be great to repeat this supplication during our prayers and at any time or place where prayers are known to be accepted.

﴿رَبَّنَا هَبْ لَنَا مِنْ أَزْوَاجِنَا وَذُرِّيَّاتِنَا قُرَّةَ أَعْيُنٍ وَاجْعَلْنَا لِلْمُتَّقِينَ إِمَامًا﴾

﴿*rabbanā hab lanā min ʾazwājinā wa-dhurriyyātinā qurrata ʾaʿyunin wa-jʿalnā li-l-muttaqīna ʾimāma*ⁿ﴾

﴿*'Our Lord! Give us joy and comfort in our spouses and offspring, and make us imāms of the Godwary.'*﴾[124]

Fortunate is the one whose request is granted.

This gift is due to Divine Graciousness and is granted to those who want it. As such, it is appropriate for a believer to repeat this supplication while in a state of beseeching and neediness, showing that they have no good virtues and are not even capable of distinguished discipline for themselves, let alone another person!

When praying to God ﷻ, believers should admit that they are ignorant, cannot influence, and cannot teach anyone else. They should add that their energy is limited, their time is divided between work and other commitments, and their happiness would be limitless if granted a distinguished child!

---

[124] Sūrat al-Furqān, Verse 74.

249. Deprivation of Some Degrees of Perfection

A young person who is entangled with sinful acts during his teenage years can still grow to become a prominent believer. When they remember their dark history, such a person will feel like they live in a condition of internal corrosion! Self-rebuke will remain with them. They will always ask themselves: how can I expect to become one of God's ﷻ closest servants when I have done all that I have done?

God ﷻ indeed forgives our sins, but how can one rid himself of the lingering subconscious effect of sins? A person mixed up in sin may be deprived of reaching certain levels of perfection, and one who does not sin is not the same as one who has sinned and asked for forgiveness!

250. Settling Scores

An excellent habit for a couple to implement in their lives is to set aside time at the end of each day to assess how they have treated each other that day. Before sleeping each night, they can review that day's folder together. If they find that it was a good day, then each of them thanks the other for that blessed day, and if it contained what upset one of them, then they discuss it to try to settle that score. This is very important to do because when negativity begins to build up, it will have two effects: distancing the hearts from each other and, more importantly, falling from the eyes of God ﷻ and becoming deserving of His wrath, such wrath that no one knows when it will befall them. When spouses clear the score and settle the matter between them, they save themselves from worrying about the repercussions that can befall them at any moment.

251. Forgive When Able

One of the best forms of mercy is choosing forgiveness when one can exact revenge. This is precisely what we noticed in the Holy Prophet's ﷺ life during the conquest of Mecca. The Prophet ﷺ was victorious in his conquest, and unlike most conquerors who enter their enemies' lands, the messenger of mercy released a statement saying:

> "Whoever lays down their weapon is safe, and whoever confines themselves to their home and closes their door is safe, and whoever seeks refuge by the Ka'bah is safe."[125]

He then called 'Uthmān b. Ṭalḥa to return the keys of the Ka'bah to him and said:

> "Today is a day of righteousness and fulfillment of trust."[126]

Do we see such an example of forgiveness and greatness in the lives of other conquerors?

252. Jealousy and Possessiveness

It has been narrated that Imām 'Alī (a) said:

> "A woman's jealousy is [tantamount to] infidelity, whereas a man's jealousy is [part of his] faith."[127]

---

[125] al-Bayhaqī, Aḥmad b. al-Ḥusayn, *Sunan al-Kubra lil Bayhaqī*, Vol. 9, p. 117.

[126] Ṭūsī, Shaykh Muḥammad b. Ḥasan, *al-Ghaybah*, p. 308.

[127] Sharīf Raḍī, Muḥammad b. al-Ḥusayn, *Nahj al-Balāgha*, p. 491.

This is because a woman naturally likes to have exclusive possession of her husband and hates to share him with another. As for a man who is jealous and possessive over his wife, he does so because he refuses to let his wife and his honor be harmed, even if indirectly.

Some men, however, stand idle and do nothing when they see their wives not maintaining their modesty. What is worse is that some men order their wives to dress up and adorn themselves in public to show them off to other men, as if they are gratified and proud when people see they have such a beautiful woman! The least that can be said to describe such men is that they have reached a level below animals!

253. Celibacy

Marriage is a part of the tradition of the Prophet ﷺ. Some claim they do not need it because they desire to remain celibate, devote themselves to God, free themselves to serve the religion, or escape marital life responsibilities.

Any blessings they think they might receive from doing so cannot make up for what they miss out on by not having children. If remaining celibate to devote oneself to God were good, Sayyidah Fāṭimah عليها السلام would have done so! Fortunate is the one who is happy in their marital life with the blessing of God ﷻ and is happy after they die because of the righteous offspring that supply them with the reward of good deeds at a time when humans are in most need of even one single reward to add weight to their good deeds!

254. Thinking About Consequences

People labor and work hard to build a life where they can enjoy eternal happiness! Yet some spend their youth and reach old age living with marital problems. They may separate from their wife, and their children may follow her. They grow older, remain alone, and may even die so lonely that no one knows until a few days have passed! What value would this life be when it can be summarized into sins committed during youth followed by a failed marriage and the continuation of problems until death? Is not thinking about this consequence before it happens called for?

255. Dissolving Boundaries

A common problem these days is the communication between members of the opposite sex over the internet. A believer should keep their eyes on the goal (of being close to God ﷻ) in their every move; if they see something that does not seem right, not to mention ḥarām, they should not move forward with it.

However, these days, religious boundaries are becoming liquid and being dissolved. A relationship between a man and a woman may start under the guise of religion in the form of advisory or missionary work and then slowly turn to sin, where, in most cases, a woman becomes victim to the weakness she may have for charming and emotional speech.

256. Trespasser

A woman who wears a ḥijāb that is not by religious specifications and shows even a strand of her hair partially violates the religious ruling. She violates it entirely if she does not wear it at all.

If a person crosses a country's borders, even by only one step, they would be considered a trespasser. Similarly, a woman who exposes a portion of her chest, hair, or leg is a woman who has trespassed against Divine boundaries.

﴿وَمَن يَتَعَدَّ حُدُودَ ٱللَّهِ فَأُوْلَٰٓئِكَ هُمُ ٱلظَّٰلِمُونَ﴾

﴿*wa-man yataʿadda ḥudūda llāhi fa-ʾulāʾika humu ẓ-ẓālimūna*﴾

﴿*and whoever transgresses the bounds of God—it is they who are the wrongdoers*﴾[128]

Therefore, we should not make light of how small sin may seem, as it is said:

> "Do not look at the smallness of the sin you committed, but look at the One you disobeyed"!

257. The Disadvantage of the Cultural Movement

Among the disadvantages of the cultural movement and the presence of institutes and universities is the increased marital disagreements arising from conflicting ideas between spouses. If a married couple are colleagues in the same field at the same university and neither holds a higher degree than the other, both having the same credentials, the closeness of their cultural and intellectual levels can lead to disputes between them. When such disputes arise and a resolution is needed, they should first accept the legitimate religious ruling and the authority given to the man since it stems from divine wisdom.

---

[128] Sūrat al-Baqarah, Verse 229.

258. Manufacturer of Righteous Generations

When a man marries a righteous woman, even if she is poor or lacking in beauty, he should take solace in knowing that he married a woman fit to give him righteous offspring. This will comfort a man who views his wife as a birther and shaper of righteous children and not as a tool for his enjoyment, as beauty serves only to give him pleasure, and being from a wealthy family would serve only his desire to take from her wealth. However, when a man marries a believing woman, he gains a woman who will bear righteous generations for him, which is the best profit that can be earned in this domain!

259. Taking the Initiative to Save the Children

Some children may not listen to their parents, mainly when they are at the age when desire and emotions are at their peak. Some even remain in a state of rebellion against their parents after they have married and passed into their forties.

Nonetheless, after calming down and experiencing the sweetness and bitterness of life, and when the surge of desire passes, many return to the laps of their parents. Some parents, however, meet them with harsh confrontations as if they were trying to seek revenge for their child! Yet, it is upon the parents to take the initiative to save a child who is disrespectful or disobedient towards them without waiting for a signal from them to do so!

260. Planting the Spirit of the Oneness of God and Wilāyah

Reciting the Adhān and Iqāmah in a newborn's ears, reciting Sūrat al-Fātiḥah and the last verses of Sūrat al-Ḥashr, placing a small amount of water from the Euphrates river and a small amount of Imām al-Ḥusayn's ﷷ turbah (with its smells of martyrdom) in the mouth of a newborn child; all these actions plant the spirit of Tawḥīd and Wilāyah in the depths of that child's existence as they are written into the first pages of their life.

This child will grow to respect his parents and hold them in high esteem as he remembers the favor they did for him in childhood. The joy and beauty of this act are completed by sacrificing an animal to share its meat with the poor, known as ʿAqīqah.

261. Poor Execution of Obligations

Some people must do better when practicing the [Islāmic] obligation of enjoining good and preventing evil. When a man sees that his wife or children have sinned, he may treat them harshly, which violates religious rulings. He may think that by doing so, he is fulfilling his obligation, and the more violent and cruel he is, the more satisfied he becomes, thinking that his actions are like those of the Prophet ﷺ when he was angry for the sake of God ﷻ. In reality, though, this man accomplishes nothing short of making the other person insist on their sin, if not lead them to commit a worse sin! Then, on the Day of Judgement, he will not be punished as a person who did not prevent evil but as one who encouraged evil instead!

262. An Engrossing Concern

The importance of children is evident in the supplications given by the prophets and righteous believers. In them, their children were an engrossing concern.

As soon as she gave birth to her blessed daughter, the mother of Maryam عليها السلام asked God ﷻ to protect her and her offspring from the cursed Shayṭān. Ibrāhīm عليه السلام asked his Lord to give his progeny success in their establishing prayers, and he thanked God ﷻ for granting him Ismāʿīl and Isḥāq despite his old age. We are also ordered to make such invocations for our offspring by repeating:

﴿رَبَّنَا هَبْ لَنَا مِنْ أَزْوَاجِنَا وَذُرِّيَّاتِنَا قُرَّةَ أَعْيُنٍ وَاجْعَلْنَا لِلْمُتَّقِينَ إِمَامًا﴾

﴾*rabbanā hab lanā min ʾazwājinā wa-dhurriyyātinā qurrata ʾaʿyunin wa-jʿalnā li-l-muttaqīna ʾimāma*^{n}﴿

﴾*'Our Lord! Give us joy and comfort in our spouses and offspring, and make us imāms of the Godwary.'*﴿[129]

263. The Benefit is One

One of the best investments a man can make to benefit himself in heaven and on Judgement Day is to strive to reform and educate his wife and encourage her to ascend the ladder of spiritual perfection.

When a man cannot perform recommended acts of worship due to his commitments to work, he can encourage his wife to perform

---

[129] Sūrat al-Furqān, Verse 74.

the night prayer (Ṣalāt al-Layl). At the same time, he sleeps or encourages her to travel to perform 'Umrah or visit the Holy Shrine. When his wife successfully performs these acts of worship, it is as if he is performing them himself. The benefit of these acts of worship is that they are partners and will remain together forever. The regard a man holds for his wife is a beautiful investment!

264. Favorable Outlets

We must do so graciously and favorably when presenting a new idea to another person. Sometimes, a word that shows love and appreciation can open the other party's heart, saving the need for much talking and preaching.

Notice how in the Noble Qur'ān, before instructing the believers to do something, God ﷻ paves the way for the request by saying:

﴿يَٰٓأَيُّهَا ٱلَّذِينَ ءَامَنُواْ﴾

﴾yā-'ayyuhā lladhīna 'āmanū﴿

﴾O you who have faith!﴿[130]

And:

﴿قُلۡ يَٰعِبَادِيَ ٱلَّذِينَ أَسۡرَفُواْ عَلَىٰٓ أَنفُسِهِمۡ﴾

﴾qul yā-'ibādiya lladhīna 'asrafū 'alā 'anfusihim﴿

[130] Sūrat al-Aḥzāb, Verse 9.

﴿*Say [that God declares,] 'O My servants who have committed excesses against their own souls'*﴾[131]

And:

﴿وَإِذَا سَأَلَكَ عِبَادِي عَنِّي فَإِنِّي قَرِيبٌ أُجِيبُ دَعْوَةَ ٱلدَّاعِ إِذَا دَعَانِ فَلْيَسْتَجِيبُوا۟ لِي وَلْيُؤْمِنُوا۟ بِي لَعَلَّهُمْ يَرْشُدُونَ﴾

﴿*wa-'idhā sa'alaka 'ibādī 'annī*﴾

﴿*When My servants ask you about Me*﴾[132]

So why don't we follow our Ever-Affectionate Lord's example in softening our speech's tone and entering hearts through favorable outlets?

265. Looking into the Mirror

A marriage is never devoid of matters that cause tension and anger. A believer should always remember a slogan in their time of anger: "Never make a decision when angry!" This is because when one is angry, they become a toy in the hands of the devil.

If people want to know their internal state when angry, they should look in the mirror and examine their exterior. There, they would see an unpleasant face that they find unbearable! If people cannot even bear themselves in anger, how can they expect others to tolerate them?

---

[131] Sūrat al-Zumar, Verse 53.

[132] Sūrat al-Baqarah, Verse 186.

266. Enduring Hard Work

A woman must appreciate her husband's effort to ensure a good life for their family. She indeed endures the hardships of pregnancy, childbirth, and breastfeeding, but her husband endures hard work lasting up to twenty-five years until his children marry and become independent.

When a mother looks at her child, who has become a young man and has an independent life with his wife, her eyes are filled with joy, and she feels happiness and comfort. Therefore, she should remember the long years of hard work her husband endured to make this dream a reality.

267. The Basis of Delegation

A man's authority over his family does not necessarily equate to control not rooted in reason and Divine law. Instead, it is the delegation of being a trustworthy ruler in managing his family's affairs; like any human gathering, two or more people need leadership and management for their affairs to run smoothly.

The verse that discusses this authority explains that the basis of this delegation is rooted in two factors: the first is the man's aptitude, natural endowment, and his position as a husband in the family according to what God ﷻ says:

﴿بِمَا فَضَّلَ ٱللَّهُ بَعْضَهُمْ عَلَىٰ بَعْضٍ﴾

﴿bi-mā faḍḍala llāhu baʿḍahum ʿalā baʿḍin﴾

﴿*because of the advantage God has granted some of them over others*﴾[133]

The second factor is the man's responsibility to strive to ensure his family's livelihood, as God ﷻ says:

﴿وَبِمَآ أَنفَقُواْ مِنْ أَمْوَٰلِهِمْ﴾

﴿*wa-bi-mā 'anfaqū min 'amwālihim*﴾

﴿*and by virtue of their spending out of their wealth*﴾[134]

268. Intermarrying of Souls

The reality of marital life is that it is essentially an intermarriage between souls and between bodies. The general public sees it as a physical union dominated by human instinct.

If a couple begins to view their marriage as an intermarrying of souls, they will naturally try to reach a psychological harmony between them. A human's instinctive side follows its psychological side, so if affection and mercy are found, the instinctive side will have an even more distinguished impact on the couple. This is how a believing family can reach a state of complete happiness, internally and externally.

---

133 Sūrat al-Nisā', Verse 34.

134 Sūrat al-Nisā', Verse 34.

269. Reviewing the Internal Information Bank

A person who wishes to prevent tension when dealing with others must review the internal information bank they use to evaluate people. A man who marries a woman while he has another woman on his mind will end up mistreating his wife for the rest of their life because he will always compare the woman he is with and the one he could not have! It is unreasonable for one to miss out on the happiness in his hands and torture himself for nothing more than an image in his mind!

270. The Mother's Influence on the Children

There is no doubt that a mother's intellect and level of spirituality influence her children's upbringing, and it is a decisive influence!

If a mother's milk can transmit traits so effectively that a child can become upset if the mother is upset, then imagine the impact that a mother's glance, behavior, and genetic composition have on her child.

Therefore, a man who wants righteous offspring must prepare their foundation: a mother who will nurture and raise his children. A righteous mother's breath, existence, and even her glances are influential; a mother can raise and discipline her child through glances and words!

271. Offering a Sacrifice

It is a parent's responsibility to raise their children and to guide them towards great matters. Congratulations to those who guided their children from the innocence of childhood to the innocence of piety through prayers, care, and observation. Their reward, as understood from the narrations, is that they will be gathered with the just Imāms.

Moreover, it is known that those who offer a sacrifice to God ﷻ are those who are interested in spreading the religion, have a good reputation, and are known for treating others well; God ﷻ blesses their offspring for them and makes their offspring outstanding in knowledge, faith, and morals.

272. Completion of the Argument

A woman has no excuse not to respect her ḥijāb if she is married to a man who is outstanding in his faith. The responsibility she carries is doubled, as can be understood from God's ﷻ words:

﴿يَٰنِسَآءَ ٱلنَّبِيِّ لَسۡتُنَّ كَأَحَدٖ مِّنَ ٱلنِّسَآءِ﴾

﴿*yā-nisā'a n-nabiyyi lastunna ka-'aḥadin mina n-nisā'i*﴾

﴿*O wives of the Prophet! You are not like other women*﴾[135]

Consider a girl born to sinful parents who lives in the West and has gone astray. Would her judgment be the same as that of a girl born to faithful parents and living in a Muslim country in a home where the Qur'ān is recited morning and night, and she still goes astray? Similarly, the judgment of a young man raised in a home filled with faith, or one whose lineage can be traced back to the Prophet ﷺ, will be different from that of a young man who grew up in a sinful environment.

[135] Sūrat al-Aḥzāb, Verse 32.

273. Caution in Interactions

A believer must be cautious in their interactions with others, especially those under their care, such as their wife and children!

They need to find out where they stand regarding their balance of deeds with God ﷻ and how many accumulated sins they have not been forgiven for due to God's ﷻ Clemency. A person does not know when Divine anger will befall them either.

A person could commit a small transgression in their interaction with others, and all of the anger that God ﷻ has held back can suddenly fall upon them, and their afflictions will be never-ending and come from where they least expect. That one seemingly small sin they committed suddenly becomes the straw that broke the camel's back, as the Arabic adage says.

274. Sweetness in the Heart

A committed believer controls his eyes and lowers his gaze out of fear and respect for his Lord, not for fear of the law, people, or his wife. It was narrated in a ḥadīth Qudsī that God ﷻ said:

> "An unlawful look is an arrow from the arrows of Shayṭān. He who abandons it for My sake, I will give him in return faith that he finds its sweetness in his heart."[136]

There is a significant difference between a person who looks at an unlawful thing and the pleasure from it quickly disappears. All that remains are negative consequences, including the pains of regret

---

[136] Rayshahrī, Āyatullāh Muḥammad, *Mīzān al-Ḥikmah*, Vol. 4, p. 3292.

that eat away at them, and between the person who avoids looking at anything unlawful for God ﷻ and finds sweetness in their heart!

275. The Blessings of a Happy Family

The blessings of a happy family are not limited to only this mortal life but extend into the hereafter, as God ﷻ says:

﴿وَٱلَّذِينَ ءَامَنُوا۟ وَٱتَّبَعَتْهُمْ ذُرِّيَّتُهُم بِإِيمَٰنٍ أَلْحَقْنَا بِهِمْ ذُرِّيَّتَهُمْ وَمَآ أَلَتْنَٰهُم مِّنْ عَمَلِهِم مِّن شَىْءٍ ۚ كُلُّ ٱمْرِئٍۭ بِمَا كَسَبَ رَهِينٌ﴾

﴾*wa-lladhīna ʾāmanū wa-ttabaʿathum dhurriyyatuhum bi-ʾīmānin ʾalḥaqnā bihim dhurriyyatahum wa-mā ʾalatnāhum min ʿamalihim min shayʾin*﴿

﴾*The faithful and their descendants who followed them in faith—We will make their descendants join them, and We will not stint anything from [the reward of] their deeds*﴿[137]

Therefore, it is an investment that cannot be measured against any other investments in this life. Regarding this matter, the Prophet ﷺ is reported to have said:

> "When a man enters Paradise, he will ask about his parents and spouse and children; it is said to him:
>
>> "Their deeds were not enough for them to reach your degree and deeds."

---

[137] Sūrat al-Ṭūr, Verse 21.

So the believer says:

> "My Lord, whatever I have done in the world was for them and me."

Then God ﷻ will order the angles to let his family join him."[138]

276. The Steadfast Mountain

The Lord of the Worlds is the most knowledgeable of what is best for a person, and He may see that some people's righteousness and perfection are attained through marrying a quarrelsome woman. Some well-known pious believers were tested with wives who were hard to tolerate. Just as God ﷻ arranges for some to marry righteous women, He arranges for some to marry wicked women to test their patience with her.

We know this life is a testing place, as God ﷻ says:

﴿ٱلَّذِي خَلَقَ ٱلْمَوْتَ وَٱلْحَيَوٰةَ لِيَبْلُوَكُمْ أَيُّكُمْ أَحْسَنُ عَمَلًا﴾

﴿li-yabluwakum 'ayyukum 'aḥsanu 'amalan﴾

﴿that He may test you [to see] which of you is best in conduct﴾[139]

Fortunate is the man who, when aggravated, remembers and fears God ﷻ so that he does not lose his temper! Indeed, a believer is like a steadfast mountain not moved by storms!

---

[138] al-Ṭabarānī, Sulaymān, *al-Mu'jam al-Saghīr*, ḥadīth 641.

[139] Sūrat al-Mulk, Verse 2.

277. Eternal Blessings

Some women refuse those who propose to them and prefer to continue with their education, claiming that their degrees guarantee their financial future and are more important than marriage and raising children. However, with time, they will discover that they were mistaken in these beliefs!

The blessings of a hardworking woman who is diligent in managing the affairs of her family and raising righteous children who will be agents of guidance in society cannot be compared to a career that may force her to do what is not suitable for her and after from which she will eventually retire. Can eternal blessings be compared to transient ones?

278. Assessing the Reason for Anger

Anger is one of the most destructive elements in the structure of a marriage. Nevertheless, it is impossible to avoid it, as it is a natural state we feel when we see something repulsive or that does not fit!

It is necessary for a person who feels angry towards another to assess the reason for their anger, if what they view as repulsive is truly repulsive, or if they only imagine it as such. They should then assess the intention behind their anger: if it is for the sake of God ﷻ, then their anger is well placed, but if it is anger for oneself and the matter was truly repulsive to them, then they should be aware of the devil taking hold of them. Therefore, it is better to delay reacting until a person calms down.

279. God Accepts Only from the Pious

Some women begin to view marital relations as animalistic when they ascend in their faith. They begin to pour all their attention to the outside of the family, claiming they are doing so for religious work! Their husbands may no longer have their needs fulfilled and resort to repression and patience until they cannot hold it anymore and resort to ḥarām acts! God ﷻ becomes angry with such a person for depriving their husband of his needs, even if they stayed up at night in worship and fasted during the day. What value do acts of worship hold anymore when:

﴿إِنَّمَا يَتَقَبَّلُ ٱللَّهُ مِنَ ٱلْمُتَّقِينَ﴾

﴿*ʾinnamā yataqabbalu llāhu mina l-muttaqīna*﴾

﴿*God accepts only from the Godwary*﴾[140]

280. Vigorous Prayers

One of the requirements for finding a righteous mate and having a happy marriage is vigorous prayer. Some marriages indicate they were divinely chosen as if God ﷻ coordinated between them and led them through incredible channels until they both received their wants. Just as God ﷻ reconciles between disagreeing spouses who wish to reconcile, it makes sense that this reconciliation is granted before disagreements arise!

[140] Sūrat al-Māʾidah, Verse 27.

281. The Complaint of Women

Some men's approach to dealing with their wives could be considered very harsh, as they try to show their manhood through it. This has become a source of complaint for many women; though it seems normal at the beginning of marriage, both spouses may be guilty of it.

A man usually tries to show his manhood excessively during the first five years of marriage. During that time, he shows jealousy, zealotry, and conservatism or speaks in an exaggerated masculine manner. However, this usually wanes as the years pass.

282. The Believer's Gentleness

A believer is gentle and filled with affection and emotions. They are affected by the problems of strangers and relatives and show concern for others in their prayers and actions; these are among the traits of prophets.

After the battle of Badr, our Holy Prophet ﷺ could not rest at night because he could not bear hearing the moans of his uncle al-Abbas, even though his uncle was still a disbeliever. This Prophet's ﷺ unrest was due to his gentleness and tenderness with his relatives, and he said:

> "When people claim to possess knowledge but do not act upon it when they claim to profess love but harbor malice in their hearts and sever relations, in such a condition God

removes mercy from them and makes them undiscerning to logic."[141]

283. Persuasion

Children, especially at a young age, often insist on things that can cause either physical or spiritual harm to them! The way to address this is not through restriction and prohibition, as it will not accomplish the desired goal. People want what they cannot have! Parents should instead practice containment and attempt persuasion until the child stops insisting on that thing alone!

For example, suppose a child pleads for a sweet with a ḥarām ingredient. In that case, the parents can persuade them to move on by speaking to them in a language they understand, engaging their minds, or showing them how repulsive the ḥarām ingredient is and making them realize it is disgusting!

284. A Woman is Not a Slave

A woman is not a slave for her husband to own and do what he pleases. She is not a tool for him to use for his benefit, only to end the relationship after getting what he wants.

Sadly, some men enjoy the company of their wives when they are young, but after they have children and they get what they want from their wives, they relegate her to a corner of the home as if she is just another piece of furniture with no one paying attention to her. These are not the actions of believers; a believer has compassion, affection, and appreciation for even his animals,

---

[141] Ṣadūq, Shaykh Muḥammad b. ʿAlī, *Thawāb al-Aʿmāl*, p. 242.

creatures with no comprehension, so how should a believer act towards his companion and life partner?

285. The Righteous Wife

Nothing benefits a believer aside from God-consciousness as much as a righteous wife! This is because the one who lives in marital tension will always be mentally preoccupied and unable to concentrate on anything. Thus, they cannot advance intellectually or spiritually!

A wife is not a neighbor that one can avoid, nor is she a company with which a contract is easily broken. Instead, she is closely tied to her husband, even if only through the children that bind them. It is necessary, therefore, to choose carefully before becoming involved with someone!

286. Protecting Marital Secrets

Protecting marital secrets and not divulging them to others saves couples many problems. As it was said, every secret that exceeds two people spreads. However, some women need to improve at concealing these secrets! When a wife complains to another believer that her husband hit her, that person may, intentionally or unintentionally, spread that information throughout the community, causing the couple to lose face. In turn, the husband can be deprived of going to places of worship with other people due to his intense embarrassment.

287. Submitting to Religious Orders

One of the most essential characteristics of a successful marriage is that both parties submit to religious rulings during every disagreement. Without a reference book with solutions to life's problems, disputes between two conflicting parties would not exist. Therefore, we should rely on religious rulings as that common reference point when disputes arise between spouses. Considered carefully God's ﷻ words:

﴿فَلَا وَرَبِّكَ لَا يُؤْمِنُونَ حَتَّىٰ يُحَكِّمُوكَ فِيمَا شَجَرَ بَيْنَهُمْ ثُمَّ لَا يَجِدُوا فِي أَنفُسِهِمْ حَرَجًا مِّمَّا قَضَيْتَ وَيُسَلِّمُوا تَسْلِيمًا﴾

﴿fa-lā wa-rabbika lā yu'minūna ḥattā yuḥakkimūka fī-mā shajara baynahum thumma lā yajidū fī 'anfusihim ḥarajan mimmā qaḍayta wa-yusallimū taslīman﴾

﴿But no, by your Lord! They will not believe until they make you a judge in their disputes, then do not find within their hearts any dissent to your verdict and submit in full submission﴾[142]

288. Lack of Self-Control

When a person finds themselves in a tense family atmosphere, it can be hard for them to maintain control over their words and actions. This is because when we are angry, the devil plays with us like a ball in his hands, pushing us to be unrestrained in our speech and actions. It was narrated:

---

[142] Sūrat al-Nisā', Verse 65.

"A man utters a word pleasing to God ﷻ, without knowing its worth, God records for him His Pleasure till the Day of Judgement. And a man utters a word displeasing to God, without realizing its importance, God records for him His displeasure till the Day of Judgement."[143]

289. Tranquility

One of the most important aspects of repairing one's relationship with God ﷻ is striving to repair your marriage. A person who lacks tranquility at home and does not live in a stable situation faces obstacles in spiritual ascension. The believer needs a calm atmosphere in the home, as well as tranquility and inner peace, to ease the burden of work and concerns of life so that they can devote themselves to the concerns of the soul and the ways to repair it to attain its perfection. The best way to ensure this is through a happy marriage.

290. The Obeyed Manager

A man's authority in organizing and managing the family's affairs is not absolute! A wife is not obligated to obey her husband's words in every minor and major situation, especially if he is controlling, unjust, oppressive, and does not know logic or religion. However, if a man were brought up in the comprehensive school of Islām, he would know the etiquette, rules, and what is recommended and obligatory. There is no doubt that such a man will not be feared. Instead, he will be trusted and automatically become an obeyed manager in his family.

---

[143] al-Ṭabarānī, Sulaymān, *al-Muʿjam al-Kabīr*, Vol. 1, p. 367.

291. Observing Religious Boundaries

When it is said that a woman should limit her activities to inside the home, it does not mean confinement and dissociation from the outside world! These days, with the abundance of means to attain knowledge and culture, a woman can study scientific and cultural courses from home. Suppose she wants to step outside the family circle and work in the community. In that case, she should try to balance her professional obligations with her religious boundaries by avoiding risky situations such as unlawful interactions with men.

292. Religion and Marital Happiness

Religion is among the foremost foundations for attaining a happy marriage. It regulates all aspects of life in a person's relationship with their Lord, family, and community. Thus, it is advised to marry one's daughter to a believer because if the love in such a marriage dissipates for any reason, the husband will unlikely oppress his wife. In other words, one should strive to be as just as possible, and justice is essentially an inner faculty that causes a person to refrain from ḥarām and commit to fulfilling one's religious obligations.

293. Seeking God's ﷻ Assistance

It is befitting for a believer to seek assistance from God ﷻ when seeking reconciliation before relying on their verbal ability and individual and social integrity. This can be done by offering two sincere units of prayer in seclusion or one of the houses of God ﷻ, in addition to reading verses from God's ﷻ Holy Book and asking God ﷻ to bless their speech. They should also frequently seek refuge in God ﷻ from the devil because when a person seeks reconciliation, the devil will try to interfere to deviate things and get matters off-track.

294. Divine Making

The divine creation of love and affection between a couple brings unity and togetherness and is capital that they will benefit from until the end of their lives. The Lord of the Worlds is the One who created the love and affection felt between a married couple, and it is in His hands to remove it if He wills! If He removes that love and affection due to a couple's negligence and transgression, you can imagine what state they will be in! Just as prayers are the pillars of religion, love and affection are the pillars of marriage. Hence, if the Lord decides to remove these pillars, the tent will no longer be able to stand and will fall.

295. Factors Influencing Upbringing

Certain factors are influential in a teenager's upbringing and behavior. Some of these factors are due to nature, such as genetic traits and mental and psychological structures. These traits, despite their differences from one individual to another (even within one family), do not mean that a person's behavior is predetermined. Other factors stem from nurture and the environment that a person lives in. Environmental factors include parents' behavior, deviant relatives, friends, school atmosphere, and various media outlets, among the devil tools that can cause our children's deviation.

296. Parents Behavior

We often observe that children are born physically sound and lack any defects. Unfortunately, however, we see that a parents' behavior inside the family, such as the presence of conflict or disputes, their non-compliance with religious teachings, or the neglect of their children inside of the home and the parent's preoccupation with their personal affairs, is what leads to the emergence of various emotional and behavioral disorders. In this way, parents are accountable and will be held responsible for the effects of their behavior on the Day of Judgement.

297. Risk-Taking

Some wish to marry a woman who is not religiously committed with the hope of being able to reform her in the future. However, this risk is not guaranteed to produce the desired results, especially if that woman stays the same and her corruption persists after marriage. He may be overcome by her sin instead of prevailing over her with his good deeds, especially when there is a strong mutual love between them! So why would he risk marrying a woman who, in her current state, is not near God ﷻ when he had the option of marrying a good woman from a good background?

298. Command of the Ship

A family is a scaled-down government; as with all governments, it must have leadership. If there are quarrels, competition, and defiance regarding commanding the ship of marital life, then it is natural that the ship will never reach the coast. Some women become worried and fearful when they hear about the guardianship of men in Islām. However, the guardianship that is meant here is wise, fair, and religiously grounded, not the guardianship of a person who is uncompromising and controlling.

299. Useful Weapon

Sometimes, anger and estrangement can be valuable weapons. Hence, the method of discipline wherein a man abandons his marital bed when his wife commits a ḥarām act. However, repeated use of this weapon, whether justified or not, will make it lose its value if it ever needs to be legitimately used!

An angry person often will find that their anger no longer acts as a deterrent. On the contrary, it can cause scoffing and rebellion from the target of that anger. Not to mention hitting and beating, a method used to deal with animals, not with humans, except within the boundaries permitted in religion.

300. Monitoring Sexual Inclinations

Parents and guardians should monitor the sexual inclinations of those under their care before they become a deep-rooted issue. It is perilous when sexual thinking becomes so dominant in a person that they begin to see their existence and what is in it from this angle. The solution is to deprive them of the tools of sexual stimulation in the media and other outlets and to keep them away from people with ḥarām inclinations. Instead, they should be guided towards permissible alternatives such as early marriage and encouraged to spend their free time pursuing permissible activities.

301. The Mirage

It is a strange phenomenon that some would give their heart, a place created to be God's ﷻ sanctuary, to someone they have only met over the internet, talked to over the phone, or communicated with through the mail. Whatever happened to loyalty and competency as the criteria for deciding who deserves your heart?

Searching for a life partner through a chat site is a mirage that cannot be relied upon! Those who put themselves on display for people are questionable, suspicious, and likely to be abnormal at their core. Look how far we have come from the Noble Qur'ān's forbidding flirtatious speech at a time when so many people have diseased hearts!

302. The Right of Parents

While transmitting the teachings of Luqmān ؑ, the Noble Qur'ān spoke of the rights of one's parents. It explained that those negligent in this area will be deprived of receiving Divine wealth, a major degree among the degrees of ingratitude for blessings!

For various reasons, negligence in this area is prevalent in today's generation. Imām Zayn al-ʿĀbidīn ؑ summed up the theoretical treatment for this in one word when he explained the right of the father with an unparalleled expression:

> "And the right of your father is that you should know that he is your root and you are his branch. And without him, you would not be. Whenever you see anything in yourself

> which pleases you, you should know that your father is the root of its blessing upon you."[144]

If a father has such rights over his children and his rights are less than that of the mother, how great is a mother's right?

303. Good Company

If the parents of a child are strong disbelievers and strive to make their child join them in their disbelief, the Noble Qur'ān calls on that child to still treat them well and to keep good company with them. If such strong disbelief is not enough to negate a parent's rights over their child, imagine the rights of a parent who is a righteous believer among those who call others to faith and righteousness. It would be great if disbelievers could see this tolerance in Islām and its appreciation for the rights of mankind.

Unsurprisingly, it is so when the Author of these laws is the Most Compassionate and the Most Kind! Is it not better for us to strive to take on the Ethics of God ﷻ so that we may call others to God ﷻ without even using our tongues?

304. An Open File

Righteous offspring are like an open file for a person who has died; they act as a means to continue to accrue good deeds in the same way that ongoing charity or any beneficial knowledge that a person has left behind would. What a great victory it is to have an open file after death, as it is a time when we are most desperate for even a

[144] Majlisī, 'Allamah Muḥammad Bāqir, *Biḥār al-Anwār*, Vol. 71, p. 6.

single good deed to swing the scales of our actions; then, blessings begin to pour in from a righteous child we left behind.

It was narrated that ʿĪsā ﷺ once passed by a grave whose occupant was being tortured, and then, suddenly, the torture stopped. ʿĪsā ﷺ asked God ﷻ what caused the punishment to cease, and God ﷻ answered him:

> "He had a righteous child who fixed a road and gave shelter to an orphan."

305. The Rights of a Child

A child's rights begin even before their parents' marriage. Therefore, believers should offer a two-unit (rakaʿāt) prayer on their wedding night, asking God ﷻ to grant them good offspring.

Among the many important rights a child has is the right to be named before birth. A stillborn baby will complain about their parents on the Day of Judgement, saying: "Why did you not name me?" The best names indicate servitude to God ﷻ and the names of the Prophets and Imāms ﷺ. It is unjust to force a child to carry a name that causes embarrassment or has no meaning, as is popular today.

306. Obedient Women

The Noble Qurʾān described righteous women as

﴿قَٰنِتَٰتٌ﴾

﴿*qānitātin*﴾

﴾*obedient*﴿[145]

Under the umbrella of obedience to God ﷻ is a wife's obedience to her husband, as long as it does not lead to sin.

A man who sees his wife as wanting her independent authority will be unlikely to continue his relationship with her for long, as the nature of a family cannot bear having two independent leaders, as is the case with countries and institutions.

The Noble Qur'ān also describes righteous women as

﴿فَٱلصَّٰلِحَٰتُ قَٰنِتَٰتٌ حَٰفِظَٰتٌ لِّلْغَيْبِ بِمَا حَفِظَ ٱللَّهُ﴾

﴾*fa-ṣ-ṣāliḥātu qānitātun ḥāfiẓātun li-l-ghaybi bi-mā ḥafiẓa llāhu*﴿

﴾*Righteous women are obedient and watchful in the absence [of their husbands] in guarding what God has enjoined [them] to guard*﴿[146]

If a man is concerned about his wife's actions in his absence, whether it is regarding safeguarding his property or honor, then this feeling will destroy the atmosphere of trust between them, which is the basis of marital harmony.

307. Punishment of Homosexuality

When the Noble Qur'ān addresses the issue of homosexuality, practiced by the people of Prophet Lūṭ, ﷺ, it records a thought-provoking situation. It swears by the life of the Prophet ﷺ that

[145] Sūrat al-Taḥrīm, Verse 5.

[146] Sūrat al-Nisā', Verse 34.

homosexuals live in a state of drunkenness and confusion. There is no drunkenness and insanity greater than treating the path of filth like one would treat the place of procreation and the continuation of lineage! That is why their punishment was turning their village upside-down; they did not deserve to walk the face of the earth due to their terrible offense.

308. Drawbacks of Development

A big problem that has resulted from the proliferation of the internet is websites that ignite the fire of temptation in the soul without offering the antidote to that fire! When temptation reaches its peak, and lawful fulfillment is almost non-existent, what else could result in repression and rushing towards ḥarām in all forms? In this context, we wonder: why waste moments of life on conversations filled with vain talk or introductions that drag one into forbidden talk?

309. Afflictions that Lead to Perfection

A believer who uses all available means to secure their livelihood may still be impoverished. For a believer who obeys their Lord, any affliction, be it sickness, poverty, or anything else, is an affliction that will lead to attaining spiritual perfection and ascension of spiritual rank instead of erasing that believer's sins.

This type of affliction is like the kind given to prophets and imāms. According to some narrations, the Commander of the Faithful عليه السلام used to have to borrow money, meaning that for him and his righteous followers, poverty is unquestionably a means to attain higher ranks hereafter!

310. The Concept of Livelihood (Rizq)

Livelihood, or Rizq, is a concept that applies to everything that comes from God ﷻ that benefits a person, whether material or moral. A believer is not concerned about a lack of livelihood or rizq because they know that when God ﷻ takes one thing from them, He will compensate them with another.

Livelihood does not just mean financial gain. In its best forms, it comes from a righteous spouse, righteous offspring, and a tender heart. It is known that cash, gold, and silver are at the bottom of the list of the rizq that a believer seeks, yet for many of us, we, unfortunately, move those things to the top of the list!

311. Asceticism

Some people who ascend in their faith decide to avoid all pleasure, claiming the practice of asceticism! However, asceticism does not mean depriving oneself of what God ﷻ made lawful. It is natural for a person to feel cheerfulness, delight, comfort, and pleasure when they eat, spend time with their spouse, or sleep in a soft bed! However, one must not become a prisoner to these pleasures, as they are temporary and could be taken away, even in this life. They are not worth becoming prisoners of! A beautiful saying to keep in mind regarding asceticism:

> "It is not asceticism that you should not possess anything; rather, asceticism is that nothing should possess you."[147]

[147] Khū'ī, Āyatullāh Sayyid Abū al-Qāsim Mūsawī, *Minhāj al-Barā'ah fī Sharḥ Nahj al-Balāghah*, Vol.13, p. 318.

312. Friendship

Forming a friendship with your children and moving away from the harsh punishment prevalent in Eastern societies is necessary for parents! Friendship will make it easier for a child to talk to their parents about what bothers them instead of resorting to strangers since parents know what is best for their child. Moreover, a father should personally choose a good group of friends for his son, the youth attending the mosque, for example, before his son chooses friends who will have a bad influence on him.

313. Drowning Offspring in Affection

We were ordered in the blessed texts to drown our offspring in affection. They advise us that even kissing your child is a good deed. The reward of a loving look to our children is equivalent to freeing a population from slavery. We are also ordered to act like a child when interacting with our children. This is further confirmed in a narration from the Prophet ﷺ that says God ﷻ does not get as angry for anything as He does over the mistreatment of women and children! However, this does not mean excessive coddling because giving in to a child's desires, big or small, will lead to their being spoiled and corrupt.

314. The Devil's Concern

Among the biggest concerns of the Cursed Shayṭān is to gain control over a believer's family. Hence, he tries to enter the family atmosphere and destroy the nest or make it unstable!

Most importantly, he does not want a believer to marry so that he can be free to tempt them. If a believer does get married, thereby safeguarding half of their religion, the devil will try to cause as much separation between the spouses as possible. If his attempts are still not successful, he begins working on distorting the matters between them by instigating suspicion and using other means to destabilize their marriage.

315. Sea Water

A person who becomes addicted to committing forbidden acts, whether through looks or action, will increase their emotional torment. It is like seawater; the more one drinks, the thirstier one becomes until it leads to one's death.

Among the Divine Punishments for those deep in the sea of forbidden desires in this life, besides not being successful in a marriage, is that God ﷻ will take away everything they seek. If they move from one woman to another, they lose the pleasure they used to feel from those forbidden acts, and eventually, they suffer psychological disorders until their death. In the end, they die in a state distant from God ﷻ.

316. Financial Means

Some young people rush into marriage and must acquire the financial means. There is a Ḥadīth that says: "One who does not have a means of subsistence does not have Hereafter either." Therefore, one who wants to get married must be able to support a family in whatever way possible, be it through gaining skills for a trade or getting an education. There is no doubt that God's ﷻ promise is true when He ﷻ says:

﴿إِن يَكُونُوا۟ فُقَرَآءَ يُغْنِهِمُ ٱللَّهُ مِن فَضْلِهِۦ ۗ وَٱللَّهُ وَٰسِعٌ عَلِيمٌ﴾

﴾'in yakūnū fuqarā'a yughnihimu llāhu min faḍlihī wa-llāhu wāsiʿun ʿalīmun﴿

﴾If they are poor, God will enrich them out of His grace, and God is Bounteous, Knowing﴿[148]

As for the young man who acquired an education, found a means of livelihood and is mature and rational, there is no reason for him to delay marriage.

317. Suppressing Anger

God ﷻ has proven to fill the heart of someone who suppresses their anger with light. People can see this clearly when they rise above their hostile nature and do not show the anger that boils inside them, fearing that they will slip in their speech and cause God ﷻ to be angry with them. Moreover, let us not forget that God ﷻ constantly forgives us despite the presence of all that would justify revenge, yet He delays our punishment so that we may return to our senses. Can we follow the example of this Divine Courtesy?

318. Thankful for the Blessings

One grounds for giving a man guardianship over his home is that he must work hard and tire to ensure his family's livelihood, while women are relieved of this responsibility. A woman should thank God ﷻ for this blessing!

When Sayyidah al-Zahrā' and Imām ʿAlī عليهما السلام, divided the household responsibilities between them, she was tasked with managing the home. At the same time, Imām ʿAlī عليه السلام cared for matters outside the

[148] Sūrat al-Nūr, Verse 32.

home. Sayyidah al-Zahrā' ﷺ was pleased with this arrangement as it relieved her from having to go out to deal with men!

319. Kindness

Some caretakers tend to show superiority when dealing with those under their care; this is a major mistake! They have gaps and vulnerabilities in their personality, and how ugly it is for a person to see the faults of others without recognizing their own! Therefore, if an adviser wants to have an influential presence in the community, they must be gentle and kind in their speech. God ﷻ even ordered

Prophet Mūsā ﷺ to use gentle words with one of the most notorious oppressors of all time! Do we remember doing that with those around us, especially our young teenage children?

320. The Motive of Instinct

There is no doubt that instinct can act as a motive for action! There are glands in the brain that release hormones that enter the blood and cause a person to become stimulated, even if that person is at the peak of moral integrity and self-struggle.

Consequently, the instinctive side cannot be denied in a believer's life, as it is like a natural stream, like the rain that falls on a farmer's fields despite him. Imagine the consequences of a person purposefully stimulating their instincts through pictures, video, and even their imagination!

321. The Issue of Raising Teenagers

The responsibility of raising a teenager causes many parents to lose sleep. Children remain under the care of their parents until a certain age, yet many times, they miss out on investing in raising their children during this period. Parents often regret this after their child has left home, either due to marriage, migration, or education. It is worth it to give this subject the time and thought it deserves, as we know now that raising a righteous child is one way to ensure one's ongoing charity, which will benefit us even after we die!

322. Emotional Movement

Some view sex in a purely animalistic sense. Those who think like this may not fulfill their marital responsibilities if they mistakenly believe that sex prevents them from reaching a certain degree of spirituality. The reality is that we must act on emotions just as we act on instinct. Together, instinct and emotions act as a safeguard for marital life and bring happiness and emotional relief to the other spouse, provided that it is done in moderation.

323. Loss of Closeness

Among those factors that can lead to the break up of a family is the loss of closeness and affection between family members. Family life turns from a gathering of humans to what looks like a gathering of animals with no bond and are only united by food, drink, and dwelling! A reason for this loss of closeness is sin, which removes a person's inner gravity, whether between them and God ﷻ or between them and the people around them. This loss of inner gravity is externalized and felt in a person's consciousness and those around them.

324. A Mother's Mercy

A mother's mercy is a miniature example of God's ﷻ encompassing mercy. It is undisputed that the highest form of mercy in human life is the mercy a mother has for her children. A mother's mercy manifests in the predatory animals we fear, where we see a female predator interact with her young just as a human mother does. She plays with them, kisses them, and ensures they are fed and safe. A mother is a mother across all existence and is one of the signs of God ﷻ.

325. The Magnet

The relationship between a man and a woman is like that between the opposite poles of magnets. This means that the attraction and adhesion between them are involuntary, and all that is needed for them to be physically attracted to each other is a private meeting.

Therefore, a woman who meets privately with a man, whether for academic research, to solve a problem, or to vent her worries, should know that her actions may lead to a devastating major sin! One thing that cannot be doubted is that private meetings between men and women will eventually lead to a person losing their choice in avoiding sin due to the strength of instincts.

326. Early Marriage

Marrying at a young age has many blessings. Those who marry young are generally more successful than others in their educational advancement, inner stability, and social maturity. Moreover, those who marry young tend to have a smaller age difference between them and their children, making raising them easier.

These days, men and women are delaying marriage until they are older, resulting in the spread of psychological disorders and addictions to ḥarām.

327. Elements of Happiness

Some people expect life to be perfect in all aspects. They want an obedient wife, a big home, a fast car, righteous offspring, abundant wealth, a good reputation, and a transparent heart. They want all the elements of happiness in this life and the hereafter.

This, however, is impossible. If it were possible, then this life would become paradise! Absolute comfort is not nonexistent in this life. God's ﷻ Prophets and righteous servants suffer the most affliction in this mortal life! Hence, one will not be surprised when facing problems and crises. Instead, they tolerate them and remain patient.

328. Translation into Practice

Love is the dominant feature of marital life. Therefore, the verse in the Qur'ān discussing marriage mentions affection (*mawaddah*), not love (*maḥabbah*). It is said that the relationship between affection and love is like that between compliance (*khudhū*) and submissiveness (*khushū'*), as internal submission brings about the compliance of external body parts. Similarly, the love felt in the heart brings about affection, which is the practical translation and a reflection that mirrors what is in the heart. Thus, in the verse calling for the mawaddat of the Household of the Prophet ﷺ:

﴿قُل لَّآ أَسۡـَٔلُكُمۡ عَلَيۡهِ أَجۡرًا إِلَّا ٱلۡمَوَدَّةَ فِي ٱلۡقُرۡبَىٰۗ﴾

﴿qul lā ʾasʾalukum ʿalayhi ʾajran ʾillā l-mawaddata fī l-qurbā﴾

﴿Say, 'I do not ask you any reward for it except the love of [my] relatives.'﴾[149]

The compensation asked for was not love, as anyone could feel love, and it might not be translated into practice, and therefore, there is no affection in it. Through this, we understand that God ﷻ made what is shared between spouses something higher than love: affection.

329. Stopping the Loss

For a person who feels as though they are suffering a loss that seems to increase as the days pass, whether the loss is in themselves or their family circle, the solution is not found in complaining, sadness, or regret! Instead, it lies in planning to reform their course and stop the loss. As it is known among merchants, stopping the loss is a profit in itself! So, if a merchant owned a store and suffered daily losses, closing the store would benefit him so that his losses would not accumulate.

---

[149] Sūrat al-Shūrā, Verse 23.

330. The Most Delightful Blessing

One of the greatest and most delightful blessings is having righteous offspring. One's offspring are companions and helpers, especially in old age, and are an extension of one's memory after dying. Whereas for one who dies alone, without a family left behind, it is as if they were never in this life as their memory faded. However, one who is blessed with a child, even if they died while the child was a newborn, their memory will live on through that child who will always think of their parents. When others see the child, they will remember the parent and pray they are shown mercy in the Hereafter.

331. The Role of Genetics

When most young men are asked about the traits they want in their future wives, they often concentrate on material matters and beauty instead of piety, religiousness, intellect, and modesty. Genetics plays a prominent role in transmitting hereditary traits to subsequent generations. By using general clues, anyone can see what a woman is like and how her offspring might be by looking at her relatives. It was narrated in a ḥadīth that:

> "Choose a proper and suitable womb for your sperm, for genes have effects,"[150]

> "Women bear children that are similar to their brothers."[151]

---

[150] *I'ānāt al-Ṭālibīn*, Vol. 3, p. 312

[151] 'Abd al-Ḥamīd, Muḥammad Muhyi Dīn, *al-Tuḥfat al-Saniyyah bsharḥ al-Muqadimat al-Ajrūmiyyah fī Qawā'id an-Naḥwi wal-I'rāb*, p. 270.

332. Leniency Towards Others

Some men are distinguished by their self-transcendence and ability to tolerate their wives. A wife can take out all her anger on her husband for the slightest reason, and such a man not only does not seek revenge and return the offense, but he thanks God ﷻ that she got out the pain inside of her and found emotional relief. The lives of our Imāms ﵇ are full of similar examples that teach us the best ways to tolerate the hurt caused by others as a way to practice leniency with them.

333. Taking Care of One's Soul

Some care about the state of their soul, and despite being young, when their desires are at their peak, they can exercise self-control. They refrain from looking at forbidden images and complain [to God ﷻ] about their involuntary thoughts. Some swear by God ﷻ and the Noble Qur'ān that they do not carry the image of an unlawful woman in their mind and do not know any women besides their closest family members. What a beautiful trait this is! When such a man marries, he will have a beautiful and happy life!

334. Hotbeds for Corruption

One of Shayṭān's biggest wishes is to create disputes between married couples. His delight intensifies when he successfully separates them, as he considers this a great accomplishment. He gets such joy because he knows the effects of a family's disintegration and the forms of deviations that manifest in the parents and children, which could lead to forming hotbeds of corruption in the community. Shayṭān does not give up on the believer until the last moment of their life, so we notice divorce cases between elderly spouses in their seventies and eighties after a long life together.

335. Belittlement

A man's relaxed attitude and pleasure in dealing with women outside of his home and his indulgence in conversation and looking is essentially a belittlement of God's ﷻ lawful blessing destined for him. The emotional abandonment and preoccupation with other than that which God ﷻ made him responsible for will not be hidden from others for very long. It is natural that, after the secret is revealed, family bonds will begin dissolving, especially with the provocation of an atmosphere of suspicion surrounding the matter in the hands of people and the devil.

336. Worldview

Adopting a worldview that sees the parents as not only people responsible for one's birth but as guardians and caretakers deepens the desire for children to be devoted to their parents and to treat them righteously. For example, a son who holds such views could not wish for the deaths of his father or mother, even if they were the reason for hardship in his life; for example, if they were physically disabled or unable to speak, think, or feel. Instead, he would wish for God ﷻ to extend their lives so that he could rise in ranks to become near to the One who does not lose count of even a tiny mustard seed, not to mention the actions of a person who treats their parents in such a noble way!

337. Monitoring Teenage Behavior

It is important to monitor the behavior of teenagers, as at that age, both sexes begin looking for a companion to fill their free time. As we know, anyone who comes forward to fill this void in a teenager's life, for the most part, is only seeking a physical relationship that will cause degradation and contempt of the soul.

One who surrenders their body to their beloved one time gets used to surrendering it every time, even if the other claims to be innocently in love without expecting anything in return. The evidence that this type of love is not innocent is the shortness of the relationship, its transformation, and the evaporation of the alleged deep love at the first sign of a quarrel between the two.

338. Her Eyes on Her Obligations

Suppose a faithful woman decides to stay home and dedicate herself to raising a family. In that case, it does not mean that she should be isolated or secluded or that her decision should hinder her intellectual advancement. She can still mingle and remain in contact with other women while keeping her attention on raising her children and tending to her other responsibilities. She is encouraged to read, study, and advance intellectually, remembering that the best knowledge helps its owner better prepare for the Hereafter! As such, a faithful woman keeps her eyes on her obligations and her role in her family and not on other matters like people's opinions because she sees managing and caring for her family as her best investment!

339. Hubristic Approach

Using a hubristic approach when treating children with a sense of superiority, condescending, and tolerating even the most minor mistakes they make can make a parent fall into oppression without realizing it.

Our Holy Prophet ﷺ ordered us to talk to people according to their level of intelligence. Therefore, dealing with adults and children should be done according to each person's intellectual abilities. Due to their age, children do not have the intellectual abilities that allow them to behave as adults would like them to.

340. Inappropriate Behavior

Women were created in part to be the source of one man's happiness, so why should they degrade themselves and turn themselves into a submissive tool for all men? A woman who displays her charm and beauty in public appears to need lustful looks and calls men to her using her appearance or words! Such behavior is inappropriate for mankind's position as God's ﷻ vicegerents on earth and reveals a state of decline in humanity. Such a woman does not understand the principles of civil socialization.

341. Zero-Tolerance

We should all adopt a zero-tolerance policy towards sinning. Our reckoning will be brutal, and only God ﷻ knows how difficult it will be! When a woman does not cover her hair and body, even if she claims to be modest and chaste, her mannerisms, charms, and seduction excite the primal instincts of every man who looks at her.

Some of those men find no issue committing ḥarām to fulfill their desires. It cannot be ruled out that such women will be brought forth on Judgement Day and given a share of the responsibility of the zīna (adultery) committed by each man who sinned due to her actions, even if she remained faithful in her marriage!

342. Hope in God ﷻ

Some young people delay marriage until late in life due to a lack of financial security. However, God ﷻ promised to enrich a person who gets married out of His bounty:

﴿إِن يَكُونُوا۟ فُقَرَآءَ يُغْنِهِمُ ٱللَّهُ مِن فَضْلِهِۦ ۗ وَٱللَّهُ وَٰسِعٌ عَلِيمٌ﴾

﴿ʾin yakūnū fuqarāʾa yughnihimu llāhu min faḍlihī wa-llāhu wāsiʿun ʿalīm^{un}﴾

﴿If they are poor, God will enrich them out of His grace, and God is Bounteous, Knowing﴾[152]

How many people who get married these days have real trust and hope in what God ﷻ promised them? Unfortunately, today, our trust, hope, and reliance are given more to insurance companies than it is to the fulfillment of the promises given by God's ﷻ, who says in His Holy Book:

﴿وَمَنْ أَصْدَقُ مِنَ ٱللَّهِ حَدِيثًا﴾

﴿wa-man ʾaṣdaqu mina llāhi ḥadītha^{n}﴾

[152] Sūrat al-Nūr, Verse 32.

﴾*and who is more truthful in speech than God?*﴿[153]

343. Objective Justifications

People who develop a strong desire for a person or an object should ask themselves their objective justifications. They should ask themselves how realistic it is to attain the given object or person! They should also ask themselves why they insist on attaining something they cannot have! When they have determined with certainty that they cannot obtain what they so strongly desire, they should seek alternatives, as persistence is always a branch of certainty.

344. Family Affection

When people feel disconnected from their roots and separated from their family origins, they are bound to feel alienated and lonely. This provides the grounds for a person to search for the first emotional shelter they can, even if it violates logic and religion. Unfortunately, this happens to many girls who feel deprived of family affection, making them an easy target that even a smile can trap!

345. Containment Methods

Using affection and love is one of the best methods to win over a loved one. Let us assume that a son disobeyed his parents, immigrated to a non-Muslim country without a solid religious foundation, and returned after a long time lacking the essential components of belief and married a woman from a different

[153] Sūrat al-Nisāʾ, Verse 87.

religion. His parents can still rescue him and help him get back on the right track by using wise words, as the Noble Qur'ān says:

﴿ٱدْعُ إِلَىٰ سَبِيلِ رَبِّكَ بِٱلْحِكْمَةِ وَٱلْمَوْعِظَةِ ٱلْحَسَنَةِ ۖ وَجَٰدِلْهُم بِٱلَّتِي هِيَ أَحْسَنُ ۚ إِنَّ رَبَّكَ هُوَ أَعْلَمُ بِمَن ضَلَّ عَن سَبِيلِهِۦ ۖ وَهُوَ أَعْلَمُ بِٱلْمُهْتَدِينَ﴾

﴿udʿu 'ilā sabīli rabbika bi-l-ḥikmati wa-l-mawʿiẓati l-ḥasanati wa-jādilhum bi-llatī hiya 'aḥsanu﴾

﴿Invite to the way of your Lord with wisdom and good advice and dispute with them in a manner that is best﴾[154]

346. Shortcuts for Stages

There is nothing wrong with consulting people with life experience before marriage. Acquiring knowledge from the hearts of experienced men can provide shortcuts through life's stages! Personal anecdotes provide valuable information gleaned from practical experiences that cannot be found in books! The secret to a successful marriage lies in several factors, including a commitment to religious worship, harmony and understanding in different matters, and accepting a man's guardianship as ordained by God ﷻ.

347. The Meaning of the Word (Mate)

The word mate means something having a shared origin, compatibility, and harmony. When speaking of unrighteous women, the Noble Qur'ān uses the phrase: the woman of. For example, the Noble Qur'ān talks about the woman of Lot and the

---

[154] Sūrat al-Naḥl, Verse 125.

woman of Nūḥ; it does not refer to them as the mates of Lot and Nūḥ. This was a way to show that those two women were essentially just a female presence, not an integral, complementary part of the lives of their husbands. On the other hand, Sayyidah Khadījah ﷺ was a complementary part of the life of our Holy Prophet ﷺ and, therefore, his mate.

348. An Impermeable Structure

At first glance, mercy and affection seem to mean similar things, yet they are different. Mercy is a noble, humane condition, while affection is the practice of mercy and, in addition to sexual instinct, reproduction, and management of life's affairs, keeps marital life going. If mercy and affection are found, they serve as a firm, impermeable structure that cannot be destroyed with time.

349. Spiritual Maturity

A husband and wife should attain at least the lowest levels of spiritual maturity, meaning they should have the inner awareness and rationality to understand the essence of this life, including marriage as one of its elements.

The reality of this life boils down to two things: that it is mortal life and that it is a prelude to a farm wherein we sow what we wish to reap in the afterlife. The belief in the mortality of this life will compel one not to become attached to it. The belief that it serves as a farm for the afterlife will lead one to invest it in the best way possible.

350. Continuous Maintenance

A marriage needs continuous maintenance. There are always new developments, both on the problems and solutions sides. Try, now and then, to solve any problems that arise. Otherwise, the devil will creep in like a worm that bores into a mighty tree until it turns and crumbles. The seeds of conflict are present in many families, but they wait for a suitable environment for germination. We should always remember the old saying: prevention is better than cure.

351. Scandal

A person struggling to overcome committing sins and entering mazes of thorny [ḥarām] relationships should remember that God ﷻ grants respite to the wrongdoers but never neglects or forgets their actions and punishment. He is The Concealer of His servants' sins. However, for anyone who goes too far in their evil and indecency, God ﷻ will uncover their faults and expose them. Again, we should practice the saying: prevention is better than cure and keep the problems at bay instead of worrying about finding solutions. This verse applies to those who have the intention of straightening up their behavior:

﴿وَٱلَّذِينَ جَٰهَدُوا۟ فِينَا لَنَهْدِيَنَّهُمْ سُبُلَنَا ۚ وَإِنَّ ٱللَّهَ لَمَعَ ٱلْمُحْسِنِينَ﴾

﴿*wa-lladhīna jāhadū fīnā la-nahdiyannahum subulanā wa-ʾinna llāha la-maʿa l-muḥsinīn*[a]﴾

﴿*As for those who strive in Us, We shall surely guide them in Our ways, and God is indeed with the virtuous*﴾[155]

[155] Sūrat al-ʿAnkabūt, Verse 69.

352. The Seeker and the Waiter

If a woman gets a marriage proposal from someone whose faith and loyalty are trusted, she should not feel confused and hesitant, as the prospects for a woman are limited compared to those of a man. Generally, a woman awaits her destiny while a man seeks his out, and the difference between the seeker and the (waiter) is not hidden! However, suppose a woman's hesitation and confusion stem from having more than one man propose to her. In that case, she can settle the confusion by performing istikhārah and asking God ﷻ to guide her to the better option. It is important to remember that when making such a crucial decision, she should pray that God ﷻ grant her a suitable husband.

353. Acting Lenient

The presence of anger and fury is noticeable in most people. Therefore, if people realize they have this negative trait and are incapable of leniency, they should act as lenient! This means that they should do their best to swallow their anger and strive to ensure that it does not show on their face or any external movements, even if they are boiling on the inside; this will keep the intensity of their anger from increasing. A believer is known not to have anger boiling inside them, as they are calmed by the remembrance of God ﷻ, even under the worst circumstances.

354. Partnership with the Devil

It is horrifying to think of having the devil as a partner in people's wealth and children. His partnership with children has been divided into two groups.

The first group of children that the devil shares with their parents are the children of adultery, conceived in an atmosphere of forbidden desires and sins. The second group includes children born to parents who are lawfully married but failed in disciplining and raising their children well, leading them to turn to sin and securing their partnership with the devil!

A partner will always seek to receive their share of the 'company' they keep, especially if such a partner is malicious and stingy like the cursed devil.

355. Contempt

Among the contributors to harshness in people's interactions is viewing others as inferior and treating them with contempt. Unfortunately, we see this in some people's interactions with those who work for them. They forget the humanity of these workers and that God ﷻ gave them their dignity. We can attribute some of the afflictions that befall people to the use of harshness with those under their control and servants who have no helper but God ﷻ.

356. Satiation

The adornment of a woman for her husband and the adornment of a man for his wife leads them both to emotional comfort and to lower their gazes, especially for men! If a man becomes both physically and emotionally satiated inside of his marital nest, naturally, he would not lean, instinctually or physically, towards other women. Suppose he does happen to pursue other women despite his wife adorning herself for him. In that case, he is doing so due to a disease or a health condition, perhaps a hormonal or psychological imbalance.

357. Convergence of Hearts

Divine blessings are something a person can rely on throughout various life conditions, even in times of disputes and conflict, as God ﷻ says:

﴿إِن يُرِيدَآ إِصۡلَٰحٗا يُوَفِّقِ ٱللَّهُ بَيۡنَهُمَآۗ إِنَّ ٱللَّهَ كَانَ عَلِيمًا خَبِيرٗا﴾

﴿'in yurīdā 'iṣlāḥan yuwaffiqi llāhu baynahumā﴾

﴿If they desire reconcilement, God shall reconcile them﴾[156]

If disputing spouses wish to fix things between them, then God ﷻ will help them reconcile. He will get involved by converging their hearts. He is the one who sparked affection between them before they lost it by misbehaving and arguing; He can bring the affection back to them out of His grace.

358. The Negatives of Marital Contentiousness

A believer might prefer to live with the negative aspects of a single life rather than deal with some of the hardships of living with a quarrelsome spouse. Contention in married life leads to illnesses and many sins, such as gossip, slander, anger, and transgressing the limits set by God ﷻ. Moreover, a person living in a contentious marriage will not be able to monitor themselves on their journey to God ﷻ, as a person who lives in constant family stress and tension will always be mentally preoccupied, even if their problems do not lead to sin.

---

[156] Sūrat al-Nisā', Verse 35.

359. Losing Control

One of the major pitfalls of being harsh and aggressive when dealing with others is that it leads to a person losing control over the decision-making centers of their mind. When that happens, they become a toy and a game in the devil's hands. Prophet Nūḥ ﷺ asked about the state in which Shayṭān can most control the children of Ādam. Shayṭān's reply, and he is an expert in his work, was:

> "At the time of anger!"

360. Pardon

Pardoning becomes even more emphasized when it involves those who have rights over us, such as parents, spouses, and those who have the right to be guided and advised by us. It is never fair to view the other side without all of their traits, and we should never allow one mistake they make to let us forget all of their rights. If we can implement it in ourselves, this ability to pardon is enough to lubricate family and social relationships and prevent various problems.

361. Dealing with the Sinners

Having pity and sympathy for sinful people was the norm for all the Infallibles ﷺ. The sympathy and compassion given to sinners was the best help for them in abandoning their evil and sinful ways. Alternatively, banishing them from the community would have led them to delve deeper into sin and disobedience. Therefore, we must treat the sinners around us with caution, skill, and an educational spirit.

362. The Weakest Link

When the devil loses hope in a believer and sees that they are like a solid mountain or a tough piece of iron, and he cannot gain control over them, he will try to move the environment around them. He will look for the weakest link in the social environment around a believer and try to agitate them through a spouse who is quick to anger, one of their children, or even their neighbor. The devil will never give up on seeking revenge from a believer who infuriates him and makes him envious of their righteous deeds.

363. Avoiding Disputes

A conscious woman should avoid falling into any disputes with her husband's family, especially his mother, and should strive to be the one to initiate conciliation and kind communication. She should understand the feelings of her husband's mother especially and understand a mother's attachment to her son whom she handed over to a stranger one night. A believing woman should remember that her husband is the fruit of his mother's love and a lifetime of care and giving and that, in the end, she loves her son and those he loves.

364. Gradual Atrophy

The biggest calamity that results from marital conflict lies in the gradual spiritual atrophy that might afflict both spouses. This is in addition to malfunctions and imbalances that occur to the nervous system, which affects even a mother's milk and, in turn, can harm her innocent newborn. A mind stretched thin with various problems and conflicts will not allow a spare moment to think about matters relating to where we came from and the hereafter.

365. The Home of a Believing Woman is a University

Islām dictates that a woman should make a university out of her home, where she raises and educates her children. Moreover, there is nothing wrong with her advising her husband and sharing any helpful information she learned in her free time while he was at work, and there is no belittlement or undermining in doing so. This is contrary to a woman who works outside of her home. Her energy is spent outside the family, and she will not be able to care for her children and husband, resulting in a growing distance between their hearts, which no salary can compensate for!

366. Anger According to Action

If a believer sees a misdeed committed by a family member, their anger should be per the degree of the misdeed. Their anger over the sin committed should equal God's ﷻ anger towards that sin. This means that a believer should not become as angry over makruh actions as they do over ḥarām actions. Similarly, they should not get as angry over a family member not doing a mustaḥabb act as they would over a wājib act not being done. Also, anger over a small sin should not be the same as anger over a major sin. One who does not observe and comply with this should know that their anger is not for the sake of God ﷻ.

367. Preoccupation with Pleasures

Some spouses do not care about anything in their marital life except for materialistic desires, their preoccupation with pleasure, and living a happy, comfortable life free from burden and responsibility. In turn, they neglect the matters of their children and shirk their educational and advisory roles in the family. They do not care about who they mingle with and remain busy with themselves and their desires and pleasures. Naturally, the attention we give our children is proportional to the desired fruits we get in return.

368. Emotional Satiation

A parent's disregard for satiating the emotional side of their children, especially their daughters, is a reason that children fall into traps of corruption and swamps of vice. They do so in hopes of fulfilling an emotional need, even if it is through someone they know to be deceitful and mischievous. Because a human is both a body and a soul, parents should put as much care into giving the soul its natural needs as they do into fulfilling their children's physical needs.

369. Beauty: A Trial For Both Spouses

Many people focus on the external aspects of beauty. Yet, it is no secret that sometimes uncommon beauty can be a trial for both spouses. A gorgeous woman may become enchanted with her beauty. In turn, her husband may feel his wife is doing him a favor by marrying him, as she sees herself in a higher place than him. This would be a trial for them both. If she were gorgeous, she could also become a seduction for others, who might try to win her over by various temptations. These days, plenty of people have a disease in their hearts!

370. The Best Form of Investment

Contemplating and planning to invest in righteous offspring is the best form of investment. The righteousness and uprightness of one's offspring have everlasting effects. It is not farfetched to think that God 🕮 will raise the ranks of a parent to the rank of their righteous child who is granted a distinguished place in heaven, for instance, near the Prophet 🕮 and his Household 🕮. So, just as Prophet Yūsuf 🕮 raised his parents to the throne, a righteous child can raise their parent's rank to the throne of Divine nearness.

371. Lack of Blessing

Most marriages that result from the communications that are common today via the internet have no permanence and no blessings, or they are often on the verge of collapse. This is usually due to a man's distrust of his wife resulting from the fact that she corresponded with him and, as such, probably corresponded with many other men. He constantly worries that she might restart her old communications while married to him. How can there be any hope of blessings for a structure raised on a ḥarām foundation?

372. A Small Government

A family is a small government, so it must have a leader and manager to organize its affairs. This leadership position is given to the man as a religious right. Therefore, as part of her obedience to God U, the wife should abide by her husband's decisions. His obedience is expected except when what he asks of his wife is a sin, as there should be no obedience to a creature when it necessitates the disobedience of the Creator. If a married couple disagrees regarding a matter in their family affairs, they can discuss their points of view, and the wife should accept her husband's judgment if she does not have a convincing argument. Thus, due to the responsibilities on his shoulders and his leadership role in the family, the last word and decision in the family's affairs belongs to the husband.

373. The Most Staunch Defender

If a man desires to add a firm, stable element to his marital life that does not change with time, he should view his wife as God's ﷻ trust in his hands. He should know that the staunchest defender of a woman is not her father or mother; it is her Lord and Creator. Especially if the woman is of excellent faith, God ﷻ will defend and triumph for her as He does for anyone who does not have an advocate besides God ﷻ.

374. Warning Against Instigation

A woman should take great caution against instigating and aggravating her husband against his mother! A husband will turn away from his wife if he finds himself between two paths: the major sin of disobedience to his mother or his wife's strongly disliked yet permissible divorce. He may let his wife go despite his love for her to please his mother. Ultimately, his wife ends up being the reason for this, instigating and pushing matters to a point that forces her husband into a decision.

375. Getting Down to the Children's Level

It is a major mistake to excessively criticize children as if they have no intellect, as every age has its world! Instead, it is essential to get down to their level, make them feel admired for their abilities, encourage them, and share with them what they like. This is important because the best way to influence children is through their hearts. If a parent successfully becomes a friend to their child, they will be more likely to talk to their parents about their problems, and no one wants the best for a child more than their parents!

376. The Sanctity of a Believer

A believer is a person who monitors their behavior and controls themselves during times of anger so that they will not make a mistake and put themselves into a position where they need to apologize. Some major unfavorable behaviors, such as aggression and physical abuse, arise in some marriages. A believer realizes that they have sanctity and dignity and, therefore, should not behave in a way that makes them lose that and their social reputation, putting themselves in a vulnerable position. Among the things that God ﷻ does not forgive is for a person to degrade and humiliate themselves.

377. Filling the Gap

A woman who grew up suffering from a conflict between her parents or lived with a single parent due to separation or divorce may have acquired the grounds for disagreement and conflict through her upbringing. As a result, she may suffer from a deficiency in her ability to deal with conflict. Therefore, a man who chooses to marry her should offer her special care to fill this gap. Since he committed himself to marry her, he needs to take on the responsibility of giving her the support she needs, whether because he is satisfied with her otherwise, because he loves her, or even because of His desire to gain nearness to God ﷻ.

378. Knowledge of Educational Methods

Knowledge and discernment of the method of education preferred by a child will make raising them easier on their parents. Some children are auditory learners and prefer to hear educational stories. Others are visual learners and learn better by watching educational programs. Others are kinesthetic learners and prefer a physical, hands-on approach to learning. It is beautiful to discern what each child prefers and present information to them in their preferred method, even if playing, as long as the desired goal is accomplished.

379. The Quality

A believer is a person who cares about the quality, not the quantity, of something. As such, a believer does not boast about the number of children he has if they are not righteous and pious because he knows they may turn into enemies on the Day of Judgement.

As God ﷻ says:

﴿ٱلْأَخِلَّآءُ يَوْمَئِذٍۭ بَعْضُهُمْ لِبَعْضٍ عَدُوٌّ إِلَّا ٱلْمُتَّقِينَ﴾

﴿al-'akhillā'u yawma'idhin ba'ḍuhum li-ba'ḍin 'aduwwun 'illā l-muttaqīna﴾

﴿On that day, friends will be one another's enemies, except for the Godwary﴾[157]

[157] Sūrat al-Zukhruf, Verse 67.

Alternatively, if a believer has only one pious child, this child will be the joy of his eyes and a delight to his heart in this life and the hereafter!

380. The Sole Purpose

Sexual deviation has been, and still is, one of the hot topics in human life. The instinct of lust was put into humans to ensure humanity's survival. However, the ignorant, tyrannical human has turned lust into a goal instead of it being a means to that goal. For some, there is no longer anything that preoccupies their existence apart from doing whatever this instinct calls for, as if it is the sole purpose a human was created!

381. Reconciliation with the Lord

A person who complains about disputes and conflicts in their marital life should first strive to reconcile between himself and God ﷻ. In turn, God ﷻ will reconcile between him and other people.

As God ﷻ says:

﴿إِنَّ ٱلَّذِينَ ءَامَنُوا۟ وَعَمِلُوا۟ ٱلصَّـٰلِحَـٰتِ سَيَجْعَلُ لَهُمُ ٱلرَّحْمَـٰنُ وُدًّا﴾

﴿ʾinna lladhīna ʾāmanū wa-ʿamilū ṣ-ṣāliḥāti sa-yajʿalu lahumu r-raḥmānu wuddaⁿ﴾

﴿Indeed those who have faith and do righteous deeds—the Beneficent will endear them [to His creation]﴾[158]

[158] Sūrat Maryam, Verse 96.

Once one reconciles with God ﷻ, they should ask Him to soften the hearts of others towards them and frequently pray to God ﷻ with:

> "I ask you for your love and also love for those who love you, and I ask you to make me love every deed which will bring me to your proximity."[159]

382. Hope

If a believer is tested by having a bad spouse, they should accept what God ﷻ has destined for him and ask that He compensate him through his children and grandchildren. A believer is full of hope in God ﷻ! How many believers were born to disbelieving parents? Some of the greatest companions of our Imāms عليهم السلام were themselves disbelievers in the past, and God ﷻ

﴿يُخْرِجُ ٱلْحَيَّ مِنَ ٱلْمَيِّتِ وَيُخْرِجُ ٱلْمَيِّتَ مِنَ ٱلْحَيِّ﴾

﴾yukhriju l-ḥayya mina l-mayyiti wa-yukhriju l-mayyita mina l-ḥayyi﴿

﴾He brings forth the living from the dead, and brings forth the dead from the living﴿[160]

383. The Devil's Entry Points

It is vital to discover the devil's entry point into family life. Devils in a human's life are like harmful and deadly germs in the air

159 Majlisī, ʿAllamah Muḥammad Bāqir, *Biḥār al-Anwār*, Vol. 91, p. 148.

160 Sūrat al-Rūm, Verse 19.

around us that we do not see. Even if they do not kill the person, those germs await the opportunity to cause damage. Similarly, the devil waits for the perfect opportunity, needing receptive grounds to thrive and destroy the family entity. Therefore, it is imperative to discover and be aware of this truth despite its invisibility!

384. Selflessness

A woman married to a man in a religious preaching role must have patience and selflessness. She must know that she is not like other women, as her role with her husband is multiplied! Therefore, she should create an appropriate atmosphere for him and become his aide and supporter to fulfill his mission. She should not think of his missionary work as a second wife for him and become jealous of the time and effort her husband dedicates to it.

385. A Purposeful Being

A believer is meant to be a purposeful, goal-oriented person responsible for managing their affairs. As such, their decision should never be made by random selection. When believers want to travel, they should choose countries without fear for their religion, themselves, and their family. What would be the value in spending their money on something that would only get them further from God ﷻ? We know our feet will only move on the Day of Judgement once we ask about our wealth and what we have spent it on!

Imām ʿAlī ؑ said:

> "The Messenger of God ﷺ said: On the Day of Judgement, each servant of God will be unable to move forward even a

single step without being questioned about the following: How he spent his life? How did he spend his youth? Through what means did he earn his money, and how it was spent? And about the love and friendship of us, Ahl al-Bayt."[161]

386. Developing a Wife's Capabilities

With his bad temper and poor manners, a husband can turn his wife into a tense being who will pour out her nervousness and tension inside the marital nest on one side and onto her children on the other. A man's wife is his life partner; he should remember that as he interacts with her. Even if from a selfish perspective, he should view his wife as a great investment, and it will benefit him to help her develop her power and capabilities. The benefits of doing so will be returned to him and will be good for her, their children, and their community.

387. Benefit and Damage

A wise person keeps their eyes on the benefit and damage that results from any movement they make. What is the benefit of a young man looking at a married woman or a woman from a social class that he will not be able to reach no matter what he does? Or even if he looks at a picture of a woman who died tens of years ago? What benefit is there to any of that to aid him against internal boiling, repression, anguish, and feelings of guilt? Doing so is like drinking seawater; the more you drink - the thirstier you become!

[161] Ṣadūq, Shaykh Muḥammad b. ʿAlī, *al-Khiṣāl*, Vol. 1, p. 253.

388. Precaution and Anxiety

We have been instructed to take precautions regarding the future. We do so by preparing for potential emergencies and necessities, whether on an individual level or a family level. However, some live in a state of anxiety and emotional distress, which makes them imagine the future as gloomy. People who do so forget that God ﷻ is the best defender and advocate for His believing servants, wherever they are and however they are!

389. Humiliation and Forgiveness

Forgiveness and accepting humiliation are phrases that often lead an inattentive person to think they have similar meanings mistakenly. Some people think that pardoning and forgiving others' mistakes imply accepting humiliation and, in turn, are driven by the devil's influence to seek revenge. However, forgiveness is a transcendence above the wrongful souls, so where is the humiliation in this position? Forgiveness makes one feel a sense of pride in achieving this height and turning away from falsehood and vanity!

390. The Known Facts

Belief in the claims that magic and witchcraft are the cause of problems, especially between a married couple, is one of the ways we fall into delusional obsessions in life. We should not be so quick to believe the claims of those who run a business out of these unlawful acts and work by extorting their victims after indoctrinating them with these unfounded claims. Instead, we should look for the origins of disputes so that we are not blaming some delusional external source instead of searching for the facts!

391. Adornment

Some women display their adornment to every person yet are negligent in adorning themselves for their husbands. Some forms of adornment are not acceptable even in the company of non-maḥram (those a person is forbidden to marry) because they draw attention and arouse lust. A woman's husband is the only person who has the right to look at her with lust. Therefore, it is only appropriate for the believing woman to save her adornments and beauty for her poor husband!

392. Sharing the Guilt

A woman who is delinquent in giving her husband his religious marital right is essentially a partner in the sins he might commit due to this negligence. This idea also applies to other situations. For example, it can be understood from narrations that a father negligent in helping his son get married will share the guilt of sin his son may incur.

393. Istikhārah

When a person intends to have a meaningful conversation with their child and give them advice about an important matter, it is appropriate for them to resort to God ﷻ beforehand. The parent can perform a two-unit (rakaʿāt) prayer to request God ﷻ point them in the right direction and grant them success.

There is also a two-unit prayer called Ṣalāt al-Istikhārah that can be performed. After finishing the prayer, a person should say: (O God, grant me what is best and choose the best for me and put goodness in it for me) one hundred times, and then act according to what they feel in their heart.

It is also recommended that whenever we find ourselves in conflict, we ask God ﷻ to put in our hearts what He wants us to do.

394. Tolerance and Patience

A person who wants to be careful in disciplining and educating their child should be able to maintain tolerance and patience. Having the tendency and inclination towards fun and play is natural for children, and often, what their parents ask them to do does not suit their mood. However, this does not mean that parents should let their children do what they feel like because, at a young age, a child does not have the intellect and the experience to lead them to what is best for them. If a parent leaves a child to their own devices at that age, that child could become an easy target for the devil.

395. Winning the Heart

When a father can successfully win over his son's heart, it becomes easier for him to educate and guide him. A son's disobedience is usually due to his lack of life experience and need to reach his full intellectual potential. However, when a son is confident in his father's love for him, he does not doubt that what his father is telling him is for his benefit, even if he does not see the wisdom behind it or it does not suit his mood. With time, it will become clearer for this child that his father was right.

396. Avoiding Woes

Viewing a wife as a weak and vulnerable being and making light of transgressing against her and undervaluing her rights is a sure way for afflictions to befall a person guilty of doing so in this life and the hereafter! Many of the afflictions and calamities people suffer for years, and some until the end of their lives, result from them oppressing their wives and transgressing against their rights! Shouldn't a wise person avoid bringing bitter woes into their lives and kindly treat those under their care?

397. Basic Law

It is common practice for companies and institutions, even small ones, to establish a fundamental law that outlines accepted procedures regarding all of its dealings and detail punishments for even the most minor offenses. Marital life is not less important than these companies. Marriage is a major company in life, and this company does not ever dissolve.

398. Threatening

Marriage is meant to be a close, intimate companionship. Even the smallest transgression one partner commits against the other can have profound effects. One adverse action that indicates a lack of reason is a husband threatening his wife with divorce as soon as disagreements arise. The effects of such an action cannot be erased from his wife's heart, even if she shows friendliness and love afterward.

399. The Importance of a Wife's Upbringing

A man must investigate the upbringing and the background of the woman he intends to marry. This includes her family, environment, and education. A woman may possess abundant beauty and wealth yet be emotionally unstable due to the turmoil and unrest she endured in her family environment. If a man marries this woman, he should be aware that he will bring that tension and instability into his family, which could eventually lead to the deviation and disobedience of his children.

400. Increased Supplication

Righteous offspring are the best fruit that can come out of a marriage. Anyone concerned with having righteous offspring should offer many supplications and requests for them beginning on their wedding night. God ﷻ wants us to always remember Him, especially during heedlessness. Thus, those who control themselves on their wedding night, a night of heedlessness and preoccupations with the pleasures of life, and take the time to ask God ﷻ to grant them righteous offspring privately are among those whose supplications will be answered.

401. The Wife is Among the Husband's Affairs

A husband's patience with the pain caused by his wife is a means for him to reach spiritual perfection. However, this only applies if he has lost hope in trying to change her and help her become a better partner. This is because his wife is among the affairs he is responsible for. As such, one of his tasks is to try to educate her and straighten her affairs, not to leave her alone and be satisfied with his anger towards her so that he reaches his spiritual perfection by swallowing his anger! The same applies to a woman who maintains her patience despite the hurt her husband causes.

402. Tasks of Servitude

When a servant of God ﷻ treats those who wrong them with kindness, they do not expect compliance from the other person. By treating others with kindness, they are fulfilling their tasks of servitude to God ﷻ, not because they want a reward from the other person. However, suppose this kind of treatment leads the other to exploit this kindness and humiliate the believer. In that case, this does not please God ﷻ! God ﷻ entrusted His servants with all their affairs, except for bringing humiliation and degradation to themselves.

403. Putting a Wedge in the Tree

Sometimes, a married couple destroys their home with their own hands! For example, a wife who insists on traveling to a certain country or going to a certain beach or restaurant with an unlawful atmosphere and asking her husband to go with her to these places is like putting a wedge in a blessed tree! No doubt, committing sins will destroy their life and the dissolution of this blessed structure.

404. Taking Responsibility

A man's lack of responsibility inside the home is another factor that may lead to the destruction of a family. At the beginning of their life together, a husband may show enormous yearning and love for his wife, only to turn with time into an unpleasant person whose presence at home does not bring comfort. Instead, he takes no responsibility, even failing to provide for his family. If his wife has a separate income, he will try to exploit what she has. Eventually, such a man turns into someone with no presence in the home besides their name.

405. The Crack

Committing some forms of immoral and shameful acts during one's teenage years causes a crack in the soul that leads a person to become disgusted with themselves their entire adult life. Therefore, we must permit any opportunity for teenagers to commit any action that has psychological repercussions that remain with them for the rest of their lives. In addition, we need to remind others not to give up on the mercy of God ﷻ.

406. Reprehensible Love

Reprehensible love is characterized by intense emotional attraction towards someone with an inclination to reach them in any way possible, even if it is at the expense of reason, tradition, and religion. Hence, it has been considered by some philosophers as a (melancholic) ailment due to the instability of the behavior.

Such love arises from covetousness and comes to a halt when joined with the loved one. Thus, it has been said that union is the burial ground of passion! In other words, it originates from the love of certain traits, and it is known that the delight one gets from something goes away with seeing it frequently.

407. True Devoutness

True devoutness means abiding by the rules and teachings of religion with genuine inner submission and acceptance. It does not mean only abiding by the prescribed and obligatory actions, such as praying in the mosque, fasting, and pilgrimage!

When a couple reaches a level of true devoutness, and religion becomes the judge that settles any disagreements, they should not lead to bigger problems if the judgment is left to God ﷻ!

408. Continual Presence

The continual presence of the husband and father in his family's environment is important to create harmony and cohesion in a family. A father's frequent absence from the home, preoccupation with others outside of the home, and distraction with personal pleasures all lead to the loss of augustness and reverence of his leadership in the family. As a result, the head of the household becomes seen only as the financier of the family, without having any educational or disciplinary role.

409. Revealing Secrets

It is a grievous mistake for a woman to reveal her husband's secrets when trying to defend herself, as her husband will automatically respond by revealing her secrets. Houses are comprised of secrets that are meant to remain inside the home. As a result of them revealing each other's secrets, their enemies may exploit their weak points and disgrace them in the community. As a result of this public scandal, there would not be any value or sanctity left in their marital life should they eventually reconcile.

410. Important Qualities

Before a young man marries, he should understand the important qualities to look for in a wife. She does not need to have the highest level of beauty. He could marry someone with an adequate degree of beauty or charm. The feminine attraction is not always limited to beauty in its physical meaning, which is one of God's ﷻ mysteries.

A young man should also heed the necessity of a woman having a pure and virtuous upbringing, as the unconscious effects of the family environment through one's childhood and adolescence cannot be denied.

411. Internal Emptiness

The root cause of falling into vain love is the emptiness of the heart and idleness. It is in the heart's nature to need something to be attached to, so if one does not fill the emptiness within their hearts with what is right, it will inevitably be filled with falsehood.

The best depiction of how internal emptiness leads to the love of mortals is this saying of Imām al-Ṣādiq (ع):

> "Hearts that were devoid of God's remembrance; so God let them taste the sweetness of the love of others besides Him."[162]

---

[162] Majlisī, ʿAllamah Muḥammad Bāqir, *Biḥār al-Anwār*, Vol. 70, p. 158.

412. The Heart's Axis

Many acts of worship begin with movement in the heart. This sincere and heartfelt movement is more honorable than the act itself, like the jihad that stems from altruism and selflessness as a principle and the presence of heart and mindfulness in prayers that arise from the love of Divine nearness. Similarly, many external sinful actions committed arise from the deviation of the heart's axis towards that which is forbidden. The forms of moral deviation we see originate from ḥarām love.

413. The Grounds

Among the most destructive effects of conflict is that it establishes the grounds for oppression and transgression. The grounds for oppression and transgression, in turn, ensure the establishment of the grounds for expulsion from Divine Mercy, according to what God ﷻ says:

﴿أَلَا لَعْنَةُ ٱللَّهِ عَلَى ٱلظَّٰلِمِينَ﴾

﴾'a-lā la'natu llāhi 'alā ẓ-ẓālimīn[a]﴿

﴾Behold! The curse of God is upon the wrongdoers﴿[163]

Indeed, God ﷻ gives respite but never neglects. A person, after a period of sinning and disobedience, could reach the dire consequence mentioned by Prophet Muḥammad ﷺ:

---

[163] Sūrat Hūd, Verse 18.

> "He becomes even further away (from God ﷻ) than the Pleiades (a star cluster)."[164]

414. Tackling the Negatives

One of the biggest factors that contribute to a family's disintegration is not addressing and tackling destructive negative behaviors of the family. Those destructive behaviors include looking at what is forbidden, which happens when each family member goes their way in life without others' supervision and surveillance. On the other hand, the presence of a state of harmony in the family brings about consistency and success in their actions, as God ﷻ says:

﴿وَتَوَاصَوْا بِالْحَقِّ وَتَوَاصَوْا بِالصَّبْرِ﴾

﴾*wa-tawāṣaw bi-l-ḥaqqi wa-tawāṣaw bi-ṣ-ṣabr*﴿

﴾*and enjoin one another to [follow] the truth, and enjoin one another to patience*﴿[165]

415. Role Models

Children look to their parents as role models in the first years of their lives. Therefore, if the parent's life together is associated with mutual oppression, with the accompanying verbal and physical sin, children will suffer an unconscious setback towards everything

---

[164] Majlisī, ʿAllamah Muḥammad Bāqir, *Biḥār al-Anwār*, Vol. 61, p. 257.

[165] Sūrat al-ʿAṣr, Verse 3.

related to religion and its followers. This occurs because the symbol representing the religion, the parents, will fall in the eyes of the children, even if those symbols' credibility was suspect from the beginning.

416. Marriage is Half of the Religion

The statement: "whoever marries has ensured half of their religion" is not absolute and unlimited! Only some people who marry fulfill half of their religion; if, for example, a wife is not righteous, then the remaining half gets lost. A man can attain and safeguard half of his religion when he marries a woman with the qualities mentioned by Islāmic teachings and narrations. One of those qualities was mentioned in this ḥadīth:

> "Choose a woman of faith [religious], so you may be blessed."[166]

417. The Countdown

If a man's eyes are set on materialistic and physical human beauty, he should know that this beauty will be gone in time. The countdown for the physical joys of marriage begins on the wedding night. With the passing of each day, beauty decreases, and the number of wrinkles increases. Add to that the effects of repeatedly looking at the same thing, which makes one get used to a beautiful face until it becomes familiar and common to the point that one no longer sees any beauty in it!

---

[166] al-Ḥillī, Muḥammad b. Aḥmad b. Idrīs, *al-Sarā'ir al-Hāwā li-Taḥrīr al-Tatawī*, Vol. 2, p. 559.

418. Sacred Structure

Marriage is a sacred structure. It is a structure because nothing built-in Islām is more beloved by God ﷻ than the building of a family. It is sacred because human generations, including prophets, messengers, imāms, and righteous believers, resulted from a marital nest. If our master 'Abdullāh did not marry Lady Aminah عليها السلام, then humanity would not have enjoyed the presence of the Seal of Prophets, Muḥammad ﷺ.

419. Change

It is tough for a wife to try to change the disposition of a husband who is of a lower level of faith than she is. This is because a man usually does not yield to his wife, even in the domain of religion!

A man could be engaged in sinful acts, and when his wife tries to deter him from doing so, he becomes prideful in his sin. The hellfire is sufficient for such a man as the Qur'ānic verse mentioned. However, changing the wife is easier as the nature of women is usually built on yielding, especially in the realm of truth.

420. The Principle of Superiority

It is wrong for spouses to consecrate and remain adherent to a belief in their family's superiority during arguments or disagreements. When they do, they ignore the principle of superiority based on piety. There is no husband's family opposite to wife's family in the Islāmic sense. Instead, there is the teaching that all believers are like one body. We should not be moving family disputes to the larger society.

421. Deterring Vices

Islām's policy on deterring moral vices revolves around keeping elements of temptations and seduction away from the individual. Those elements include anything that leads to temptation, be it a look, a conversation, a touch, seclusion, joking, and the mixing of sexes. Tackling what leads to temptation is preferred over trying to treat the repercussions of that temptation, such as being in an aggressive or offensive state due to the failure to attain the desired goal or the frequent replacement of lovers due to boredom caused by meeting similar people.

422. Thankful for the Blessing

There is no doubt that a marriage based on Islāmic principles leads to the safeguarding of half of one's faith as well as emotional stability. Such a marriage is a blessing, and part of being thankful for that blessing is not denying the favor of one's family that embraced them for the entire duration of their life before marriage. Unfortunately, some people break away from their environment and annul the rights of their family upon them as soon as they build their own nest.

423. Marital Disputes

Rarely do marital disputes remain only between spouses. Instead, they spread, even unintentionally, to their families, causing a wide rift in the community. This, in turn, prepares the grounds for various social vices such as backbiting, gossip, slander, defamation, vilification, and other things that we consider insignificant but are grave sins in the eyes of God ﷻ.

424. The Believer's View on Pleasures

A believer does not view this world's pleasures from the scope of sheer pleasure and satisfaction but as a means of providing for their Afterlife. It was narrated in a Ḥadīth that:

> "A believer attains their provisions, and a disbeliever seeks their pleasure."[167]

A believer does not seek the pleasure of this world for the joy they get from it but as a requisite for another matter. For example, there is no denying that a husband finds joy and pleasure in his wife, but a believer does so intending to bring righteous offspring into this world, which would be a source of ongoing charity for him after his death.

425. Attraction and Gravitation

Everything that exists in this universe is based upon and revolves around gravity. The attraction between sexes is like the gravitation seen between the constellations and planets. If we let go of an object we hold, it would automatically fall to the ground due to the earth's gravity. The One who made this gravity is the One who made the power of attraction and gravitation in women. Thus, to prevent falling into a forbidden gravitational field, we have been instructed to keep our distance from members of the opposite sex.

---

[167] Majlisī, ʻAllamah Muḥammad Bāqir, *Biḥār al-Anwār*, Vol. 75, p. 112.

426. State of Acceptance

When discussing a wife's obedience to her husband, we are not referring to some blind obedience that gives a man the feeling that he lives in a camp and represents the leader of that camp. Instead, what we mean by a wife's obedience is her acceptance of her husband's decisions after discussing the matter and alternative solutions. If a man senses the wise judgment of his wife, he will automatically refrain from trying to control her and forcing her to do what he wants.

427. The Alternative

The intensity of affection and the passionate, emotional relationship between spouses in the first years of marriage does not last forever. This could be due to their growing age or preoccupation with complicated family problems. Establishing a state of mercy and compassion would guarantee the continuation of their relationship. This is referred to in the verse:

﴿وَجَعَلَ بَيْنَكُم مَّوَدَّةً وَرَحْمَةً﴾

﴾*wa-ja'ala baynakum mawaddatan wa-raḥmatan*﴿

﴾*and He ordained affection and mercy between you*﴿[168]

Maintaining this compassion and mercy will provide a foundation for an Islāmic family that will not be shaken despite all the obstacles.

---

[168] Sūrat al-Rūm, Verse 21.

428. The Limits of Jealousy

Jealousy should be contained within reasonable limits. Watching a man's every step, big or small, will only cause him to develop an aversion to his home life and seek other alternatives outside the home. He may turn to sinful and destructive relationships outside of the home or abandon his marital home altogether. This, in turn, will cause his children to become lost, turning them into prey in the hands of fate because a mother often cannot maintain the same control over the home.

429. Reciprocity

It is wrong for a husband to deal with his wife based on reciprocity, wherein he refuses to improve his moral character and behavior unless his wife does the same. The principle of

﴿لَا نُرِيدُ مِنكُمْ جَزَآءً وَلَا شُكُورًا﴾

﴿lā nurīdu minkum jazā'an wa-lā shukūra^{n}﴾

﴿We desire no reward from you, nor thanks﴾[169]

should be applied in this situation. There is a big difference between good morals to please God ﷻ and achieving the highest ranks of excellent character. Good morals are practiced to attain the benefits of this world.

---

[169] Sūrat al-Insān, Verse 9.

430. Spiritual Attraction

Spiritual attraction can be achieved even without the presence of remarkable external beauty. If a man finds this attraction in his wife, in addition to her acceptance of his guardianship as ordained by God ﷻ, along with the most essential element: her religiosity, then such a man's life will have a happy life. Even if his wife has a relatively common level of beauty.

431. The Consequences

It is wise for a person to think about the consequences of their actions. There must be mutual respect between spouses, and they must avoid exposing each other's faults in front of others, especially their children. Children have emotions towards both parents. When they see a lack of disrespect and the hurt inflicted upon one parent by the other, they naturally feel an aversion towards the hurtful parent and become partial to the one who is hurt.

432. Uprightness

A parent's uprightness greatly influences the blessing of their offspring. One of the most prominent examples of this is what came into play in the life of Ibrāhīm عليه السلام when he fully submitted to the Divine order and began to sacrifice his son. God ﷻ rewarded him with the best reward; He brought Muḥammad ﷺ out of Ibrāhīm's lineage.

433. Polluted Environments

It is necessary to maintain close supervision of children and teenagers when accompanying them to lands that are overcome by immorality and vice, as some deviations begin from exposure to these polluted environments. It would be harrowing for a father to realize that he pushed his child, even if unintentionally, into a swamp of vice, especially using the money God ﷻ entrusted him with!

434. Moral Dissolution

It is unfortunate to witness the spread of moral dissolution due to the expansion of corruption. We see some parents who do not care if they discover that their daughter is deep in sin, justifying their carelessness by saying that we are in an age of modernization. Sadly, this has become the norm today; parents are silent about the sins of their children instead of those sins igniting their protectiveness and instead of losing sleep worrying about their offspring.

435. Fairness

A believer is not infallible; therefore, they are prone to making mistakes occasionally. A man may be mindless at one point, and Shayṭān takes over, leading him to utter a bad word towards his wife. In such a case, it would not be fair for this man's wife to forget all the good things her husband has done for her and all the beautiful words she heard from him only to remember this terrible word he said. It is unfair for her to keep using it against him and revealing it to relatives and strangers.

436. Raising Children is a Specialty

Most things require educational and scientific specialization to guarantee desired results. Striving to raise righteous offspring is no exception. Raising children is also a field within the programming of existence and is not less worthy than other specialties. Dealing with children is one of the most complicated matters; thus, it also needs studying and planning.

437. Innate Mercy

A mother's mercy towards her child is something innate and inherent. She would be compassionate towards her child even if she knew that the child was going to die months after being born. Her compassion towards such a child might even be more intense, and her efforts towards the child more sincere because she does not expect any reward or thanks from this helpless child. When a child is inflicted with diseases, especially chronic and malignant ones, we see mothers show emotions that we do not see in others. This is what qualifies them to care for their children with great patience.

438. The Ambitions of a Believer

Forming a family that pleases God ﷻ and His messenger ﷺ is the ambition of every believer. A believer wants to form a family consistent with the family of our Holy Prophet and his wife, Sayyidah Khadījah, Imām ʿAlī, and Sayyidah Fāṭimah ؑ. Nothing prevents believers from making these transcendent entities their role models as they form and build their families. Indeed, one will not reach their rank; however, one who aims to reach high stations will reach, with great effort, a level that is close to them.

439. Giving Thanks for the Blessing

God ﷻ is the One who created a woman's beauty and ordered it to be covered. Therefore, a woman should not think she is doing God ﷻ a favor by obeying His orders! Instead, a woman to whom God

ﷻ has given distinguished beauty should be careful and mindful of her ḥijāb. She should even be more cognizant of her modesty and conceal her beauty from others to give thanks for this blessing.

440. Facilitation

Among the significant problems in this era was the delaying of marriage resulting from increased complications by both men and women. This is not how it was in the past, and temptations then were not as widespread as they are today. This combination makes the affliction even greater! Blessings are found when there is facilitation and alleviation, and whoever is content with less will attain more than they want with time.

441. Arguments

A rational person knows only to get involved in important and decisive arguments. So, when a husband sees that his wife has committed a sin, he should convince her that what she did is forbidden and sinful. However, when it comes to trivial matters such as furniture in the home, food, or travel, it is unreasonable to argue about such matters. A home with plenty of arguments and disputes will quickly become dominated by resentment, spitefulness, and hatred.

442. Compliance with the Rules

A person needs to show serious concern regarding their food and drink in non-Muslim countries. If the body grows from consuming ḥarām food or drink, it becomes a sinning machine. The rules set by God ﷻ should be adhered to in every matter, big and small. We never know if God ﷻ has concealed His punishment in a sin that His servant underestimated, such as in a meal or a drink!

443. Scrutiny When Choosing

Before getting married, a young man may be afflicted with moral deviation. His parents may hope that their son will finally rid himself of his previous problems by getting married. However, the precursors to disagreement and conflict usually arise between a man and his new bride within the early weeks of marriage. Being afflicted with this consequence can be avoided by practicing scrutiny when choosing a spouse and asking God ﷻ to grant such a man a suitable, righteous wife.

444. Divine Mercy

One who shows mercy to others and forgives the wrongdoers among them puts themselves more prone to receiving God's ﷻ-encompassing mercy. It is only natural for the Merciful, Most Loving to look with love and mercy towards those who have planted this divine quality within themselves so that it becomes a deeply rooted trait. So let us all show mercy to those on earth so that we may be shown mercy by the One in the Heavens!

445. Divine Sunnah

One of the divine sunnahs (laws and practices) is that a person's sustenance and livelihood come according to a specified measure and amount, which correlates with the effort spent by the person seeking it. Therefore, one who is lazy in their work, neglects to acquire life skills or wastes what God ﷻ bestowed them with must endure the divine predestination of a decrease in their sustenance due to their deeds. It is the way of God ﷻ that these matters should follow their natural course.

446. The Counselor

When a disagreement arises between a married couple, they should remove the thorns between them on their own. If they cannot do so and it becomes necessary for them to consult with others, they must be careful who they choose as a counselor. The counselor they choose must have both wisdom and a deep understanding of the religion and its laws. As the arbiters of their dispute, they must be extremely just and precise in their decisions and impartial to ensure they will not side with one party at the expense of the other.

447. Family Hypocrisy

An example of family hypocrisy is when a husband showers his wife with words of love and affection while he is disloyal to her in her absence with his ḥarām looks or ḥarām meetings. It is as if this man does not know that if God ﷻ wants to expose a person, He could, even if they are inside their own home. Just as God ﷻ covers our faults for a purpose, He also uncovers them for another purpose!

448. Adherence to the Ḥijāb

When some people travel, they absolve themselves from many restrictions. Yet, God ﷻ is Ever Watchful and observes His servants in every state. A chaste woman remains attentive to everything that safeguards her femininity even if she is not in a Muslim country. She adheres to her ḥijāb and does not participate in what corrupt men and women are involved in.

449. Intellectual and Educational Tourism

It is great to take advantage of a family's relaxation when traveling to propose the concepts and programs that need a cheerful and pleasant atmosphere. Hearts and minds are usually more receptive to advice during travel. Therefore, we can turn tourism into an intellectual and educational program to achieve an ideal, believing family.

450. Harshness

Harshness and roughness in interactions have become a widespread phenomenon these days. We see it, especially in people's dealings with those without defenders or helpers besides God ﷻ. Sometimes, people find it easy to treat their spouse or child harshly due to their long companionship. Consequently, that person will eventually face the anger of The Most-Exalted Protector.

451. Heart Break

A man who does not monitor his behavior and transgresses against his wife in speech or action can create a wound in her heart that will never heal. Even if he wants to reconcile with her and expresses his affection through a gift or similar gesture, she will still remember the past. Wouldn't it be better for him not to break her heart in the first place instead of going through much effort to mend it, an effort which might never heal no matter what he does?

452. Looking for the Cause

Some women complain that their husbands address them with demeaning words that bother them. This goes back to a lack of harmony between spouses. Therefore, a wife should consider the roots of her husband's lack of respect for her to treat this problem. It is wrong to attempt to solve a problem by concentrating on the symptoms while remaining negligent of the causes.

453. The Manager of the Institution

The family is one of the most important institutions. As such, it needs a manager to direct its affairs and settle matters. Therefore, spouses must agree that the husband is the manager and that it is his religious right as the guardianship of the family was given to the man. Otherwise, a couple's disputes over this matter will dissolve the family.

454. The Most Sacred State

Among the most sacred states is that of becoming a spouse and parent. These heartfelt emotions are sacred and beautiful and push one towards giving to the point of sacrifice. Because of these emotions, we see a father wishing his son would be better than him! This giving spirit distances a person from themselves, which in turn leads the person towards reaching their perfection.

455. Going to Extremes

When it comes to raising children, neglect and lack of supervision are equivalent to strictness in prohibition. Excessive discipline and lack of discipline are both misleading. Therefore, it is necessary to identify what children should be prohibited from doing. The prohibition that must be emphasized is a prohibition from what is ḥarām in Islām. For other matters, parents need to convince their children and attempt to change their inclinations and habits, which may require time and mental and spiritual maturity. The use of admonition and restraint will not be effective in this case.

456. Family Ties and Bonds

The family entity is founded on ties and bonds that cannot be denied. If the affection and passion disappear after a period of marriage, there remains a strong basis to keep that relationship together. The remaining basis includes the state of mercy between spouses and viewing the other spouse as a spiritual being that represents a divine trust in this existence.

457. The Best Woman

The best woman that can be chosen as a partner in marriage is a woman who finds comfort in home life and does not have the desire to leave the home, to mingle with men, or to acquire material possessions except out of necessity. When a wife is mentally preoccupied with things other than her husband and children, she is naturally less likely to give her husband his rights, as she would if her family were her sole concern.

458. The Flock

Children are essentially a flock. Their parents oversee them for a limited time as they are under their parents' control due to their need for care and financial support. However, some parents do not take advantage of this time and misuse their opportunity. When the time comes, and children leave home, whether because of marriage or other reasons, many parents regret and lament the opportunity they let slip by!

459. Reunification

Many parents work very hard to raise a righteous child. Some of them might not see the fruit of their labor in this life as a result of the child's death not long after they mature. However, they should remember that they did not lose anything because their reunification will happen in Barzakh and the Hereafter in the best way possible!

460. The Principle of Trust

The primary basis for a happy marital life is for both spouses to sense trust when dealing with the other. A husband should view his wife as the trust that God ﷻ placed in him and feel the weight of this trust and the greatness of this responsibility placed on him. The wife should also do the same, strive to be her husband's best wife, and respect and appreciate him.

461. The Worst Suffering

Divorce often leads to a mother being deprived of the comfort and joy of caring for her children and causes the emotional bond between them to become weak. As they grow, and with the arrival of the day that every mother dreams of, the day she would feel the joy of seeing her child get married, she may find herself a stranger at her child's wedding. What a terrible suffering that would be! That suffering could have been avoided had she been more patient during marital conflicts!

462. The Ease of Injustice

If a man wanted to swear at a person in the marketplace or on the street, he could think of a thousand reasons why he should not. After all, this person is a stranger and could complain about him and cause a scandal! However, his wife is under his control, so he finds it easier to cross the line with her and wrong her. However, the greatest injustice is against one who has no defender besides God ﷻ!

463. Anger for the Sake of God ﷻ

A believer should save their anger for matters worthy of it and not get angry over every small and big thing. This will ensure that their anger maintains its value and remains effective, so it is said: "Beware of the level-headed person when they get angry." When a believer who suppresses their anger and only gets angry for the sake of God ﷻ becomes angry, their family becomes attentive to what caused their anger and will be less likely to do it again.

464. Warding off Hellfire

A man should not seek his pleasure and comfort outside of the home at the expense of his wife. God ﷻ has instructed us to ward off the Hellfire from ourselves first and then from our family:

﴿يَٰٓأَيُّهَا ٱلَّذِينَ ءَامَنُواْ قُوٓاْ أَنفُسَكُمۡ وَأَهۡلِيكُمۡ نَارٗا وَقُودُهَا ٱلنَّاسُ وَٱلۡحِجَارَةُ﴾

﴾yā-ʾayyuhā lladhīna ʾāmanū qū ʾanfusakum wa-ʾahlīkum nāran waqūduhā n-nāsu wa-l-ḥijāratu﴿

❨*O you who have faith! Save yourselves and your families from a Fire whose fuel will be people and stones*❩[170]

A man leaving his wife at home in seclusion and loneliness, especially at night while he enjoys the company of his friends, is committing a kind of unintentional torture.

465. Moral Fluidity

Islām opposes and strongly rejects the concept of moral fluidity. This is especially emphasized for females, who possess an instinctive ability to attract the opposite sex. Imām ʿAlī 🕮 once commented when a beautiful woman passed by his companions, and they stared at her:

> "Verily, the eyes of these virile males are covetous, and this glancing is the cause of their lust."[171]

466. The Deeds of the Offspring

There are some people who, while in Barzakh, double the rewards and rank they had at the time of their death. Counting only their deeds during their life, they might have attained the level of being guests or visitors in Heaven. However, if such a person left behind righteous offspring, they might elevate their rank to become among the neighbors of the Prophet 🕮 and his household 🕮 only as a result of the deeds of their offspring.

---

[170] Sūrat al-Taḥrīm, Verse 6.

[171] *al-Manāqib*, Vol. 2, p. 113.

467. Leniency

The Holy Prophet ﷺ used to emphasize the need for leniency in our interactions, especially with the weak among God's ﷻ creatures and those we ought to show mercy towards, such as children. Once, when the Prophet heard the crying of his young grandchild, al-Ḥasan ﵇, he asked Sayyidah Fāṭimah:

> "What happened to al-Ḥasan? Didn't I tell you that his crying hurts me?"[172]

468. Romantic Gestures

Expressing emotions and showing romantic gestures when interacting with one's wife is required in Islām. It has been narrated that the Prophet ﷺ said:

> "The man who tells his wife: "I love you", never leaves her heart."[173]

This behavior should not be restricted to the first few years of marriage. Instead, it is necessary always to keep hydrating marital life with such gestures.

---

[172] al-Nuʿmān, al-Qāḍī, *Sharḥ al-Akhbār fī Faḍā'il al-A'imma al-Aṭhār* ﵈, Vol. 3, p. 77.

[173] Kulaynī, Shaykh Muḥammad b. Yaʿqūb, *al-Kāfī*, Vol. 5, p. 569.

469. A Perfection Attained only by Marriage

There are degrees of perfection a person cannot reach except through marriage. For example, when added to another, number one changes from being described as a single odd number to becoming a part of a pair, forming an even number. If one of those numbers is removed, the description of a "pair" is also automatically removed. The situation is similar regarding a man and a woman; when they are united, they attain a distinction, a perfection not found in their singular state.

470. Family Breakdown

Family breakdown is one of the matters that concern modern societies. It arises from the increased complications of daily life. We have reached a point where a person's main concern is to do away with their problems. Thus, due to their lack of emotional and mental space, a person cannot think of the problems of those closest to them, let alone distant people!

471. Rising Above

One of the ways that help with being able to forgive others is to rise above petty and insignificant matters. Believers are preoccupied with their celestial world and spiritual well-being and hardly allow trivial matters to distract them. After all, what value is there to the words of others that do not show reality? Why would one give those words any weight and take a hostile stand against them, depriving themselves of the blessings of forgiveness and leniency?

472. Compulsory Dealings

A person who must deal with compulsory interactions with the opposite sex at work and other places should pay extra attention to the laws of jurisprudence dealing with the interaction between members of the opposite sex. They should strive to implement the rules in their interactions, which include avoiding doubtful and suspicious private meetings, not being involved in unnecessary conversations, and not having an appearance that draws attention and leads to temptation. Necessity must only be answered proportionately and should not be overestimated.

473. The Balance

A woman should always strive to balance the negative outcomes of stubbornness and insisting on a certain position and the positive outcomes of tolerating some deprivation to decrease tension in her marital life. It would not be logical for a woman to acquire all the materialistic possessions she wishes for in this world in exchange for losing some of her faith and religiosity or her emotional wellness.

474. Excusing

The desire to reform others and help them become righteous often makes one forgiving and lenient. Excusing and overlooking others' mistakes is a practical lesson for one who wishes to attain the best morals. People are naturally attracted to and become compliant towards moral excellence and towards the one who possesses this trait without asking for this compliance.

475. Man's Guardianship

God ﷻ said:

﴿ٱلرِّجَالُ قَوَّٰمُونَ عَلَى ٱلنِّسَآءِ﴾

﴿*ar-rijālu qawwāmūna 'alā n-nisā'i*﴾

﴿*Men are the managers of women*﴾[174]

The Arabic word used to describe a man's role is "qawwam," an intensive (exaggerated) form of "qā'im." The root verb for both, aqam, means one who stands or makes something stand. Thus, "qawwam" means continuously standing or making something stand. Concerning the verse, this means that men are responsible for supporting and managing the affairs of marital life in the best manner possible. The man was given this responsibility due to his distinguished qualities, including physical strength, decisiveness, and emotions that are not predominant over logic, and because he was given the responsibility of financially supporting his wife.

476. Knowing the Obligations

When spouses know their obligations and responsibilities, they avoid many problems. Housework, though necessary for the continuation of life, is not among the wife's obligations. Yet, some men resent their wives if they fail to manage the household affairs with the same resentment for one who commits a sinful act or fails to fulfill an obligation!

---

[174] Sūrat al-Nisā', Verse 34.

477. Acquiring the Divine View/Outlook

A transparent and divine view of women is important for a happy life. A woman was also created in this life to reach her perfection. Therefore, we must view her as a creature on a journey to reach nearness to God ﷻ, just like a man, and we should not be an element that slows her down or discourages her in her march to perfection.

478. Cleanliness

A believer who feels like they are in the presence of God ﷻ will strive to maintain a pleasant smell and dress in pure, clean clothes. So, what if his wife also desired this pleasant appearance from him and gets emotional satisfaction whenever she sees that her husband beautified himself for her?

479. The Hastening of Divine Vengeance

The Holy Prophet ﷺ said:

> "Fear God regarding the two vulnerable groups,"[175]

about women and orphans. It is known that oppressing those with no supporter and defender except God ﷻ brings about the hastening of Divine Vengeance. From this, we can derive that a person who is unjust and oppressive towards his wife will not be able to advance toward the ladder of perfection. After all, how can he come near The Master when he deserves His wrath?

---

[175] al-Ḥillī, Aḥmad b. Fahd, *'Uddat al-Dā'ī wa Najāḥ al-Sā'ī*, p. 91.

480. The Deposited Instinct

The sexual instinct that was deposited in and entrusted to human beings, both male and female, is not to be intended and sought for itself. Instead, it was made to serve as a means of achieving the necessary attraction between the sexes. The lawful union between the spouses brings about a state of companionship, affection, and mercy. Eventually, the lawful application of this deposited instinct leads to forming a righteous family, which is the nucleus of a righteous society.

481. The Current

Traveling to Western countries can be likened to a person put in a sweeping river current and asked to wrestle the waves. Such a person has two options: either resist and swim against the current and become an internationally known expert swimmer, or surrender to the violent waves and be taken by the water.

482. Realism

A wife must be realistic in her financial dealings with her husband. Overburdening and asking him for more than he can offer will likely lead to disputes and estrangement between them. This is especially true when a husband is unsatisfied with his spending. A wife should know that what is taken through embarrassing the giver or out of the giver's surrender to keep problems away is like that which is taken by force!

483. Deviation

A believing father may be tested with a deviant son who causes his heart to suffer from sadness and concern for that son, especially if the father is distinguished in knowledge and faith! Likewise, a believing son can also be afflicted with a deviant father! His trial and suffering would be huge as he would be torn between being a good son to his father and trying to deter him from sinning, all while his reputation is tarnished in the community!

484. To Each their World

It is normal for a difference in interests and directions between fathers and their sons, as each lives in their own world due to their age difference. Unfortunately, this can create emotional distance between the father and son. However, a wise father will bring himself down to his son's level to be close to his heart, making it easier to guide him to what is better for him.

485. Behind Every Great Man, there is a Woman

A woman who monitors her behavior and strives to reach her perfection, behaviorally and intellectually, will be more capable of giving and caring for her husband and children. She will not only be raising distinguished children but will also have a great role in influencing her husband's betterment and distinction. From here, it was said:

> "Behind every great man, there is a woman."

486. Caring for the Soul

A human being has both physical and spiritual composition. Just as there is a body that moves, there is also a soul that grows. Therefore, just as we care about the physical growth of our children, we must also care for their souls and growth. This spiritual growth reaches its peak, whether height and perfection or lowliness and degradation, during adolescence.

487. Child Care

When parents take on the responsibility of caring for their children by themselves, it does not have the same result as if they delegated that responsibility to someone else, such as a maid or others. The affection and care they give their child in their childhood will become ingrained in the child's memory, and the child will remember their love and kindness when they grow up. Those feelings of appreciation and gratitude will deter the child from committing acts of disobedience towards them!

488. Specifications List

One who insists on finding a spouse that fits their ideal specifications will remain without a spouse in this life. After all, God ﷻ did not put perfection in it! One who wants beauty and perfection should wait for the Houris of Paradise, but first, they will have to wait until Judgement Day! Hence, we should be realistic and figure out our top priorities!

489. The Greatest Means to God's Nearness

One of the greatest means to seek God's ﷻ nearness is to achieve reconciliation between spouses. Solving disputes between a married couple might even be dearer to God ﷻ than helping someone get married! This is because the repercussions of separation and divorce cannot be compared to the negatives of not being successful in helping others marry, just like the destruction of a tall building is not like building a home that does not yet exist.

490. Avoiding Injustice Towards the Wife

Injustice and oppression towards one's wife should be avoided at all costs, especially if she has no defender or helper except God ﷻ, for "she could hit him with an arrow of the night!" (A proverb meaning she could pray against her oppressive husband during the night, a prayer that is sure to be answered) Even if she were to forgive him, God ﷻ might not forgive him due to the graveness of his injustice. The Common Right belongs to God ﷻ, and as such, He can inflict punishment on the husband from which he will suffer bitterness for a long time due to the injustice he committed for just a few moments!

491. The Institutional Government

The government can be divided into two: a realist government, which is the government of the Lord of the Worlds, and from it, the government of the prophets and imāms branches off... and a constructivist government, like the family government. In the family government, a wife views her husband as the ruler of the home, and if she notices a shortcoming or a defect in him or his rule, she brings it to his attention in a polite manner.

492. Supplication and Thankfulness

It is highly recommended for a married couple to intensify their prayers and supplications for their child during pregnancy. This is because, during pregnancy, the child's situation is uncertain. The child might come out into this world deformed and handicapped. When the child is born safely and without any deformities or handicaps, they should offer thanks to God ﷻ for the end of a stage full of anticipation, fear, and anxiety.

493. Thinking About the Hereafter

Preoccupation with managing the affairs of the family should keep a person from thinking about the matters of the Hereafter. They could waste their life trying to gather wealth and enduring the most demanding jobs, only to have their child squander their wealth after their death while the poor parent is in dire need of one good deed to save them from painful suffering!

494. Bringing Delight

Bringing delight to the heart of a believer is among the matters emphasized in Sharīʿa, and wives fall under the category of believers! When a man sees his wife sad and needing him by her side, and he leaves the congregational prayer to be by her side, he brings joy and delight to her heart. Would such a man be a loser by doing that, or would he have gained a great reward?

495. Affection

It is noticed that as soon as the marriage contract is finalized, a state of affection is introduced between spouses. Unfortunately, with time, this affection begins fading away due to disputes and incorrect practices. However, one should not despair and instead ask God ﷻ to return the affection they lost during their marriage.

496. A Man's Suspicion

One of the biggest destroyers of marriage is when the husband is suspicious about his wife's chastity! How could this poor, innocent wife live with a man while he is slandering her chastity and honor at every moment with his mistrust and the false signs he imagines? What a terrible life that would be!

497. The Map

The mental and emotional composition differs from one child to another due to the differences in their genetics. It is wrong to deal with all of them using the same method and to compare them. Instead, a child's inner map should be identified and learned to assist and supply parents with a suitable method to deal with the child and raise them best.

498. A Daughter's Role Model

A mother who wears a ḥijāb but does not monitor her behavior when dealing with others is not a good role model for her daughter when it relates to adherence to the ḥijāb. Instead, her daughter might be deceived by the slogan that religion is in the heart, especially when she sees a woman who does not wear a ḥijāb but has a high level of morality in her speech and actions!

499. Affability

A believing woman feels a state of affability and enjoyment as she works on caring for and teaching her children despite the exhaustion she faces as a result. She does not complain about this great responsibility, which has been more prominently placed on her shoulders than the father. Instead, she is overjoyed that the greats graduate from the mother's hands!

500. The Intelligent Woman

An intelligent woman does what is needed to attract her husband to the home, creating a calm, romantic atmosphere. A man who does not find a woman who embraces him with her affection and lightens the burden he carries from life and its problems will dislike coming home and turn towards anything else that will give him comfort.

501. Reasonable Expectations

Among the mistakes some parents commit when raising their children is having unreasonable expectations from them. Often, parents' expectations are not suitable for a child's age. We should not expect a child or a teenager to do the tasks of adults! Bearing down heavily on them and obliging them with serious matters at the age of playfulness has significant negative implications for them.

502. The Golden Opportunity

One of the golden opportunities in the life of a believer is the time of bachelorhood. During that time, a man has free time and a lack of responsibility towards a wife and children. It is unfortunate, though, that many youths need to make the best of this great opportunity. Instead, while single, they keep thinking about marriage, and when they get married, they long for the days of bachelorhood!

503. The Awaiting Community

Tightening family bonds is a way to show support and loyalty to the Imām عجل الله فرجه الشريف. The assembly of all the happy, connected, believing families forms the ideal awaiting community. This, in turn, leads to the hastening of our Imām's عجل الله فرجه الشريف reappearance and our awaited relief.

504. Family Foundation

An individual's spiritual and emotional perfection cannot be attained except through a happy family. However, if one does not secure and strengthen their family's foundation after marriage, they might collapse even in their spiritual relationship with God جل جلاله.

505. Methods of Deterrence

One effective method of deterrence is for a person to pay attention to how they look and behave when they are angry. They can do so by looking into a mirror or asking someone to take a picture of them when angry. Upon seeing how they look when they are angry, they will realize that they cannot stand their look, let alone for others to stand to look at them!

506. Declaration of Sins

It is considered a major crime for a father to openly declare and speak about his sins in front of his young children. If he is addicted to some reprehensible act or substance, then do it in secret! If he is drowning in vice, then why would he drag those innocent souls into it with him? Woe to him from the judgment of God ﷻ!

507. Recitation of Qur'ānic Verses and Wisdom

Islām ordered women not to flaunt and display their beauty in front of strangers (non-maḥram) and to not go out in a manner that attracts other's attention. At the same time, they were instructed to read the Qur'ān. Through this, a woman is encouraged to be an element of radiation for thought and righteousness in the marital home instead of becoming a tool men exploit and use!

508. Marital Life Maintenance

Married life certainly needs continuous maintenance. There are always new developments, both on the problems and solutions sides. It is best to solve any problems that arise. Otherwise, the devil will creep into this existence, like a worm that bores into a mighty tree until it turns into ruins.

509. Exceeding Beyond the Circle of Dispute

A marital dispute is not only confined to a couple. Instead, it exceeds and reaches out to include their families. This, in turn, causes a wide rift in the community and prepares the grounds for many social vices, such as backbiting, gossip, defaming, and other evil acts that we may consider insignificant but are mighty in the Eyes of God ﷻ!

The Bottom Line for a Happy Family

As stated in the Noble Qur'ān, these three elements form the basis of marital life: tranquility, affection, and compassion.

Thinking about righteous offspring should begin on the wedding night, though such offspring only emerge from the laps of spiritually mature ones.

There are degrees of perfection a person can only reach through marriage, and this might be understood by considering that marriage is the completion of half of one's faith.

When one views their spouse as the other half that completes them, they would be cautious when choosing their spouse.

The wife trusts in the husband's care, and the higher her level of faith, the deeper and greater the responsibility of safekeeping this trust is on the husband.

Kind treatment of the wife is one of the traits of a believer, even if she is unappreciative of it or denies her husband's good actions.

One who wants distinction and excellence for their child should plan for it early on, meaning before marriage and afterward.

Some forms of children's deviation and disobedience result from the mother's cruelty, aggression, and tension.

Some mothers' mere existence and looks are enough to discipline their children; even their breaths are blessed and effective in ensuring their children's righteousness, even if they have not spent much effort disciplining them.

Children's deviation can happen due to external influences, such as a corrupt environment, even if their parents put much effort into raising and disciplining their children.

If a dispute between the spouses arises from an objection to a religious ruling, they should not be lax about it, and both sides should abide by it.

If a dispute between the spouses stems from a personal matter, then it can be solved by convincing the wife in a gentle, emotional manner that does not make her feel that her husband is trying to have absolute control over her.

One of the best ways to be effective with the other party, such as the wife, is through emotional containment and showing love.

If one deals with a child that deviated, one should commit to praying for children, asking God ﷻ for the child's righteousness.

A believing woman can bring her husband back to his senses with proven educational methods and supplications.

When a woman improves herself in terms of spiritual purity and intellectual development, she does a service to herself first and to her husband second.

Beauty has two dimensions: external beauty, which is subjective and temporary, and internal beauty, which is lasting and does not become boring.

A religious wife is the best helper for a man in matters of his religion and life, and she is not to be mistrusted as long as religion is the law in all circumstances.

A believer blessed with a believing wife has also attained the mother who will give him righteous progeny, the best gain a person can secure.

A believer does not view worldly pleasures from the scope of sheer pleasure and satisfaction but as a means of providing for their Afterlife! Their intention for marriage is to have righteous offspring to ensure that they will have ongoing charity after death.

A wise man would not care for the beauty of a woman who grew up in a corrupt family, no matter how breathtaking her beauty was!

Marriage leads to enrichment unless it impedes receiving the wealth, such as committing sins.

Just as the survival of affection and mercy in a marriage is contingent on not committing what causes their loss, the couple's divinely predetermined livelihood is also contingent on not committing sins that would cause its decrease.

Livelihood (rizq) is not confined to money but includes all that comes from God ﷻ, and the best kinds of rizq are a righteous wife, righteous offspring, and a gentle heart.

A believer does not get angry, except in two cases: when God ﷻ would get angry and if his anger would effectively deter a wrongdoer.

Inner preoccupation with important and serious matters effectively prevents one from becoming angry, even if exposed to considerable hurt from others.

A person wishing to avoid feeling tense and anxious when dealing with others should clear the mental images and judgments they have created to assess others.

Anger and lust are two dark clouds; if they overcome a person, they block the sun and prevent them from seeing it.

When Shayṭān gives up on corrupting a believer, he will try to attack them instead through any vulnerable relatives they have.

Among things that bring extreme happiness to Shayṭān, causing him to boast to his devils, is his success separating a believing man from a woman.

One of the strong foundations that help create a solid marriage is acquiring knowledge in marital and family life.

The secret of success in marital life is commitment and obedience to the commands of the Transcendent Master and the state of harmony in accepting a man's reasonable guardianship that God ﷻ ordained for him.

The reality of marital life is that it is a mating of the souls, not just a physical union dominated by instinct. Therefore, a couple should increase the emotional and spiritual harmony between them.

If a couple can agree on these two judges, religion and intellect, their marital life will be stable and happy.

The marital relationship is eternal. When one of the spouses seeks to elevate the other spiritually, this elevation will determine the rank in Heaven.

One of the factors that help stabilize marital life is avoiding contact with the opposite sex, except for a compelling necessity.

The attraction of a female is something that cosmetics and a coordinated appearance cannot measure; it is enough for her to be a believing woman with acceptable beauty to have this hidden attraction and allure.

It is of the believer's good fortune to have a wife who is compatible with his principles and goals in matters of his religion and life and is his helper in accomplishing them.

When wishing to marry a girl, please do not limit yourself to looking at her beauty only, but investigate her traits and disposition, genetics, ability to raise children, and mental and intellectual capacity.

Having control over the believer's family situation is a major concern for the devil. Therefore, he will strive to enter the family atmosphere to destroy it or at least cause tension between family members.

Naturally, a woman has limited energy; therefore, the more she constricts her activities outside of the home, the more concentrated her efforts will become inside in raising her children and caring for her husband.

When a believing woman rejects a marriage proposal of a competent believer due to his lack of wealth, she may be subjected to some divine punishments because this shows her carelessness about the trait of faithfulness present in that man.

It is necessary to provide a safe means of entertainment for kids to be occupied with during their free time so the parents can stop worrying about their kids' preoccupation with the wrong materials. Alternatively, they can take them to recreation centers.

Disobedience to parents is among the destructive matters in a person's journey towards God ﷻ; it is not just the cause of decreasing one's life! It causes one to grow even further away from God ﷻ because the parents represent the external reason for a person's existence!

A wise man enters his wife's heart with subtle and nice ways of convincing her of what he wants because harshness and forcefulness will not get him what he wants, even if he appears to have control.

Both spouses beautifying themselves for the other brings about psychological satisfaction, instinctive and emotional satiation, and stops the inclination to look and seek forbidden relationships.

One of the spouses may feel inferior to the other's financial or educational excellence, but these matters hold no weight with God ﷻ; the best and superior of the two is the more pious and spiritually perfect person!

A man's lack of responsibility inside the home, even in terms of obligatory spending, is cause for the demolition of the marital entity.

A person addicted to looking at unlawful images, besides committing a sinful act, will become less inclined to seek what is lawful from his wife and will treat her unjustly and harshly, which in turn causes his loss to be multiplied!

When parents are tested with having sick children, their hearts break, the grief and worry they feel for them, and the hardships they endure caring for them are the expiation for their sins and a means for them to reach spiritual perfection and gain closeness to God ﷻ.

Simply being a woman holds no value; if a woman is righteous, then she is better than gold, and if she is wicked, then she is inferior to dirt!

The best method to plant virtues in children's souls is their upbringing in a believing family, as they see their parents as a righteous role models.

A woman who wears the ḥijāb is more attractive than one who shows her beauty to others because the latter's beauty is enjoyed by all, leaving nothing special for her husband!

A woman without a ḥijāb is like a body without skin, with no protection from germs and harmful microbes!

A ḥijāb does not prevent a woman from performing her educational and social role because her work is concerned with the mind and the heart, which have no veils; the ḥijāb is only for this external body.

A mother should accustom her daughter to the ḥijāb at a young age and provide her with convincing introductions so that she does not rebel against the ḥijāb when she reaches the age when it becomes obligatory.

It is no secret that the personality of a working woman is different from that of a woman who stays at home, with the first losing much of her femininity, which attracted men towards her.

One of the primary duties of a wife is to be a source of relief for her husband's instincts, so if she refrains from fulfilling her religious obligation towards him, it is natural for him to seek another alternative.

One who does not maintain close monitoring of their delusions and misconceptions will live with an enormous number of mental images that do not match reality, which in turn causes discord and confusion between spouses.

A family relationship is eternal; according to narrations, when a person enters Heaven, they will look for their family members and even ask about their servant who was with them in this life.

A woman's main mission is to create a righteous family, and the appropriate uniform for her job is the ḥijāb, just like every job; medicine, for example, has its uniform.

Parents should pay attention to developing their children's religious education and teach them prayers before puberty so that they adapt and get used to it before it becomes obligatory.

If a believer is in a situation where they must have contact with the opposite sex, then with dignity and reverence, they should make the other person understand that they are a serious person who is over trifles.

One who loves his wife for her external beauty should know that it is naturally destined to vanish. However, for one who loves the beauty of her soul, the soul is eternal and never vanishes.

The optimal marriage is the mating of the souls, not the bodies. When souls are joined, many daily shortfalls will become easier to tolerate.

One of the factors that lead to the family's breakup is having illogical expectations, such as when the man expects his wife to be ideal in her every move, but is he that ideal?

When a woman suffers from an aversion to her husband due to their deep differences, she should make a sacrifice if children are present and supplicate to God ﷻ and invoke the Prophet's household's help in this matter.

A believer can sacrifice their desires and marry a woman who does not have a distinct level of beauty or wealth because she is righteous, and God ﷻ destined that a righteous progeny will come out of her womb.

If a woman is intelligent and clever, she can convince her husband of what she wants without an argument.

The affection between spouses at the beginning of a marriage is removed due to committing religious violations. Piety and extending kind treatment to others can change the enmity to harmony between the two.

Having useful knowledge of family dynamics and relationships opens the horizons for spouses, enabling them to solve their problems and overcome tribulations independently.

A married couple should choose an appropriate time to hold truth sessions, discussing family problems objectively and without blame and provocation.

To strengthen a family's relationship, there should be mutual respect for viewpoints between the members, as it is natural for the personalities, attitudes, and perceptions to be different.

Some forms of children's disobedience stem from the parents' misconduct and arguments in front of their children so that a child judges one parent as an oppressor and sides with the other parent.

To solve the problems of children, it is necessary to combine two methods: the use of disciplinary and educational methods and resorting to God ﷻ for help and guidance.

The jihad of a woman is to take care of her husband, but her encouragement of her husband to face life's demands and provide him with warm, kind companionship is also a means for her ascent and reaching her perfection.

One who envisions their family to reach the nearness of God ﷻ will find happiness in caring for them, all while relishing the wafts of breeze sent from the Divine.

The marital nest is a sacred establishment founded on tranquility, affection, and mercy, without which there is no guarantee against family dissolution.

The backbone of a happy marital life is for the husband to feel the depth of the trust placed in his hands by his wife and children.

When marriage becomes a woman's primary concern and biggest wish, then she will accept anyone who proposes to her, even if he is a lunatic or a sinner.

When a man sees marriage as only a means to fulfill his instincts and desires, he will marry even a disbeliever and one who is a known sinner.

A person who suffers from an unstable marital life should use this affliction to get closer to God ﷻ, as this affliction could be their means of reaching spiritual perfection.

A wife is a trust placed in the hands of her husband and is his life partner. Therefore, he should not view her as a prisoner or a hostage under his control!

With his misconduct and mistreatment, a husband might push his wife away from her femininity and natural disposition, as it is known that when a being is altered from its natural form, it will be difficult to change it afterward.

When there is a state of spiritual and cultural harmony between spouses, the affection and intimacy between them will last until the end of their lives.

If marital love and spiritual love combine, marital life will be wonderful.

Even if a believer happens to hate his wife for some reason, he will not be unjust to her because he fears God ﷻ. Instead, he conceals what he feels in his heart and shows her intense warmth and love.

A believer's attachment to his wife increases with time because he appreciates the care and assistance she has offered him over the years and for giving him righteous offspring who are the joy of his eyes.

One who wishes for a happy marital life should acquire the same characteristics as God ﷻ from the first day of marriage and try to win over his wife's heart.

It is wise to conceal the secrets of marital life and to only present marital problems to an advisor who is trustworthy and rational, one who possesses faith and piety, so he can guide the couple towards what is in their best interest.

Before marriage, a believer should enroll in educational courses on family management, spousal relationships, child-rearing methods, and discipline.

Religious violations committed before marriage are one of the causes of family disputes and dissolution. Therefore, caution should be taken with this matter, and a man and woman should remember that they are strangers to each other until the marriage contract is finalized.

Love is a heartfelt emotion, and its practical expression is affection. Love without affection is not enough in marital life, as both are needed to strengthen the relationship between spouses.

A spouse and children are the closest people to a person, but they can also be one's enemies if they distract them from remembering God ﷻ, and this hostility appears on Judgement Day.

Failing to practice equality of treatment and giving between children instills grudges and hostile feelings in their hearts against each other, and this is reflected in constant disputes between them that disturb the parents' lives.

Some men use money to solve their problems with their wives; eventually, their wives learn to blackmail them with a new request daily! Yet if a husband works on winning her heart, he would have won everything about her, even if he did not give her anything!

Mutual respect and politeness between spouses deactivate the mines found in a marriage, so even if the husband does something that enrages his wife, she should suppress her anger and avert conflict.

It is a believer's wish to have a son who is innately distinguished and not only obedient to God ﷻ but is also pious, devout, and God-fearing; he feels joy and comfort whenever he sees his son! This is more important to a believer than having a beautiful child, as external beauty is short-lived.

A believer cares equally about reaching their spiritual perfection and helping their offspring reach theirs and do not advance one at the expense of neglecting the other.

A father who monitors and is mindful of his behavior is the best role model for his children, even if he does not spend much effort disciplining them. There is no use in trying to direct children when they see their father committing a violation right before their eyes.

Being unnecessarily elaborate in conversations with non-maḥram relatives can be an introduction to interactions influenced by the devil. Therefore, a wife's sister should not be treated like a wife or a husband's brother like a husband.

Raising a child with a strong foundation of faith and piety helps them form a self-shield that protects them from the hotbeds of corruption, which has spread everywhere and beyond the control and watch of parents.

One should be careful of arguing, especially in insignificant matters, as it sows grudges and bitter feelings in the hearts of family members to such a degree that a son wishes for his father's death. A daughter wishes for her mother's death!

A man who sees his wife and children as weak overpowers them and dares to be unjust to them. Does he not think that they have a Lord who will seek victory on their behalf from him when he least expects it?

A husband who shirks his responsibilities and is lazy in managing his family's affairs risks losing his wife's respect, and the opposite is true, as one's value is in what one does well!

One's children are entrusted to him and are his ongoing charity and the joy of his eyes, so how many hours does he give them?

One of the ways we show our support to our Imām عجل الله تعالى فرجه الشريف is by contributing to the hastening of his reappearance. This can be done by raising righteous offspring who will be his helpers and supporters.

Some men direct their efforts and concerns outside the family, claiming to be spreading the religion and fulfilling the needs of other believers, which could make their own family turn away from the religion.

Exaggeration in spoiling and indulging a son makes him weak and incapable of social confrontation. He will then break at the slightest shock he faces from others because he expects that everyone will treat him like his parents do.

A man who looks at beautiful women a lot naturally will become less interested in his wife and thus end up destroying his lawful nest with this destructive pickaxe.

One of the ways the devil tries to gain control over a person is to get to them through their marital life. His exploitation of the women's emotional nature makes this easier for him; he attempts to create an atmosphere of tension and disputes between spouses.

A believer tries to reap the fruit of married life to achieve happiness on that lonely night through righteous offspring who will supply him with gifts and great rewards during a stage where one most needs a good deed to tip the scale in his favor.

Suppose there is a state of compassion and mercy between spouses, in addition to affection, instinctive desire, and management of the family's affairs. In that case, this paste becomes an impenetrable structure that cannot be destroyed with time.

The instinctive side follows the emotional side; if affection and mercy are present, then the instinctive side of the relationship will have a distinct impact on spouses. Therefore, a believing family lives in complete happiness, internally and externally.

Marriage is sought for matters that could become weak or disappear with time, but what makes the marital life a solid element that does not change with time is for the husband to view his wife as a trust God ﷻ placed under his care.

Each of the spouses must view the other from an angle of faith, not a physical one, meaning for the wife to view her husband as the servant of God ﷻ and for the husband to view his wife as the servant of God ﷻ as this trait does not go away with the passing of days. Instead, it increases in strength and clarity.

It is necessary to provide a child with continuous care that suits their stage of life, as the method followed during their childhood is unsuitable in their adolescence, and this requires a high level of knowledge of education methods.

Guardianship is a trust God ﷻ gives to the man, and he must know its worth and never try to misuse it. Instead, he should turn it into a positive element of control in his marital life.

It is wrong to limit marital happiness with money. Although living in poverty, some people have a high level of stability and happiness, righteous offspring, and are successful in performing worship acts in ways the wealthy cannot dream of.

Financial difficulties can cause worry and turbulence in marital life. In such a situation, a believer should turn to God ﷻ and ask Him to enrich them with His bounty, howsoever, through whatever, and wherever He wishes, as He is the Most Knowledgeable of His believing servants and what protects their faith.

Both spouses should become psychological experts on the moods of each other so each spouse would know the emotional fluctuations of the other so that they can use the correct way of dealing with them, thus getting what they want and avoiding disputes.

A marital nest is a sacred structure; occasionally, it needs maintenance and renovation as the passing of time will cause some wear that makes it lose delight and joy. Therefore, it is important to hold honest meetings to discuss family issues calmly and purposefully.

Indifference and overlooking sins committed by one spouse, and not enjoining what is good and forbidding what is evil, leads to the destruction of the marital nest. The best guarantee for the safety of marital life is abiding by religious laws.

For the first years of a child's life, they do not see any educator besides their parents. Therefore, the parents should make sure they are showing the best behavior in front of their child so that they maintain the child's respect and do not expect them to make a mistake.

It is necessary to take practical steps towards reconciliation to solve marital disputes that influence the children's upbringing and ask God ﷻ to bring the hearts closer. Commitment to praying for the children's righteousness is not a substitute for striving to educate and discipline them.

A person who sees precursors of goodness in their children should not destroy their marital life because of a small dispute or unreasonable expectations. This is unfair; instead, it is considered ingratitude for this major blessing!

Some blame black magic or Jinn as the cause of their marital disputes. However, a believer should not follow these feigned delusions. Instead, they should review their behavior and look for the real causes.

A mother breastfeeding her child is in one of the most sacred human states. It is beautiful for the mother to instill high human emotions in her child through her looks or her voice through frequent remembrance of God ﷻ.

It is natural for a woman to be jealous of her husband. Therefore, a husband should not give her any reasons for doubt and should be careful not to put himself in a position of accusation. He should also elevate his wife's level, especially if she sees him as her everything in this existence.

Having a deep sense of responsibility towards children and knowing that they are a trust in our hands helps both parents and children avoid the consequences of negligence that escalate with time until they reach a point wherein one wishes they were not given children due to the greatness of the suffering they are going through.

When one holds a superficial view of marital life and that it is a means for his worldly pleasure and social prestige, then it is natural that he would limit his efforts to those aspects and not bear the burdens of marital life.

The basis of marital happiness is these three elements mentioned in the Noble Qur'ān: tranquility, affection, and mercy! Happiness is not from cohabitation, offspring, or other material things.

This life is a limited place, and every distinction has a shortage opposite it. Thus, we should be realistic and not idealistic! If people do not see idealism in themselves, they should not expect idealism and perfection from others. If the Lord of the Worlds wishes, He will make the wife better than the husband wants.

A marital relationship is eternal, and God ﷻ will unite the spouses in Heaven. No matter how bad one might think of their wife's looks, she will be of utmost beauty and perfection in Heaven, and none of the Maidens of Heaven will rival her in beauty.

A wise believer invests in his wife; he guides her toward spiritual perfection and encourages her to perform different acts of worship. That way, he will be a winner on the Day of Judgement because the higher his wife ascends, the more they will benefit, and the higher the expected rank they will reach in their eternal life!

A mother who produces the best scholars from her school is better than one who is content with a salary from a job that might not be suitable for her and that she will retire from after some years but will not be able to see the genuine delight and the lasting fruit of life.

It is necessary to hold dialogue sessions to discuss any new family issues. However, the dialogue must be done logically to reach solutions, not merely for argument and gaining victory over the other.

Anyone wishing to support the Imām of the Time عجل الله تعالى فرجه الشريف must ensure the proper upbringing of their children. This way, one can ensure they are at the top of a chain of good offspring, and one of their grandchildren would be a helper of the Imām عجل الله تعالى فرجه الشريف. May God ﷻ hasten his reappearance, even if they did not get the chance.

God ﷻ takes special notice of some homes, making these homes the landing place for abundant Divine Mercy. We can qualify our homes to receive this Divine Mercy by purifying the home from ḥarām, having mutual respect between spouses, and safekeeping family secrets.

When a man loves his wife for her beauty, his love will fade with her beauty with time. However, one who loves his wife for her beliefs and internal beauty then his love for her will increase as her faith increases, even if she loses her beauty or becomes paralyzed and unable to leave home.

A believer does not do anything in this life without intending to gain nearness to God ﷻ. Even a believer's wish for his children is done with this intention. As a believer, he wants a guaranteed investment that will be profitable after death. Therefore, he works tirelessly to discipline and educate his children to reap the eternal fruits hereafter.

Children should be given space to freely have fun, play, and discover, as long as they are safe from danger and sin. Unjustified strictness in preventing them from doing so has many negative consequences.

Some parents need to ensure that their children know the religious rules that pertain to them when they reach the age of puberty. The child has to redo many years of prayers and fasting, causing them to resent their parents for not teaching them the rules properly and as early as possible.

When a parent is careless about guiding and advising their children, what is the value of their acts of worship in the eyes of God ﷻ, even if they were among those who perform many acts of worship?

They are responsible for teaching and guiding their children more than performing extra acts of worship!

Some children's mistakes cannot be ignored, and it is important to address them adequately and choose a suitable punishment to deter the child from repeating the same mistake. Some forms of punishment include avoidance and coolness, showing anger by raising their voice or depriving them of money.

Some parents exaggerate in their care of their children: their appearance, education, and recreation. They make their children their main concern, even at the expense of their worship! However, moderation must be practiced even in the care of children.

A righteous father brings himself down to his son's level, acts childish with him if he is a child, and when he becomes a teenager, he speaks with him in a language he understands. He enters his son's heart through his preferred method. If a father can win over his son's heart, he will win everything about him.

Pride in being obedient to one's parents is not as much of an achievement if the parents are intellectually and religiously distinguished. However, if a child is tried with contentious parents who are hurtful, and they still treat them with kindness, it is here that the child achieves levels of perfection!

A believer could be dealing with an unrighteous wife due to his poor choice of a partner, his destiny and fate, or the woman changing from her former righteous state. In such a situation, a believer should accept what God ﷻ has destined for him and remain patient and tolerant of his situation, as this could be the means to reach his spiritual perfection.

A husband should avoid looking at his wife with belittlement. A woman was also created to seek her spiritual perfection and achieve nearness to God ﷻ. Some women have the determination and resolution that men cannot compete with, like Āsiya, who asked God ﷻ to build her a home near Him in Paradise.

Among a man's obligations is to provide financial support for his family without negligence or holding it over their heads. However, some do not prioritize their spending; even if they are well off, they offer their money to charitable projects and donations while neglecting to care for their family.

Winning over children's hearts is the best way to influence them. When children are comfortable with their parents and view them as nurturers and role models, they are more likely to heed the parents' orders no matter what they are, as happened with Ismāʿīl ﷷ and his submission to his father Ibrāhīm ﷷ when he intended to sacrifice him.

Righteous offspring bring joy to a parent's eyes, not for their beauty or prestige, but by seeing them as effective and influential community members who add weight to the earth with their words of "there is no god but God." The Holy Prophet ﷺ takes pride in them on Judgement Day.

One way to get children accustomed to performing righteous acts is by encouraging them after every good act and motivating them financially until these acts become faculties they take pride in and cannot abandon. They will have nothing but gratitude and appreciation for those who were the reason they acquired those faculties.

Some parents do not show concern for their children's religious commitment. For example, some mothers pour their anger on their daughter for breaking a vase, yet do not care about their daughter not praying, listening to music, or befriending a bad group of girls!

A parent's deviation is one of the elements for the deviation of children. Children see their parents as role models from a young age and cannot differentiate between the religion and those who practice it. This makes a parent's guilt a major one as they are the reason for their children's corruption!

A couple's disputes and criticisms of one another in front of their children are a major crime! By doing so, they are unknowingly destroying their innocent children's psyches. What is the children's fault for having to endure such suffering? Is it not more appropriate for the parents to solve their disagreements away from their children?

Obliging children to religion is another area where parents can make mistakes, such as excessive restrictions and holding something undesirable at the same level as something that is prohibited. Dealing with children watching entertaining shows should not be the same as dealing with them watching pornography! The deprivation that is baseless and unreasonable will only cause them to develop an aversion towards religion and those who practice it.

Some parents exaggerate in spoiling their children, even at times of seriousness and work. Instead, they should practice moderation between excessive leniency and harshness. Playing and joking with the child has a certain time, only some of the time.

Some women, due to their preoccupation with social services or religious studies, neglect some of their obligations towards their husbands and children when they should be their priority to care for more than others.

When a believer desires righteous offspring, he does not rely only on his efforts in disciplining and educating them because he realizes his inability to deal with the most complex beings! Instead, he asks his Lord to give him righteous offspring as this blessing is given as a favor from God ﷻ and is not something a person is entitled to due to his worthiness.

Spouses are not two identical parts of one thing that become united with marriage. Therefore, they naturally differ in their attitudes, moods, and thoughts, and no family is free from tension and problems.

If a dispute happens between a couple and they want to solve it, God ﷻ will reconcile between them no matter how deep the dispute is. As God ﷻ says in the Qur'ān:

﴿إِن يُرِيدَآ إِصۡلَٰحٗا يُوَفِّقِ ٱللَّهُ بَيۡنَهُمَآۗ إِنَّ ٱللَّهَ كَانَ عَلِيمًا خَبِيرٗا﴾

﴾*'in yurīdā 'iṣlāḥan yuwaffiqi llāhu baynahumā*﴿

﴾*If they desire reconcilement, God shall reconcile them*﴿[176]

This will happen if they agree to make religious laws the basis for judgment between them.

---

[176] Sūrat al-Nisā', Verse 35.

Assigning family guardianship to the man does not mean a man is intrinsically superior to a woman. Instead, it is simply giving the family a form of government. The basis for superiority is a person's innate faculties and closeness to God ﷻ.

A woman may be more capable than a man in gaining nearness to God ﷻ. This is due to their advantages, such as free time, the absence of many problems a man must deal with, emotional nature, and patience in raising children.

A wise woman does not complain about her husband's mistakes in front of others because he may have gone too far in his foolishness. Instead, she waits for the appropriate time, and using a warm and intimate approach, she affects his heart and corrects his mistakes with tenderness and gentleness.

It is surprising how some women turn their lives into constant misery by insisting on what their husband does not want or does not suit them. Due to things that may not be worthy, they ignite the fire of arguments and may destroy their lives with their own hands!

A woman who worries about losing her husband should win and own her husband's heart! However, this cannot be accomplished by snooping, yelling, scolding, rebellion, and threatening. These methods will only push him further away from her! With her bad behavior, a woman can push her husband towards what she is afraid of.

A woman captures her husband's heart by dressing up and beautifying herself for him. However, some women only dress up for weddings and visits and never for their poor husbands! Therefore, part of the believing woman's duties is to prepare an atmosphere that completely preoccupies her husband with seeking anything forbidden.

It is best for spouses not to expose their marital secrets to anyone, especially family, as the wife's family will defend her, and the husband's family will defend him. As a result, disputes and arguments will ensue, and judgments that do not follow God's ﷻ rules will be made!

A young man who cannot marry should keep himself chaste and ask God ﷻ to grant him patience. One who remains patient in avoiding ḥarām, the appropriate doors of fortune and destiny will open for him. If he is not patient, he might be deprived of happiness in this life and the hereafter.

A believer should always be cautious about falling into the devil's traps and never belittle unlawful violations. These violations could start from a look and a smile, only to end in a way that has undesirable consequences. Then, the devil may wipe this person's face while saying: this is a face that shall never prosper!

Striving to help single women and men get married is one of the greatest acts that bring one closer to God ﷻ. So, just as parents put effort into helping their son marry, why don't they do the same for their daughter instead of leaving her at home waiting for her destiny to come knocking?

A believer must commit to the religious rulings and duties, including his responsibilities towards his family. As it is known, there will be questioning for every religious ruling, so one should be careful in this area.

A believer seeking to build his family nest should remember that the more faith, respect, and worthiness a wife has, the bigger and more profound the responsibility of safeguarding that trust is on the husband! This is because God ﷻ made his wife a trust in his hands.

If a woman finds that someone is trying to instigate her against her husband, she should not take anything they say and instead treat her husband even better! When that person sees this, they will stop what they are doing either due to embarrassment or lost hope in influencing her!

Resorting to physical violence or using profanity and insults in marital life represents the peak of spiritual decline that erases the joy and delight of marital life. It also causes a deep gash that is hard to heal, even if peace returns.

A man with bad behavior and an ill nature can turn his wife into an anxious, tense being. In turn, she will pour her tension and anxiety into her marriage on one side, and it will reflect on the children's discipline and upbringing on the other!

A wife is one's partner in life and is the best investment for one who wants to grow their capabilities and powers. Doing so will have a good return and benefits for the husband, children, and community.

The seeds of disagreement are present in many families and await suitable circumstances to germinate and sprout. Therefore, we should remember the old saying:

> "Prevention is better than the cure."

The blessings of a happy family are not limited to this life only; instead, they extend to the Hereafter, as God ﷻ says:

﴿وَٱلَّذِينَ ءَامَنُواْ وَٱتَّبَعَتۡهُمۡ ذُرِّيَّتُهُم بِإِيمَٰنٍ أَلۡحَقۡنَا بِهِمۡ ذُرِّيَّتَهُمۡ وَمَآ أَلَتۡنَٰهُم مِّنۡ عَمَلِهِم مِّن
شَيۡءٖۚ كُلُّ ٱمۡرِيِٕۭ بِمَا كَسَبَ رَهِينٞ﴾

﴿*wa-lladhīna ʾāmanū wa-ttabaʿathum dhurriyyatuhum bi-ʾīmānin ʾalḥaqnā bihim dhurriyyatahum wa-mā ʾalatnāhum min ʿamalihim min shayʾin*﴾

﴿*The faithful and their descendants who followed them in faith—We will make their descendants join them, and We will not stint anything from [the reward of] their deeds*﴾[177]

[177] Sūrat al-Ṭūr, Verse 21.

www.ingramcontent.com/pod-product-compliance
Lightning Source LLC
Chambersburg PA
CBHW021702120626
46545CB00004B/1364
9781956276459